S0-CJM-429

SPORT DIVING

SPORT DIVING

THE COMPLETE MANUAL FOR SKIN AND SCUBA DIVERS

A. P. BALDER

COLLIER BOOKS
A Division of Macmillan Publishing Co., Inc.
NEW YORK

COLLIER MACMILLAN PUBLISHERS
LONDON

FOR
STELLA
who touched upon
the sorcery of it
at Ras Mahamad, Sinai,
in the Red Sea

Copyright © 1968, 1978 by A. P. Balder

All rights reserved. No part of this book may be reproduced or transmitted in any form or by any means, electronic or mechanical, including photocopying, recording or by any information storage and retrieval system, without permission in writing from the Publisher.

Macmillan Publishing Co., Inc.
866 Third Avenue, New York, N.Y. 10022
Collier Macmillan Canada, Ltd.

Library of Congress Cataloging in Publication Data

Balder, Alton Parker.
    Sport diving.

    Edition of 1968 published under title: The complete
manual of skin diving.
    Bibliography: p.
    Includes index.
    1. Skin diving.   2. Scuba diving.   I. Title.
GV840.S78B25   1978   797.2'3   78-6717
ISBN 0-02-028140-4

First Collier Books Edition 1978

Sport Diving is a revised and updated edition of *The Complete Manual of Skin Diving* originally published in hardcover by Macmillan Publishing Co., Inc.

Printed in the United States of America

CONTENTS

Boyle's Law * The Breath-held Dive and Squeeze *
Charles's, or Gay-Lussac's, Law * Lung Damage in
Diving * Dalton's Law * Henry's Law * Air and
Pressure * The Lungs and Air Consumption

4

OPEN-CIRCUIT SCUBA EXPLAINED

Tanks * Harness or Backpack * Regulators * Octopus Rig
* Reserve Valves * Useful Tips for Annual Regulator
Maintenance * Safety Rules for the Use of Compressed-
air Cylinders * Recharging Cylinders with Air *
Assembling Breathing Apparatus for Divers * Pressure
Gauge * Depth Gauge * Underwater Watch * The
Compass and Underwater Navigation * Underwater
Slate * Diving Light * Line * Decompression Meter

5

DIVING TECHNIQUES

The Buddy System * Communication Among Divers *
Plan Your Dive, Dive Your Plan * Calculating Your Air
Supply * How to Breathe * How to Relax Under Water
* Hints for Diving Expeditions * The Safe Depth Limit
for Open-circuit Compressed-air Diving * Dive Site
Equipment Preparation: General Checklist * Dressing
for the Dive * The Dive * Predive Anxiety * Fear of
Surfacing * Claustrophobia * Entries and Exits from
Dives * Fresh Waters * Tips for Freshwater Diving
* Ocean Waters * Choosing a Dive Site * Coral Reef
Diving * Currents that Concern the Diver * Surfacing
* Postdive Inspection * Postdive Procedures * Postdive
Maintenance Care and Stowage * Practical Suggestions
for Field Maintenance and Repair

6

DECOMPRESSION AND DIVING

No-Decompression Limit * Single Dives * Repetitive
Dives * Examples of a Typical Repetitive Dive Situation
* How to Use a Dive Profile * Symptoms of the Bends

Warning * Hunting Lobster * Turtles * Marine
Mammals * Features that Identify Fresh Fish *
Handling, Preparing, and Storing Fish * Cooking
Fish Indoors * Cooking Fish Outdoors * Shellfish
Cookery * Batter, Butter, and Sauce

11

DIVING HAZARDS, PREVENTION, REMEDIES

Potentially Dangerous Marine Life * Sharks * Shark
Defense Systems * Killer Whales (Orca) * Sea Snake *
Grouper (Sea Bass) * Sea Lion * Stingray * Moray Eel *
Great Barracuda * Octopus * Giant Clam * Sea Urchin *
Cone Shells * Barnacles * Abalone * Jellyfishes
(Coelenterates), Sea Nettle, Portuguese Man-of-War,
Sea Wasp * Coral * Marine Plants * Fish that Inflict
Venomous Stings * Special Precautions in Tropical
Waters * Dry-suit Squeeze * Face Squeeze * Intestinal
Squeeze * External-ear Squeeze * Middle-ear Squeeze *
Sinus Squeeze * Thoracic Squeeze * Toothache
(Aerodontalgia) * Shallow Water Blackout * Anoxia *
Asphyxia * Carbon-dioxide Poisoning * Carbon-monoxide
Poisoning * Nitrogen Narcosis (Rapture of the Deep) *
Oil-vapor Poisoning * Oxygen Poisoning * Air Embolism
* Decompression Sickness * Spontaneous Pneumothorax
* Subcutaneous and Mediastinal Emphysema * General
First Aid * Bleeding * Wounds * Loss of Consciousness
* Shock * Fractures * Burns * Seasickness * Panic * Leg
Cramps * Stomach Cramps * Exhaustion * Drowning *
Fainting * Strangulation * Injury from Lightning * Fish
Poisoning—General * Fish Poisoning, Most Usual
Specific Varieties * Chills * Suggested First Aid Kit *
Flying After Diving * Loss of Consciousness During or
After Dive * Emergency Assistance Plan (EAP) *
Fouling and Entanglement * Self-rescue * Rescue of
Another * Tips on Rescue * Artificial Respiration

ACKNOWLEDGMENTS

Thanks to Joe Dorsey of Divers Den, Baltimore, for sharing once again his full-ranged diving experience; to Curt Marshall, M.D., for meticulously reviewing the medical and technical side of the manuscript; to many professional divers who lent an ear to my queries: Brett Gilliam and his associates at V. I. Divers, Brian Max Friedman, all in St. Croix; Andy Whitehouse in Maryland, and others too numerous to single out individually. My thanks go out to Ruth Dugan for her comments and encouragement; to Charlotte Schisler for typing neatly, speedily, and attentively. And a special thanks to my friends Marc Trupp and Wolfie for giving shelter to a grumbling author in their cozy country home down in Maryland.

A. P. Balder

INTRODUCTION

Some kindly critics have labeled *The Complete Manual of Skin Diving* (the original edition of this book) encyclopedic. As with the first edition, in *Sport Diving* I have included comprehensive essential information for divers with any amount of prior' diving experience—from beginner to advanced.

But the first edition grew out of the early sixties when sport diving was in its infancy. Diving, as a sport, has since matured and achieved the sophistication and precision of modern aviation. Now, just as a pilot needs a license, scuba divers must pass an accredited course and be certified before they can buy or rent equipment. Just as the sport has expanded, so has my text.

Updated and extensively revised, this edition of my manual is directed at any diver who wants to make safe round-trips to the fascinating world under water. It remains a working field manual, organized for ready reference so that information can be located quickly, when even seconds count.

All the basics are still here, but now I have incorporated the latest advances in equipment and technique. I have added more detailed discussion of emergency and safety procedures, expanded the chapter on exciting diving activities, and included new charts and tables for the more sophisticated divers among you. A personal diving log has also been added.

This manual is here to lure you away from chlorinated pools and littered holiday beaches to a new world of unsuspected beauty under oceans, lakes, quarries, rivers, and even flooded meadows. Once you have gained basic competence, the range of underwater activity for amateurs and professionals is broad; it includes nature study, marine biology, treasure hunting, archaeology, salvaging, volunteer police work, sea rescue, live tropical fish collecting, gold prospecting, photography, film-making, and dive instruction.

Unfortunately, not all dive education can be committed to memory or retained with indelible accuracy even by those who are lucky enough to dive with regularity the year round. Much of what was learned and grasped at one period of a year can be forgotten in another unless you can honestly brag that you remember everything about equipment, body and pressure, marine dangers, and the nature of the underwater environment. Can you?

A lot is forgotten between the bookshelf and the sea. This book will serve as an aide-memoire for those whose memories do falter and are wise enough to know it. It is as much for the beginner who is having difficulties with skills already learned and wants to correct bad habits or overcome fear, as it is for the C-card holder who won his or her certification last year but hasn't dived since. It is also for the intermediate who wants to advance, for the diver who has reached the cocky stage of diving and thinks he or she knows it all and will never get into a jam, for any diver who wants to improve, and also, for those who have not tried for certification but want to develop a feel for the sport. If you feel that you are any combination of these, then this manual is for you.

I believe that any healthy swimmer can learn to skin or scuba dive. There's no wizardry involved, although there is certainly a kind of otherworldliness about it. There are some facts, formulas, and figures to know, and I offer these for reference as needed, for either applied field use or leisurely study. This book is a tool, a unit of equipment, meant to be taken with you. Keep it conveniently near, not tucked away and forgotten in your gear bag. Keep it topside or bunkside to bone up on things it wouldn't hurt to remember. It's meant to be leafed through, read, left, picked up again. Don't let complicated charts, diagrams, tables, and polysyllabic scientific terms throw you. Most of these are simple enough (you've probably covered them in class). Study them. Some day, who can tell, they may concern you or a buddy. Mind you, they are all part of the driving force behind this handbook—the joy of diving. Or, for some of you—a way of life.

SPORT DIVING

1

DIVING INSTRUCTION
AND FITNESS

A WORD ABOUT YOUR UNDERWATER EDUCATION

Your basic training is merely the beginning of a larger diving education. What it takes to remain a qualified diver depends on the individual's frequency of diving. To become a seasoned diver with the necessary wisdom and water sense requires two years of steady diving, at first under close supervision; that is, a couple dives a month, mostly open-water descents.

The various diving schools are ponderous establishments, each bent on turning out divers. But, in the final analysis, one learns by diving, not by reading and listening to an instructor speak. By whatever method you earn your certification, remember, if you have not trained under close supervision, you cannot hope to engage safely in any kind of diving activity involving scuba. After that, there's no substitute for experience. Your quality and the quality of your experience is determined by several things: how you make ready for a dive, your comportment in action, and your ability to prevent accidents.

Experienced divers should not be afraid to relearn techniques that they have not used for a long time or to face the fact that their standard of diving efficiency may have noticeably deteriorated. In diving it is dangerous not to admit limitations and no diver should force himself or be forced beyond his own capabilities.

WHERE TO OBTAIN ADDITIONAL TRAINING

A certified diver, that is, one who holds a C-card, is qualified in the use of a mask, snorkel, fins, and open-circuit scuba. The following agencies offer introductory, intermediate, and advanced instruction, as well as diver instructor courses:

† Association of Canadian
    Underwater Councils
    (ACUC)
National Sport & Recreation
    Center
333 River Road
Vanier City, Ontario, Canada
    K1L8B9

† Los Angeles County
    Underwater Unit (LACO)
155 West Washington
    Boulevard
Los Angeles, CA 90015

* National Association of Skin
    Diving Schools (NASDS)
1757 Long Beach Boulevard S.
Long Beach, CA 90802

† National Association of
    Underwater Instructors
    (NAUI)
22809 Barton Road
Colton, CA 92324

* Professional Association of
    Diving Instructors (PADI)
P. O. Box 177
Costa Mesa, CA 92697

* Professional Diving Instructor
    College (PDIC)
320 Hoffman
Monterey, CA 93940

* Scuba Schools International
    (SSI)
1634 South College
Fort Collins, CO 80521

† Young Men's Christian
    Association (YMCA)
YMCA National Scuba
    Program
1611 Candler Building
Atlanta, GA 30303

---

* Programs by these agencies include courses in equipment repair, retail salesmanship, and dive-store operation. They are business-oriented.
† These agencies offer complete scuba-diving programs, instructor-certification courses.

Send away for information on courses near you by writing directly to the above-mentioned addresses and/or consult local dive stores (see yellow pages).

DIVING CLUBS

Wherever you find a beach, a water hole, an old quarry, or a creek, chances are you'll find a diving club nearby. For that matter, clubs exist that are based far from bodies of water, and their members travel thousands of miles annually to find good diving. Diving clubs are plentiful throughout the world; there are more than nine hundred in the United States alone. Their members convene to dive or, when diving is unseasonable, to plan future expeditions, to train one another, to hear lectures by famous scientists, explorers, and adventurers, to talk about what's old and what's new, and to outspin one another's yarns.

The Advantages of a Good Club: A good club reports the latest in equipment, literature, legislation, training methods, and dive areas. A good club provides a place to go, companionship, a source of diving buddies, and training for newcomers. Clubs organize public service activities and promote conservation.

Whereas an individual may not be able to afford to rent or charter expensive gear such as an air compressor or a boat, a club can. A good club will impose upon its members a sense of responsibility. As a diver, you already belong to a worldwide fraternity; but club membership is your passport to adventure throughout the world, where new-found comrades far from home will give you a warm welcome and valuable time-saving tips on local conditions. You and your club can do the same for divers visiting your area.

COMMUNITY RELATIONS: A CODE OF CONDUCT FOR DIVERS

A diver must acknowledge that he or she has a responsibility not to come into conflict with other users of waters, as well as the general public. Wherever you dive don't crowd out other water users.

Park cars so as not to be inconsiderate. Keep equipment out of people's way and keep wharves and docks clear. Keep the peace. Avoid making noisy nuisances of yourselves.

Don't litter. Don't damage property and crops.

Obey National Park rules, local bylaws, camping regulations. Remember, divers are conspicuous and bad conduct invites resentment and hostility. Ask locals where to launch boats. Stay clear of buoys, pots, and fishermen's markers. Find out from locals where not to dive. Avoid channels and areas of heavy surface traffic. Never use a speargun with an aqualung. Fly the diver's flag when diving. Remove it when diving is finished. Take only mature fish or shellfish and only for nourishment. Don't show off your catch.

Be conservation-conscious. Do not disturb bathing beaches or crowded anchorages with your boat wake.

Don't be a wreck scavenger.

Don't let your sport or your club down. Keep diving's reputation at a high level.

BASIC PREPARATION

Stay fit. Be in especially good form when you anticipate strenuous dives or long diving vacations. Stay well within the limits of your physical endurance. Pace yourself, use minimal energy. Always breathe normally.

Be equipped for the specific kind of dive planned. The hardware you would need for a cave dive will differ from what you would need for spearfishing. That applies to the training. Look to your diving school for specialized instruction.

Keep your gear in good repair, always washed in fresh water after diving. Precheck everything at least two days before your planned dive. Know where you are throughout the dive. Be a navigator, making mental notes on landmarks, currents, the direction and velocity of currents, your time spent down. Always return with at least 100 pounds per square inch (psi) in your tank; 300 pounds or more per square inch in cave, ice, and wreck dives.

Never dive alone. Maintain constant contact with your buddy by sight and sound. Begin together at an agreed-upon rendezvous point and stay together. Have a prearranged plan for regrouping if separated or lost.

Be vigilant against environmental factors which could trouble your dive: increasing surf, rising sea, increase in current, bad weather, poor visibility, excess surface traffic. Revise plans accordingly or abort. Cancel dive plans if your physical condition is poor.

MORE ON FITNESS

Concern with good health and fitness should not end with the doctor's stamp of approval; they should be a continuing condition all year round, and annual checkups are advisable. Be frank and open with the examining physician. You may know of symptoms he can't detect without your cooperation, so bring him up to date on your total condition. If you conceal any unsoundness of health you will be a hazard to yourself and to your diving companions.

MEDICAL REVIEW FOR YOUR EXAMINING PHYSICIAN

	(Yes or No)
Frequent cold or sore throat	_____
Hay fever or sinus trouble	_____
Trouble breathing through nose (other than colds)	_____
Painful or running ear, mastoid trouble, broken eardrum	_____
Asthma or shortness of breath after moderate exercise	_____
Chest pain or persistent cough	_____
Spells of fast, irregular, or pounding heartbeat	_____
High or low blood pressure	_____
Any kind of heart trouble	_____
Frequent upset stomach, heartburn, or indigestion; peptic ulcer	_____

	(Yes or No)
Frequent diarrhea or blood in stools	_____
Bellyache or backache lasting more than a day or two	_____
Kidney or bladder disease, blood sugar or albumin in urine	_____
Syphilis or gonorrhea	_____
Broken bone, serious sprain or strain, dislocated joint	_____
Rheumatism, arthritis, or other joint trouble	_____
Severe or frequent headaches	_____
Head injury causing unconsciousness	_____
Dizzy spells, fainting spells, fits	_____
Trouble sleeping, frequent nightmares	_____
Nervous breakdown or periods of marked depression	_____
Dislike for closed-in spaces, large open places, or high places	_____
Any neurological condition	_____
Train, sea, or air sickness	_____
Alcoholism or any drug or narcotic habit (including regular use of sleeping pills)	_____
Recent gain or loss of weight or appetite	_____
Jaundice or hepatitis	_____
Tuberculosis	_____
Diabetes	_____
Rheumatic fever	_____
Any serious accident, injury, or illness not mentioned above	_____

Keeping Fit When Not Diving: If a swimming pool is available, use it often. Swim laps and practice holding your breath. Don't try to break breath-holding records without proper supervision. Practice breathing exercises to increase breath-holding capacity. Engage in such athletic games as tennis, handball, and squash—anything to maintain good muscle tone and endurance.

2

EQUIPMENT REFRESHER
FOR ALL DIVERS
BASIC THROUGH
ADVANCED

The debate over what equipment is best and safest goes on. Competition among equipment manufacturers is keen and divers of every degree of skill argue, and, I suppose, will continue to argue, the pros and cons of hardware. Don't knock it. A crossfire of claims and counterclaims is healthy, all for the greater good of a restless diving technology. I could add a tree-felling page or two to the ongoing debates, but why? Such is not the purpose of this manual. The manual offers information rather than arguments. While recommendations are inevitably sought by curious readers, I restrict these to a minimum. The choice of brand is a personal preference as well as a question of dollars and cents. Certainly, well-made, well-maintained equipment is not to be understated, but my emphasis is on personal performance. Nor should we forget the gift of mind and muscle, the underwater environment itself, and the immutable biological and physical laws associated with diving. The ultimate measure of our performance as divers hinges on these fundamentals and equipment combined.

Stick to tested, proven equipment. Buy at reliable, well-established dive stores. Avoid homemade gear. Before buying, seek the advice of an instructor or someone whose diving experience commands respect. Take good care of your property. Label it with your name and address. Follow the manufacturer's instructions and your equipment will last longer.

EQUIPMENT PREPARATION

Prior to any dive, all equipment must be carefully inspected for signs of deterioration, damage, or corrosion, and must be tested for proper operation where required.

Every diver must always check his own equipment and must never assume that any piece of equipment is ready for use unless he has personally verified that readiness. If you can't trust your own judgment, ask others.

FACE MASK

Purpose and Use: The purpose of the mask is to give the diver clear, full vision under water. It has the additional use of protecting the diver's eyes from injury, salt water irritation, and pollutants. Bear in mind that everything under water will appear about one-quarter larger and closer than normal when viewed through the mask.

Selection: The best type of mask covers eyes and nose, not the mouth, and never the eyes alone. With the mouth free, it is easier for the diver to gasp for much needed air when he surfaces, and if in distress, to shout for help. The faceplate should be of shatter-proof safety glass firmly encased in a rubber frame; in many masks this frame is secured by a stainless-steel rim. The mask should have a properly contoured soft skirt with feathered or sponge edges. The head strap should be of good-quality rubber with adjustable buckles and should not be tight. Wear the strap high on the back of the head. A plastic faceplate is not recommended because it is too easily scratched, is susceptible to prolonged condensation, and offers poor-quality visibility.

To test for correct fit and air leakage, hold the mask properly placed on your face and begin to inhale, then let go of the mask. If it stays on without being held by the hand but because of the suction while you are inhaling, the fit is good and no air is leaking in. If the mask leaks air, then it can leak water no matter how tight the head strap, and the head strap must not be worn too tightly. If it is, the skirt may fold and admit water, you may suffer fatigue and eyestrain, and your blood circulation may be cut off. Do not allow hair, bathing cap, or diving hood to come between the mask skirt and your skin or you will not be able to seal properly.

Never plunge headfirst while wearing a mask. Always hold the mask firmly to your face if you are jumping in; otherwise, the mask will rip from your face.

If you wear glasses, you can dive with contact lenses or you can have an optician incorporate your prescription lenses or lens right into the faceplate of your mask. Finally, there are lens holders that will fit many of the masks now on the market. Check with your dive shop. Glasses with thin frames over the ears can be worn inside a mask and the mask can seal right over them.

Never wear goggles in place of a mask. You can't blow air into them in order to equalize (counteract) the pressure of the water.

Purging a Mask of Water While Using a Breathing Apparatus: A mask other than the self-purging type is purged in the following ways:

Position 1. From a horizontal swimming position, turn your body sidewise horizontal to the bottom. With the hand nearer the surface press against the side of the mask nearer the surface. Exert firm but mild pressure only. Inhale deeply from your air supply and blow through your nose. The resulting buildup of air pressure in the mask will force the water out of the low side of the mask skirt.

Position 2. From an upright or vertical position, tilt your head back so that it faces the surface. Put both hands firmly against the top of your mask. Do not press too hard. Inhale normally and then exhale through the nose. Water will flow away by gravity through the skirt of the mask.

There are excellent masks, known as self-purging masks, equipped with a one-way flutter valve in the faceplate or lower skirt for easy purging of water. If any amount of water gets into the mask, all you need to do is position the head and the valve and blow through the nose; the water will escape through the valve. If your mask is pulled off and must be put on again while you are submerged, you can purge it via the one-way valve. To do so simply lower your head as though nodding and exhale through the nose.

Clearing Condensation from Mask: You must prevent your mask from clouding up with condensation, and the best anticondensation is saliva. Rinse the mask. Spit inside it, rub the saliva all over the glass, then rinse it out with a little water. Put your mask on. Glasses or lens holders too can be cleared of condensation (can be "defogged") in the same manner.

Care and Maintenance: Wash and rinse your mask with fresh water after dives. Keep it out of the sun. Do not store it in a hot, dry place such as a car trunk or a boat locker.

SNORKEL

Purpose: The snorkel is a major item of safety equipment. For surface swimming the snorkel allows breathing while your face is submerged, and you can use it whether you are carrying compressed-air tanks or not. You can breathe with the snorkel to conserve your compressed-air supply while engaged in searching from the surface, especially when your air supply is low or you have a long swim home. When you are covering long distances back to shore or boat, when your air supply is gone, the snorkel enables you to swim without lifting your head out of the water, thus minimizing exertion and the chance of your hitting your tank or regulator with the back of your head. The snorkel in skin diving can be used for short breath-held dives of moderate duration.

Selection: The best snorkel is the simple J-type with a plastic or semirigid rubber spout; the latter is preferable for snorkel diving, especially in kelp waters. Because of its flexibility there is less chance of entanglement when using the rubber spout. It has a mouthpiece at one end and is open at the other. Snorkels with Ping-Pong balls or corks are toys and not for diving. The ball or cork often sticks when it shouldn't, especially in choppy surf. Snorkels with bellows are designed primarily for use with self-contained air-breathing equipment so that the mouthpiece will hang out of the way.

How to Use: Insert the snorkel under the mask head strap, preferably in a snorkel holder ring just at the temple. When submerging with a snorkel take a breath first. Submerge holding your breath. Water will fill the snorkel tube, and sometimes some water will trickle into your mouth. You can prevent this by placing your tongue in the mouthpiece or by biting down hard to seal the mouthpiece altogether. When you surface, blow forcefully into the tube, expelling water at the other end to clear it for breathing. Careful! Don't "blow" too soon. Otherwise water may flood the tube and you may not have enough breath left to blow it out at the surface, where you may gag and panic. Once the tube is cleared, just breathe normally.

Care and Maintenance: As with all rubber goods, wash your snorkel with fresh water, rinse, dry, and keep it out of the sun.

SWIM FINS

Purpose: Swim fins are designed to increase swimming efficiency, power, and ability with minimum muscular exertion, especially in prolonged swims. Mainly your feet and fins will do the job of propelling you, since your hands will often be filled with equipment.

Selection: The most preferable fins are the buoyant, soft-rubber fins that enclose the full foot and have an open or a closed toe. They provide maximum comfort. Be sure, as with all equipment, of a comfortable fit. If the fins are too tight, they hinder circulation, causing discomfort, cramps, and coldness of the feet. If too loose, they can cause blisters and chafing or can fall off and be lost just when most needed. A good idea when buying fins is to fit them while wearing rubber "booties." The latter afford protection while diving and, incidentally, after the dive if you have a long walk across rough terrain. If you are wearing a rubber suit, use a larger-size fin, just as you would with booties. When neither booties nor a suit is used, smaller-size fins work better.

Other than the soft, floating fin, there is the nonbuoyant fin. Nonbuoyant fins are less flexible and sink if detached in water. Thus they are not as easily retrieved as the floating, soft-rubber fins. Soft fins require less kick power but offer less forward thrust. Advanced divers usually prefer large-surfaced, rigid fins. For dives around coral, use full-foot fins fitted like shoes for best protection against lacerations. Otherwise use rubber booties. Accessory safety straps are a must in heavy surf unless your fins fit perfectly.

How to Use: To don your fins, wet them or use talc to ease them on. Talc is sold at dive shops. Swim moderately, kick at an easy pace, minimize your effort. Do not try speed (water resistance will only tire you). If you use your hip and leg muscles, the rest of your body can remain relaxed. Don't overexert. The whole purpose of fins is to increase swimming efficiency and forward thrust without strain.

Care and Maintenance: Rinse your fins well with fresh water. Keep them out of the sun.

WEIGHT BELT AND LEAD WEIGHTS

Purpose: Ideally a diver should be able to maneuver underwater as effortlessly as possible. He need not expend energy to prevent rising or sinking involuntarily. If he rises involuntarily (he is lighter than the water) and an effort is required to prevent rising, he is in a state of *positive buoyancy*. He hasn't enough weight added to his person to counteract the tendency to rise. If, on the other hand, he sinks involuntarily or is heavy in the water and an effort is required to prevent sinking, he is in a state of *negative buoyancy*. He is weighted down too much. Of course, there may be occasions when he may require negative buoyancy or positive buoyancy. A diver working on the bottom would want to be heavy in order to stay on the bottom. Under normal circumstances, however, the ideal state of buoyancy is neutral, and to be neutral, neither rising nor sinking, is to be weightless. The purpose of the weight belt is to help the diver achieve the weightless state. Let's examine the simple science of buoyancy so that you will understand what the weight belt is all about. Most people float quite well in sea water (less well in fresh water) but a few cannot because their average body density is greater than that of the water and is thus heavier than the water it displaces. Two factors determine whether a man's body will have negative or positive buoyancy: (1) fat, muscle, and bone, and (2) lung capacity.

Fat is lighter than muscle and bone and weighs less than water. Therefore, fat people float better than lean people. As to the second factor, the air space of a man's lungs buoys him like a pair of inflated water wings. Almost everyone has noticed that he is more buoyant with a full breath than when he exhales. When a man skin dives (holding his breath), the air in his lungs is compressed as he descends, so that he becomes decreasingly buoyant the deeper he progresses. If he starts with a full breath at the surface, the average man will become negatively buoyant after descending 15 or 20 feet. Some breath-holding skin divers taking breath-held dives (without air rig) may find themselves as much as 10 pounds "heavy" at their maximum depth and may have to swim energetically at the start of the ascent.

A self-contained diver wearing a foam neoprene exposure suit is buoyant because of the air trapped between the suit and his body. He may have to use 5 to 30 pounds of diving weights in order to off-set this buoyancy. When he descends the trapped air is compressed and he becomes progressively heavier, passing from positive to neutral buoyancy, and finally even to a definite negative buoyancy. In some cases the diver may have difficulty returning to the surface without dropping some of his weights. Anyone who dives with some regularity should get to know his weighting requirements under all circumstances.

The laws of flotation based on Archimedes' principle can be summarized as follows: (1) a body sinks in a fluid if the weight of the fluid it displaces is less than the weight of the body; (2) a submerged body remains in equilibrium (weightlessness), neither rising nor sinking, if the weight of the fluid it displaces is exactly equal to its own weight; (3) if a submerged body weighs less than the volume of liquid it displaces, it will rise and float with part of its volume above the surface. A floating body displaces its own weight of a liquid. (The volume of a liquid displaced by a floating body has the same weight as the body itself.)

Selection: A nylon belt is better than cotton because it resists the corrosive effect of sea water. Lead weights are ideal because they are corrosion resistant. They come in sizes of 1, 2, 3, 4, 5, 6, 8, or 10 pounds and in square, rectangular, or rounded shapes. A quick-release safety fastener on the belt is a *must*. In an emergency ascent, the belt may be the first piece of equipment to jettison, although it is debatable whether jettisoning your weight belt is the best course in an emergency that requires a fast and free ascent. If you are wearing a wet suit, the sudden detachment of your belt may free you to rise at a dangerously rapid rate, causing a serious air embolism.

How to Use: Weight requirements vary with individuals. Some divers are able to achieve a state of weightlessness without using a weight belt at all. Others achieve an ideal state of weightlessness, enabling them to descend and ascend without overexerting, by attaching enough lead weights to their body. Weighting should be determined in a safe place before proceeding with a dive. To determine how much weight you need in order to arrive at correct neutral buoyancy, enter the water with your weight belt in your hand and submerge to the bottom, which should not be more than 10 feet down. Start with enough weight to pull you down; be sure some of the weights are small. Then remove small weights one at a time. Put them on your float. After each weight is removed, test your buoyancy by taking a deep breath, then blow it out. You will have achieved neutral buoyancy when your body rises each time you inhale and sinks each time you exhale. You should have positive buoyancy near the surface because submerging will compress you and provide the negative buoyancy to neutralize the positive, creating weightlessness. You may discover that you don't need any weights at all. But if you do need them be sure that you wear your weight belt on the outside of all equipment, straps, and clothing, and that it is held on with a quick-release device within easy reach. You should be able to jettison the belt instantly with either hand alone.

Weighting While Wearing an Exposure Suit: When wearing either type of exposure suit you will need to add more lead weights to your belt. With a wet suit start with positive buoyancy at the surface. This means at first you will rise rather than sink. The wet suit will be compressed the deeper you go, and positive buoyancy will soon become neutral—another term for weightlessness. If you lose or jettison your belt in an emergency ascent, guard against the possibility of a sudden, rapid rise by using legs and arms to check your speed upward. A premature or overly rapid ascent may cause air embolism, decompression sickness, or both (see Hazards of Ascent, pages 225–28.

FLOAT

Purpose: The float is a device for rescue, self-rescue, rest when fatigued, stowage of gear, and deposit of speared fish.

Types: An inner tube, a small inflatable life raft, paddleboard, small boat or skiff, an inflatable surf mat (preferably compartmentalized)—all are practical.

Selection: Selection depends on circumstances and the purpose of a dive. Should you use an inner tube, don't use one you would not consider safe enough for your car. Get a good one. If you elect to use a paddleboard, it should be about 6 feet long with a broad beam.

Skiffs are ideal for short-range marine transportation to and from a dive site, for rest, for gear stowage, and for holding speared fish, as blood does not leak into the water to attract predatory fish. If it is lightweight, the skiff can be carried on your automobile. It should be equipped with a small outboard motor and oars. Remember that powerboat users should exercise extreme caution to avoid divers in the water, and divers should be especially alert and cautious where powerboats are used. Have adequate anchors and anchor line. An anchor can be towed by a diver or, as the diver travels away from the point of origin, by a topside tender. Under unfavorable conditions, use a lifeline attached to your float and to yourself and tow as you go. Use the shortest line that will permit swimming and freedom. Do not attach it to your weight belt. Take care to avoid fouling.

BUOYANCY COMPENSATOR (BC)

Purpose: A BC is an inflatable ballast tool designed as a personal flotation device (operable at the surface and at depths to 200 feet or more) and as a system to control and trim your buoyancy while under water. A BC can be used any time during a dive. It is a portable, flexible air ballast system which operates like the ballast system of a submarine.

Control of buoyancy is essential because you want to stay off the bottom to prevent stirring up the mud or silt and reducing your visibility, particularly in fresh water or caves. In both fresh and salt water, you want to maintain neutral buoyancy at all times. If an emergency does occur and you must make an ascent with neutral buoyancy, you have only to start toward the surface and you'll continue ascending without any effort on your part.

Buoyancy Control at Depth: When wearing a wet suit, if you descend, your suit compresses and becomes heavier. The deeper you descend, the more you will be affected by the increasing water pressure. By admitting just enough air into your BC, you can prevent sinking and attain neutral buoyancy. Upon ascending, the air can be removed by holding the corrugated tube above your head and depressing the mouthpiece valve or by operating a special dump valve.

Surface Use: After surfacing, inflate the BC via the mini cylinder or low-pressure hose from the regulator; or by orally inflating the unit, the unit will keep you afloat, reduce fatigue. To descend again, deflate the vest and make your second dive. Inflation and deflation are instantaneous. Monitor carefully until you get the hang of it.

Buoyancy Ascent: The BC is inflatable at depth—even at the 100-foot level. In the case of an extreme emergency, you can fully and quickly inflate a BC and make a rapid ascent to the surface. *Warning:* Rapid ascent increases the chances for an accidental air embolism or a case of the bends. The rate of ascent is 60 feet per minute. This rate can be easily controlled with most BCs by carefully regulating the amount of compressed air put into the vest. As soon as lift begins, shut off the air supply. As you rise toward the surface, the air trapped inside the vest will expand, thus providing more buoyancy but increasing the rate of ascent. You then regulate the speed of ascent by venting off excess air via the oral inflator valve or dump valve.

The best design for keeping your head supported clear of the water, should you become unconscious, is the doughnut or horse-collar shape. The bulk of the bag should be in front of your chest and upper stomach. The portion going around the back of the neck should also be capable of being filled with air like a life ring around your head.

It must be inflatable orally. It must be mechanically inflatable, either by an attached refillable air tank, or by way of a low-pressure hose off the main scuba system. It must have an overpressure relief valve. The CO_2 cartridges are an effective emergency backup system to be used at the surface for instant inflation.

A CO_2 cartridge at average diving depth will not furnish the buoyancy required. Adequate inflation by gas cartridge is more effective at shallower depths.

The advantage of BC inflation directly off regulator is that the vest can be inflated without removing your regulator from your mouth. You have at least one hand free instead of two hands occupied. However, there is the possibility that a defective mechanism of inflation could jam and you can't deflate fast enough. It is probably best to inflate orally. Avoid overinflation as this will be the most common way of achieving positive buoyancy throughout an ascent. Ascent rate can be controlled with conscious monitoring.

Care and Maintenance of BC Vest: After each day's use, CO_2 cartridges should be taken out and the mechanism and cartridge sprayed with silicone prior to putting them back together.

Fill the vest half way with warm water. Inflate fully. Shake vest well. Drain water out of oral inflator. Taste water; if salty, repeat rinse. To check BC for leaks, inflate fully and dunk BC in tub of water. Escaping bubbles will reveal source of leaks. Store vest inflated.

BUOYANCY CONTROL PACK (BCP)

As with the BC vest, the pack allows you to arrive at neutral buoyancy at depth and be capable of compensating for heaviness, as pressure increases with increased depth. The BCP works on the same principle as the BC vest. It can be inflated and deflated, at will. It is worn as a backpack, incorporating a weight belt, tank regulator, inflation device, and back pack, all in one heavy unit. Hard-shell types are designed to doff and don in or out of the water. Generally speaking, the BCP's lift capacity is slightly greather than that of the BC vest.

How to Use: This pack may be fully inflated on land. Make your entry with fully inflated pack. You will remain afloat without effort. From a beach entry, this is especially advantageous if you have a long swim to the dive site. Remain on the surface, kicking yourself backwards. It feels as if you were relaxed in an easy chair. When ready to descend, hold exhaust hose above your head, push exhaust button only enough to descend slowly. (You must of course allow time to equalize pressure on your ears.) If you sink too fast, check your descent by pushing your inflation button slightly or by finning or leveling off with a little body control.

DIVER'S FLAG

Purpose: A diver's flag afloat is a marker that warns surface vessels that a diver is operating within a radius of 100 feet or so of the flag. Boat users should therefore navigate well outside this radius, but divers must be discreet in selecting a dive site. The flag should be floated during all dives, at least 3 feet above the surface of the float, or displayed from your boat. Use as large a flag as possible. The color is red-orange, generally known as international orange. A diagonal white stripe runs from the upper left- to the lower right-hand corner. The size of the flag is usually four units by five units, and the stripe is one unit wide.

EXPOSURE SUIT

Purpose: Because it protects you against the cold and chills, an exposure suit enables you to prolong your dive time. In addition, it can protect you from cuts and abrasions from coral, but since you may also tear an exposure suit on coral, a pair of old trousers and a sweat shirt should be adequate for coral exploration.

Selection: For best service, the exposure suit must be a good, snug fit. There are two types of suits, the wet suit and dry suit. In addition to the suit itself there are a separate hood, boots, and mittens of similar material to outfit you completely.

The Wet Suit: The foam neoprene wet suit lined with four-way stretch nylon is recommended for sport diving. It is strong, easy to put on, and simple to repair with neoprene cement when torn. Suits of a thickness of $3/16$ inch, $1/4$ inch, or $3/8$ inch offer the best protection. As you submerge, a layer of water will soak into the suit. This layer of water will soon take on your body temperature, and you will have experienced cold only momentarily. The foam neoprene nitrogen bubbles blown into the suit when it was manufactured act as a dead air space, which prevents the cold water from conducting the heat from the body. Wet suits are popular with water skiers, surfers, and swimmers wherever the water is chilling.

The Dry Suit: The dry suit made of watertight thin rubber is designed for ice diving, but having no insulation itself, it should be worn over long underwear and socks or over a wet suit. A sweater or sweat shirt under the dry suit will suffice when water temperature is not less than 60° to 70° F. A duck-bill valve on a dry-suit hood allows excess air to escape during ascent, thereby reducing the tendency to rise too fast.

Disadvantages of the Dry Suit:
1. Tears or punctures can be a serious matter.
2. Although the suit is designed to be watertight, water can enter the sleeve and neck openings or tears and completely reduce the insulation, chilling the diver.
3. The admission of water can seriously affect buoyancy.
4. Trapped air in the dry suit could subject you to suit "squeeze" as you descend. There is no "squeeze" in a wet-suit hood.

Care and Maintenance: Give your suit a good freshwater rinse, dry it, and sprinkle it with talc or hydrous silicate of magnesia. Keep your suit clean. A skin rash called "diver's rash" can result from an unclean suit. Avoid heat and keep out of sun, turned inside out. To store, hang on a wooden hanger. Lubricate metal fittings with a silicone spray to keep corrosion-free.

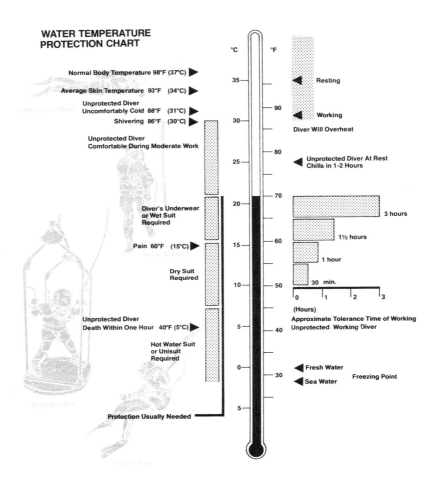

WATER TEMPERATURE PROTECTION CHART

Normal Body Temperature 98°F (37°C) ▶

Average Skin Temperature 93°F (34°C) ▶

Unprotected Diver
Uncomfortably Cold 88°F (31°C) ▶

Shivering 86°F (30°C) ▶

Unprotected Diver
Comfortable During Moderate Work

Diver's Underwear
or Wet Suit
Required

Pain 60°F (15°C) ▶

Dry Suit
Required

Unprotected Diver
Death Within One Hour 40°F (5°C) ▶

Hot Water Suit
or Unisuit
Required

Protection Usually Needed

°C   °F

35

90

30

80

25

70

20

60

15

50

10

5

40

0

30

5

◀ Resting

◀ Working

Diver Will Overheat

◀ Unprotected Diver At Rest
Chills in 1-2 Hours

3 hours

1½ hours

1 hour

30 min.

0   1   2   3

(Hours)

Approximate Tolerance Time of Working
Unprotected Working Diver

◀ Fresh Water

◀ Sea Water   Freezing Point

KNIFE

Purpose: The knife is an indispensable all-purpose tool. Some uses include freeing a fouled propeller, freeing oneself from entanglements of any kind, killing wounded fish, preparing game for cooking, and dislodging biological specimens.

How to Carry: It is best to buy a knife and sheath with straps to tie to your leg or to your tank harness in such a way that the knife

22

can be safely and quickly drawn in emergencies. Do not wear your knife on or in your weight belt.

Care and Maintenance: Rinse your knife thoroughly after using it. Unless it is rustproof, apply a thin coat of light oil after each use. Keep it sharp.

GLOVES

Purpose: Wear cotton or leather-palmed work gloves to prevent abrasions from fish spines, coral, and debris. The gloves should be dark-colored, as bright gloves may attract dangerous fish. Neoprene gloves, which prevent chilling, are recommended for cold water. They can be worn with or without an exposure suit.

3

UNDERWATER PHYSICS
REFRESHER

Physics is the science that deals with the properties of matter and
the way matter behaves under different conditions. To understand
compressed-air diving and its effects on the body and equipment, a
diver ought to understand the principles of physics as they relate to
diving.*

COMPOSITION OF AIR

The air we breathe (the same air we breathe in self-contained
compressed-air diving) is not a chemical combination but a simple
mixture of the following gases:

	Approximate Percentage by Volume
Nitrogen	78.09
Oxygen	20.95
Argon	0.93
Carbon Dioxide	0.03
Rare gases: neon, radon, hydrogen, helium, etc.	Traces

* Much of the material in this chapter is derived from material supplied through
the courtesy of the U.S. Navy.

For ease in calculating we will hereafter express the above figures in round numbers.

Gases for Breathing: The gases most important to the diver are the two main components of air—nitrogen and oxygen. Oxygen (O) alone is capable of supporting life, and it forms 21 percent of the atmosphere by volume. Nitrogen (N) is the other main component of air, comprising 78 percent of it by volume. In its free state nitrogen is inert and incapable of supporting life or pressure, but under a pressure of 4 atmospheres or more, nitrogen has a dangerously intoxicating effect (details of which are discussed later in this chapter and in Chapter 11).

There are two harmful gases with which you should be familiar. One is carbon dioxide (CO_2), colorless and odorless and tasteless except for a faint, pungent smell and a slightly acid taste. It becomes harmful if a large concentration of it builds up in the diver's breathing medium, though with open-circuit scuba (which you will be using) you will be unlikely to encounter problems.

The other harmful gas is carbon monoxide (CO), which is colorless, odorless, and tasteless but highly poisonous. Carbon monoxide is found in dangerous concentration in engine exhausts and during the filling procedure could contaminate a diver's air supply with serious results. (See Chapter 11.)

PRESSURE

Pressure is the amount of force per unit area. Force is any push or pull that tends to produce motion. Force is commonly expressed in pounds. Area is the surface upon which the force is executed, usually measured in square inches. Thus pressure is commonly measured in pounds per square inch (psi). In diving computations, pressure is often expressed directly in feet of seawater. It can also be expressed in atmospheres (atm) (see below).

TYPES OF PRESSURE

Atmospheric Pressure: Atmospheric pressure is the result of the weight of the earth's atmosphere producing a force in all directions on the surface of the earth. Almost all structures on earth are exposed to the same atmospheric pressure both inside and outside. Atmospheric pressure is so normal to us that we seldom notice its effects. However, if we remove the air from a container, the pressure as the container becomes a vacuum—about 14.7 psi—acting on its walls would crush it. (Remember the experiment in your high school physics class of the collapsing gasoline can?) In other words, the miles of air above one square inch of surface area at sea level weigh about 14.7 pounds. The term "atmosphere" is used to denote a pressure of 14.7 psi. For example, a pressure of 147.0 psi can be expressed as 10 atmospheres (10 atm) in diving.

Gauge Pressure: Gauge pressure indicates the difference between the pressure being measured and the surrounding atmospheric pressure. Gauge pressure equals depth in feet times .445 psi. It is that pressure alone; it does not include the atmospheric pressure present at the surface. The .445 psi is the weight of a column of seawater one inch square by one foot high; in other words, seawater pressure increases .445 psi for every foot of depth. The amount .445 psi equals about ½ psi or $1/33$ of 14.7 psi. Gauge pressure is measured in either pounds per square inch or atmospheres. It is registered by an instrument known as a pressure gauge (see pages 53–54). If pressure is doubled as it is at 33 feet, density of the gas doubles, as does its weight, and the volume of the gas is halved.

The gauge pressure at 33 feet is determined as in the following example: $.445 \times 33$ ft. $= 14.7$ psi $= 1$ atm of gauge pressure. Gauge pressure at 50 feet would then be 22.25 psi. At 70 feet, 31.2 psi.

Absolute Pressure: The absolute pressure of any depth is the pressure of the atmosphere above the sea, 14.7 psi, plus the increase of pressure with depth, which is 1 atm for every 33 feet. It is the true or total pressure being exerted on the diver. To obtain absolute pressure, multiply the depth in feet by .445 psi and add 14.7 psi (the atmospheric pressure). Example: $.445 \times 33$ ft. $+ 14.7$ psi (the gauge reading) $= 29.4$ psi, or 2 atm absolute pressure. Absolute pressure is commonly expressed as pounds per square inch absolute (psia). If the pressure is being expressed in atmospheres, one atmosphere is added to the number. Always use absolute pressure rather than gauge pressure in equations describing the behavior of gases.

Liquid Pressure: Liquid pressure is the pressure the diver is most directly concerned with. Liquid pressure is exerted by the surrounding water at diver depth. The pressure produced by water is the direct pressure transmitted equally in all directions and distributed evenly over all the area of any container regardless of its shape. The pressure at any level in a container is directly proportional to the depth at that level. We express the weight of water in terms of *density*. For example, the density of fresh water is 62.4 pounds per cubic foot. The density of average seawater is 64 pounds per cubic foot because of the added weight of salt. Water is practically incompressible, so its density remains virtually unchanged regardless of pressure applied to it. As a result, the pressure exerted by 20 feet of water will be twice that exerted by 10 feet, and so on. It takes 33 feet of water to get a pressure equal to the weight of the atmosphere in pounds per square inch. If a tank 33 feet deep is filled with seawater, the pressure on one square foot of surface area on the bottom will be equal to the weight of the column of water above it. You can think of this column as a stack of 33 1-foot cubes of water, each weighing 64 pounds. The total weight would itself be 33 ft. $\times$ 64 lbs., or 2112 lbs., acting on 1 square foot of surface area. Since there are 144 square inches in a square foot, the pressure on each square inch in this case would be 2112 divided by 144, which equals approximately 14.7 psi, or 1 atm of pressure. This is the pressure exerted by the water above. But then, as previously stated, the air above the water is exerting an additional 14.7 psi of pressure, so that the absolute total pressure at a depth of 33 feet is 29.4 psi, or 2 atm. Each additional 33 feet of depth will add 14.7 psi, or 1 atm of pressure. Each additional foot of depth will add $1/33$ of 14.7 psi, or .445 psi of pressure. To repeat: The depth in feet multiplied by .445 gives the water pressure at that depth in psi. Adding 14.7 to this gives the absolute pressure at that depth in psia. Example: (40 ft. $\times$ .445) + 14.7 = 32.5 psia.

BOYLE'S LAW

Boyle's Law states that if the temperature is kept constant the volume of a gas will vary inversely with the absolute pressure while the density varies directly. It is expressed in the equation $CV = C$. In easier language this means that, for example, if the pressure on a gas is doubled, the density too is doubled but the volume is decreased to one-half the original volume.

Vital to the diver, Boyle's Law defines the nature of compression exerted on air spaces by the pressure of depth and the relationship between pressure and the volume in the air spaces we carry below with us. It relates also the quantity of air in the cylinder with the depth and duration of dives. Let's explore some of the ways Boyle's Law affects your diving with self-contained compressed air.

You now know that in seawater each 33 feet (34 feet for fresh water) is equal to one additional atmosphere of pressure. For this reason, when we have completely filled our lungs with air at 33 feet, our lungs are holding twice as much air as when filled at surface. For each 33 feet additional in depth, the volume of air we need to fill our lungs is increased accordingly. At 66 feet, the water exerts additional pressure of 29.4 psi, so that the total pressure is 44.1 psia, or 3 atm, absolute, and our lungs will hold three times as much air as when filled at surface. The density is, therefore, actually three times greater than it was at the surface, but the volume is one-third less.

If you fill your lungs with air while at depth to the size they are normally on the surface, and then ascend, they will progressively expand. Rupture of membranes and capillaries results, permitting air to enter the bloodstream. On leaving 99 feet, fully inflated lungs will arrrive at the surface four times larger. You can understand how lung damage could be serious, even fatal, if you held your breath while surfacing. (See Air Embolism, pages 225–26.)

Warning: Always remember with great caution that the relative changes in pressures and volume are greater near the surface than at depth. For example, while a descent to 33 feet from the surface doubles the liquid pressure on any flexible container of gas such as your lungs, and reduces the volume of the gas by a half, the descent from 99 feet to 132 feet reduces the volume of a gas by only $1/5$. Although in each descent depth is increased by 1 atm for every 33 feet, the pressure and volume changes are progressively less the deeper you go. The nearer you are to the surface, the greater the danger of lung damage and air embolism.

Boyle's Law and Your Air Supply: For normal breathing, the volume of air needed by a diver at depth will be greater than at surface. Therefore, at 33 feet, where a diver's air is required at 2 atm of pressure, 1 cubic foot of air is equivalent to 2 cubic feet at the surface pressure of 1 atm. Proportionally greater requirements apply at greater depths. This means that the supply of air in the cylinder is reduced as the depth increases. To provide, for example, 1 cubic foot of air at 33 feet requires a mass of 2 cubic feet of atmospheric air, and a cylinder which would supply a diver with air for half an hour at the surface would last him only 15 minutes at a depth of 33 feet. For a diver breathing at a normal rate of 1 cubic foot per minute (cfm), a 71.2-cubic-foot cylinder would last 90 minutes at sea level but only 45 minutes at 33 feet (2 atm, absolute). The same 71.2-cubic-foot cylinder would last 30 minutes at 66 feet or $1/3$ as long; 22.5 minutes at 99 feet, or $1/4$ as long, and so on. The effect of Boyle's Law on the duration of your air supply is vitally important. Take special care to allow for this shortened duration of your air supply as you descend. Figure the allowance in the predive stage of your plans.

To find the volume of air needed at a given depth, use the following formula:

where:

$$P_1 V_1 = P_2 V_2$$

$P_1 = 1$ atm pressure at surface

$V_1 = $ vol. of compressed air, in cu. ft.

$$V_2 = \frac{P_1 V_1}{P_2}$$

$P_2 = $ pressure at a given depth in atm

$V_2 = $ vol. of air needed at a given depth

Problem: Remaining air time at 66 ft. (3 atm pressure) using one 72-cu.-ft. tankful which lasts 90 min. at surface?

$$V_2 = \frac{1 \times 72}{3} = 24 \text{ cu. ft.} \frac{24}{72} \times 90 = 30 \text{ minutes}$$

Answer: At 66 ft., one 72-cu.-ft. tankful supplies air for 30 minutes.
Note: Since temperature change is negligible, it is not considered in the formula.

Word of Caution: Formulas and arithmetic are only guides and cannot be relied on except hypothetically since all individuals and the circumstances of each dive are different. For example, one diver at a given depth and working hard may use up a full tank in half the time it would take another diver who is relaxed.

THE BREATH-HELD DIVE AND SQUEEZE

The air held in the lungs on a breath-held dive will undergo change. The pressure pushes the air outward against the inside wall of the chest at a force of 14.7 psi. As we swim down, the pressure against the outside of the chest is also increasing. The chest is hollow and contains gas so that with the increase in pressure there will be, according to Boyle's Law, a proportional increase in compression of the lungs until their own pressure has increased to equal the pressure that is being exerted on it. That is, as the pressure of water is added to the normal atmospheric pressure exerted against your chest, the air in the lungs in a breath-held dive will be squeezed into a proportionately smaller space. The muscles and bones of the chest wall are at first able to resist the extra pressure, preventing the chest from being squeezed inward. But if we could swim to an unlimited depth, we would soon reach a point at which the muscles and bones could no longer resist the extra pressure. The chest would collapse as if crushed in the vice-like grip of a giant hand. (See the various types of squeezes, pages 216–19.)

CHARLES'S, OR GAY-LUSSAC'S, LAW

Temperature affects the action of gases. Charles's Law (known also as Gay-Lussac's Law) states that at a constant pressure the volume of a gas will expand when heated. The volume increases when temperature increases. If the temperature is doubled, the volume will double. If the temperature is decreased, the volume will decrease. It follows that if volume rather than pressure is kept constant, as by heating air in a rigid container like a high-pressure cylinder, then the absolute pressure will increase in proportion to the absolute temperature.

A diver's cylinder of air exposed to the hot sun will increase in pressure approximately 5 psi for each degree Fahrenheit of temperature rise. Heat is produced as gases are compressed, and cylinders will heat when being charged with air. If a cylinder is not cool while being filled, the subsequent drop in built-up pressure when the cylinder cools will result in a partially filled tank. For obvious reasons therefore, a cylinder should be submersed in cold water when being filled and kept out of direct sunlight.

How Pressure Can Hurt—Squeeze: Normally, pressure itself and the mechanical compression of gases under pressure have very little effect on your body. However, when for some reason transmission and equalization of pressure do not occur owing to failure of your air supply or inability to clear your ears, destructive differences in pressure can develop. The consequences of failure to equalize occur mainly during descent and can be classified under the term "squeeze."

I previously stated how vital it is for you to notice that the relative changes in pressure and the relative changes in volume of any gas (according to Boyle's Law) are greatest near the surface. To repeat, a certain length of descent near the surface causes greater compression of gas than the same length of descent at greater depths. A diver who descends a given distance during a relatively shallow dive is therefore in a greater hazard with respect to squeeze than one who descends an equal number of feet during a deep dive. These same depth relationships apply to the ascent phase of a dive but not in connection with squeeze. Th reverse would be expansion or, more seriously, the overexpansion of gases. (See Air Embolism, pages 225–26.)

Squeeze can occur on a smaller scale when one of the body's air spaces, such as lungs, sinus, ears, or any cavity of air attached to the surface of the body—ordinary goggles or a face mask, for example—fails to equalize with the ambient pressure. In the latter case, you would suffer eye squeeze. Never wear goggles; there is no way by which the pressure on the inside can be equalized. Goggles contain air at normal pressure at surface, and no air is available to add for the purpose of equalizing during descent. As the pressure increases outside (ambient pressure), a difference in pressure develops between the inside and the outside of the goggles. Since the goggles are generally rigid, the difference will simply increase as the diver descends, and something will have to give. The external pressure is being transmitted freely throughout the body, so the diver's eyes and external tissues are not under the same pressure as the air with which they are in contact. The difference in air is acting across them much as if a suction cup were being applied. This may cause bleeding, rupture of vessels and membranes, and possibly more serious damage.

LUNG DAMAGE IN DIVING

The most serious damage the lungs can suffer in diving is from the expansion of air as a result of pressure reduction. If air is taken into the lungs and held in at a depth of 125 feet, it will increase five times in volume if carried quickly to the surface, where the external pressure is proportionately reduced to one-fifth. An ascent from lesser depths may cause serious consequences. The diver must be trained to curb the natural impulse to hold his breath under water. He must exhale continually during any rapid ascent.

The free diver using self-contained breathing equipment who gets into trouble may have to return to the surface as quickly as possible. Under such conditions inducive of panic, an untrained and inexperienced individual is sure to hold his breath to the last possible moment—with dire consequences.

Occasionally, even when the diver exhales as he ascends, he will suffer serious lung injury because a bronchial obstruction (such as a pneumolith) prevents rapid equalization of air pressure in some

localized portion of the lung. As the diver ascends, the intrapul-
monic pressure progressively distends the alveoli. If sufficient air
has not been exhaled, some alveoli will rupture.

DALTON'S LAW

Dalton's Law states that in a mixture of gases, each gas asserts a
partial pressure proportionate to the percentage it represents of the
total gases. This means that if air contains 21 percent oxygen, the oxygen exerts 21 percent of the total pressure by air. Or, since air contains 78 percent nitrogen, the nitrogen exerts 78 percent of the total
pressure exerted by air. (We are still using round figures.) In a mixture of gases the pressure of each component depends on its concentration in the mixture. On descent, increasing pressure will increase
the pressure of each component almost in the same proportion. To
determine partial pressure of any gas, multiply the percentage of
that one component gas by 14.7 psi.

Let's take as an example nitrogen, which constitutes approximately 80 percent of the air. $14.7 \times 80 = 11.76$ psi. Such is the partial pressure of nitrogen at surface. So at 2 atm the partial pressure
will be 23.52 psi. At 3 atm partial pressure will be tripled to 35.28
psi, etc. When calculating partial pressures, the absolute and not
the gauge pressure of the gas should be used.

HENRY'S LAW

If a gas is brought into contact with a fluid, for example, as the
air in the lungs is brought into contact with blood, some of the gas
will be absorbed by the fluid. Henry's Law deals with gas absorption
under pressure. Henry's Law states that the amount of gas which
will dissolve in a liquid (go into solution) at a given temperature is
directly proportional to the partial pressure of that gas. What this
means is that if the pressure on a gas is doubled, a liquid will absorb
twice as much of that gas. Conversely, the liberation of a gas from a

fluid will vary in porportion to the decrease of pressure. Dalton's and Henry's laws explain the causes of such pressure-induced illnesses as bends (decompression sickness), oxygen poisoning, CO_2 poisoning, and nitrogen narcosis. (See pages 222–27.)

Let's look at the physiochemical effects of pressure which form the basis of these laws. We now know that approximately four-fifths, or 80 percent, of the air we breath is nitrogen. Normally at surface pressure, nitrogen, being a neutral gas, has no effect on our bodies. At sea level we pass it off without incident. No chemical action occurs with nitrogen or the other inert gases making up air; however, when subjected to pressure we have another matter. As we go down deeper in water, we breathe multiples of nitrogen, and it is increasingly harder to bail out. At 33 feet, a diver is under twice the surface pressure. The partial pressure of all the components of air inhaled is doubled, and the body tissue, especially the fatty tissue, will absorb twice as much of them. Of these gases, only nitrogen goes into solution in the bloodstream slowly, although in its cycle on the surface, nitrogen is simply inhaled, circulated, and exhaled without combining with body tissue.

Now, if a diver whose body has been subjected to sufficient underwater pressures over a long period of time (expressed as depth-time ratios) is saturated with nitrogen and is suddenly (and here is the dangerous part) brought rapidly to the surface, the tension of the dissolved gas in his body will be lighter than the total pressure surrounding him. With the reduced pressure of the water as he ascends and therefore the lowering of the air pressure from the regulator, the blood in contact with the air introduced by his lungs is unable to hold as much nitrogen in solution as it did at the higher pressure. The gas would be in a supersaturated solution, and some of the excess nitrogen would literally boil out of solution in the form of bubbles throughout the circulatory system, muscles, and joints, causing great pain and blocking the arteries. This condition is known as the bends, that most dreaded of all diving illnesses, with its crippling, perhaps fatal, results. The amateur diver should stay within the limits of depth-time ratios which don't form a basis for the bends. (See pages 109–10.)

However, there is a preventive known as stage decompression

for amateurs who wish to conclude long, deep dives safely and sanely. Stage decompression is a way of "uncorking" slowly in stages, taking stops prescribed at certain depths and for set times in order to permit the body to purge the nitrogen overload naturally.

To understand the principle of decompression, nitrogen saturation, and its subsequent elimination, think about a bottle of champagne. When the champagne is being made and bottled, carbon dioxide gas is dissolved in the liquid at high pressure. The liquid is then sealed in its bottle so that none of the carbon dioxide can escape. The gas in the small space between the liquid and the cork in the bottle is at a very high pressure. When you uncork the bottle, the high pressure on the liquid instantly drops with a "pop" to the 14.7 psi of our atmosphere. At this lower pressure, the liquid can no longer hold the carbon dioxide gas in solution. The excess pressure of the dissolved gas is freed with a rush in the form of bubbles fizzing upward and escaping into the air. When pondering this analogy, think of yourself as the bottle, the champagne as your blood. The water over your head is the cork, the weight of the water is the pressure space between the cork and the champagne. So long as the "cork" remains on and the total pressure under it matches the tension of the dissolved gas—no problem. With the removal of the water above by your ascent, the pressure instantly drops, and the excess pressure of dissolved gas is released freely in bubble form throughout your bloodstream. The removal of pressure by rapid ascent (the suddenly removed cork) releases the gas, in this case nitrogen, which bubbles painfully in the blood, blocking the circulatory system. The painful condition that results is known, as we have already stated, as decompression sickness or the bends, so called because early sufferers of the condition were observed to double up, to bend over, in their agony.

We spoke of sudden release or uncorking (coming up too quickly, causing a rush of bubbles). Now, if the pressure in the champagne bottle is released very slowly, the excess gas will diffuse itself out of the liquid so gradually that no (or almost no) bubbles will form. By analogy, a diver can be brought up safely from depths if in his ascent he manages to "uncork," or decompress, in steps or stages so that the nitrogen can come out of the solution slowly and harmlessly.

Fortunately our blood and tissues can hold gas in a subsaturated solution to some extent without the serious formation of bubbles when we rise. This factor permits diving and ascent without harm. It has been discovered that blood and tissues can hold gas at a partial pressure equal to twice the total exterior pressure. Example: The diver saturated at 33 feet can return directly to the surface without serious nitrogen bubble formation because the pressure is reduced by only half. A diver saturated at 100 feet can ascend to 33 feet (½ the pressure) without bubbles forming. However, the diver must stop at 33 feet and decompress until his blood and tissues are sufficiently desaturated before he can ascend another step. This process is called "step" or "stage" decompression. The U.S. Navy decompression tables show the decompression stops necessary for various depths and duration of dives. Full instructions accompany the tables. But I state now, and I will repeat it throughout this book: *Avoid dives to depths or for durations such that the combination of both factors forces you to resort to these tables.* If, however, you have passed the allowable limits, you will have to know the instructions, and follow them carefully. There is no margin for error. Maintain a rate of ascent of 60 feet per minute. A slower ascent is unwise, for it permits additional absorption of nitrogen into body tissue. A faster ascent causes too rapid an expansion of gas in the system, resulting in air embolism and the bends. A rule of thumb is to stay behind your smallest bubbles in the water. To play it safe, stop the ascent at about 10 feet from the surface for a few minutes if possible, breathing normally before surfacing.

Another effect of nitrogen is nitrogen narcosis, or rapture of the deep, a state of euphoria resembling alcoholic intoxication and occurring at depths beyond 130 feet. Its effect is unfelt before reaching 100 feet, but for every 50 feet of depth thereafter the increased partial pressure of nitrogen will give about the same effect as one dry martini on an empty stomach. The sensations vary with the individual, and the effect is govered by what divers call "Martini's Law." For example: 99 ft. = 1 martini; 132 ft. = 1½ martinis; 165 ft. = 3½ martinis, and so forth. At 10 atm (330 ft.) a diver would become totally helpless on pure air. The effects of nitrogen narcosis vanish as soon as the diver ascends to a safer-pressure level.

AIR AND PRESSURE

Water is practically incompressible. Air *is* compressible. The human body is not compressible, because it is composed mainly of liquid. Only the air cavities therein are compressible. Think of yourself as a mass of water sealed in a flexible man-shaped rubber bag. We have a problem with water pressure not because of our "too too solid flesh" but because of the air we carry within. The body transmits the external pressure freely, and at every point the pressure outside would be almost exactly balanced by an equal pressure inside the body. If no difference of pressure existed in any part of the body, there would be no mechanical effect or damage. But the human body is more complicated than a simple bag of incompressible water because it contains cavities of air spaces such as lung, sinuses, and the middle ear, on which water pressure has an effect of singular importance to divers. If the pressure exerted on these spaces is balanced by air of equal pressure inside (we call it "equalization" or "equalizing"), the net result is practically the same—no damage. At sea level we are in a perfect state of equilibrium with the atmosphere. This is called "equalization of pressure"; at depths, we cannot enjoy this perfect state unless we obtain air from some source with which to equalize the water pressure bearing in on us. The wellspring of air that accomplishes equalization is supplied at the proper pressure by your air-breathing apparatus. Thanks to the regulator, you can maintain your normal lung volume by continuous regular breathing. The air pressure will thereby remain exactly equal to the surrounding (ambient) water pressure whatever it is, whatever your depth. Thus if you go down to 33 feet, where the absolute pressure is about 29.4 psia or 2 atm, an equal amount of air pumped into your lungs by way of the regulator will create a pressure to equalize the surrounding pressure.

Air pressure in the lungs is transmitted to other air spaces in the body, and with continuous normal breathing this air pressure maintains pressure equalization, preventing squeeze in these other air spaces. When we fail to maintain an equilibrium of our air with the surrounding water, certain symptoms of "squeeze" will appear.

With the knowledge you should now possess about diving we can go on to show you how the self-contained air-breathing apparatus is built to make diving a safe, pleasant, and useful experience—provided the apparatus is properly employed and well maintained.

THE LUNGS AND AIR CONSUMPTION

With each breath, we inhale about a pint of air. Resting lungs hold six pints. When hungry for oxygen as a result of exercise, lungs will take in ten or more times the oxygen supplied during rests. The lungs are not simply inflatable bladders; they are complex structures and look something like a cross section of a bath sponge when dissected. Each lung has its own duct from the windpipe. Each duct enters near the top and branches like a tree. The branches are called bronchial tubes. The job of the bronchial tubes is to deliver air to the functioning part of the lung, that is, to 750 million microscopic air sacs called "alveoli." Each alveolus has a covering of capillaries so tiny that red blood cells must pass through them single file. Through their walls the blood gives up waste carbon dioxide and takes new oxygen. Every few minutes the entire blood supply of the body passes through these capillaries. It enters one side a blue-black, and when it leaves the other it is a bright red. The work of the lungs must proceed without interruption.

The Breathing Process: The lungs hang loosely in the chest, each in a separate compartment surrounded by a partial vacuum. When the chest is expanded the vacuum pulls the lungs outward, thus sucking in air. Expansion of the chest is activated by one or both of two methods: The diaphragm, a muscular tissue located between the chest and the abdomen, may drop downward and bring about the expansion; or the ribs hinged to the spine may swing outward.

Expiration is simply a recoil mechanism. Lack of oxygen stimulates respiration, but carbon dioxide is the main chemical regulator of respiration.

Normally we breathe between 12 and 18 times a minute. Energy renews itself by each exhalation of breath. While you are diving under exerting conditions, your power will be enhanced so long as you concentrate on the slow expulsion of air from your lungs. The management and husbanding of breath will be of as much practical value to the diver as it is to a track man or opera singer, to whom breathing is everything. Be conscious of breathing at all times. Practice walking with your shoulders back, shoulder blades as close together as possible without straining. Make a consistent effort to enlarge your vital capacity by prolonging your outbreathing. Deep-breathing exercises, letting out air slowly, will pay off in longer dives that use fewer cubic feet of air per minute.

4

OPEN-CIRCUIT SCUBA EXPLAINED

Three basic conditions are necessary to enable a person to swim underwater for an extended time, move about freely, and make a safe round trip to the surface:

1. he must be in a state of hydrostatic balance, i.e., weightlessness;
2. he must be able to equalize pressure;
3. he must have an air supply.

The equipment designed to provide the air supply and to enable the diver to equalize pressure is the self-contained open-circuit (or demand-type) underwater breathing apparatus that we shall discuss in this chapter.

The term "self-contained" means that the diver carries his breathing medium with him in one or more cylinders and thus is not dependent on air supplied from the surface. The self-contained unit you will use is the open-circuit, or demand, type normally charged with compressed air—for you, *only* compressed air. A special type of regulator supplies your air on demand when you inhale. When you exhale, air is discharged into the water. There is no rebreathing of the same air. The duration of the air supply in this system is limited according to your inhalation requirements and the capacity of your cylinders.

Only an open-circuit (demand-type) self-contained underwater breathing apparatus is recommended for sport divers. No other. Let it be clearly understood that this book is based upon the use of air as the breathing medium in diving. The breathing apparatus referred to consists of a tank to carry the air, a regulator to dispense it, hoses and a mouthpiece to carry it to your lungs, and a backpack in which to carry the apparatus.

TANKS*

The fuel we use for keeping us alive below is air, compressed into tanks, then strapped onto our backs and carried down. Tanks are of rugged steel construction built to withstand high internal pressures. A galvanized steel tank is adequate for amateur diving. Usually a tank sinks slowly when full and floats when empty.

The 71.2-cubic-foot tank is at present the most popular tank. Its capacity can give a diver about 45 minutes of sport diving at an easy pace at 33 feet of depth. *Caution:* Under difficult conditions an increased breathing rate due to exertion will exhaust your air supply sooner.

Twin or Triple Tanks: Users of a twin- or triple-tank combination with capacities of 80 cubic feet or more must be especially alert to depth-time ratios. These higher capacities of combined tanks permit dive durations that can lead to decompression problems because these higher capacities are a temptation to remain below for prolonged durations. The heaviness of twin- or triple-tank blocks makes them impractical for women and children. Twins and triples are not advisable unless you are an advanced amateur or professional.

---

*Also known as bottles, flasks, scuba tanks, cylinders, and high-pressure cylinders.

How the Compressed-air Self-contained Breathing Apparatus Works: The air in the cylinder is stored under very high pressure. As the breathing cycle starts, the regulator admits air from the cylinder and automatically reduces its pressure to equal the pressure of the surrounding water. The air flows from the tank through the hose into your mouth and lungs, where the oxygen content of the air goes into solution in the bloodstream and carbon dioxide comes out of solution. As you exhale, the carbon dioxide is exhaled into the water. Water pressure varies with depth as you go down or up, but the demand regulator automatically adjusts and equalizes the pressure of air being breathed. The result is that perfect equilibrium is maintained between the surrounding water pressure, the breathing apparatus, air spaces, and body tissue so long as you breathe normally. You should descend at a maximum rate of 75 feet per minute to avoid squeeze.

As you ascend from the depths the ambient pressure (surrounding water pressure) decreases so that the air in your lungs expands and if not exhaled will overinflate your lungs. Because your lungs are delicate, this unnatural ballooning can cause serious injury, even death, by rupture. However, there is a simple way to avoid lung overinflation: Breathe at a normal rate.

Ascend no faster than 60 feet per minute in order to permit absorption of nitrogen into the system. A faster ascent invites a too rapid expansion of gas in the body. The new air you breathe from the tank as you rise will be supplied at less pressure by the regulator. You will, therefore, arrive at the surface with air of normal pressure in your lungs. *Never hold your breath and never rise faster than your smallest bubbles.*

HARNESS OR BACKPACK

The tank harness or backpack should have operable quick-release buckles and should fit snugly with adjustable straps holding your tank in its proper place at all times in the water. After all dives, rinse the harness in fresh water and keep it dry.

REGULATORS

Used with the tank is a regulator assembly consisting of a yoke for attaching the assembly to the tank, the automatic demand regulator, single or double hoses, and a mouthpiece. When the regulator assembly is attached to the tank block and the tank valve is opened, your breathing apparatus is ready for use as soon as you place the mouthpiece into your mouth and breathe. The regulator will deliver air regardless of the position of your body.

Selection: There is a wide selection of regulators from a number of manufacturers. Your preference is a personal one. There is the two-stage regulator in which the high-pressure air from the cylinder is reduced to a lower pressure before contact with the diaphragm. The purpose is to provide a constant pressure against the mechanism of the demand valve regardless of varying pressures in the cylinder.

The single-stage unit eliminates the high-pressure reduction valve and consequently can be produced for a lower cost. In the single-stage unit high cylinder pressures are reduced for breathing by action of the demand regulator. It gives a dependable performance. Single or two-hosed units are two-staged with the high-pressure reduction taking place in a valve in the cylinder. From this valve, air is conducted through a single hose to a demand regulator attached directly to the mouthpiece. Water cannot enter this type of air hose because the pressure remains in the cylinder and the necessity of an exhalation hose is eliminated by attaching the regulator and exhaust valve directly to the mouthpiece.

How to Place the Regulator Valve on the Cylinder: The yoke fits over the valve. Before opening the cylinder valve, make sure the yoke fits snugly and the reserve lever is up. Beware of a leaking O-ring. Improper placement of the regulator may be the cause of the leakage. Carry spare O-rings to replace those worn. Your dive shop should supply them.

How to Remove the Regulator from the Cylinder: Turn off the cylinder valve and breathe the air remaining in the regulator. Then loosen the yoke screw and remove the regulator.

How to Wear the Regulator: Wear the regulator level with the shoulders so that the mouthpiece demand and exhaust valves are at the same pressure level for comfortable breathing. If the regulator box is placed lower with two-hose equipment, air will overflow; if it is placed higher, breathing will be harder and you will constantly hit the regulator with the back of your head.

Maintenance and Servicing: Always wash your regulator with fresh water after each dive. When rinsing it, do not permit water to enter the high-pressure air-intake opening. Press your thumb over it to use the dust cap supplied with the regulator. Run fresh water into the mouthpiece and blow it out to rinse the exhaust tube and exhaust valve. Occasionally detach the intake tube and flush it out. Rinse the cylinder and valve after each use. If water repeatedly enters the breathing tubes during normal operation, there may be a leak in the tube's exhaust valve or in the regulator diaphragm. To test, install the regulator on the cylinder, leaving the valve shut. Inhale deeply from the mouthpiece. There should be no air. If any air seeps in, you have a leak. Holes in the hoses usually occur near the clamp at the regulatory housing. These holes are usually caused by bumps and careless handling of the regulator. Leaks are also caused by punctures or an unseated diaphragm when assembling the regulator. Never dismantle your regulator unless you are trained to do so. Keep a manual on the maintenance of your regulator. Never leave your equipment out in direct sunlight.

Breathing Hoses: Breathing hoses should be so fitted as to permit normal movement of your head. A good rig has a nonreturn valve in the mouthpiece to prevent water from spilling into the inhalation hose. The hoses are made of rubber and deteriorate from normal exposure. Replace them when they are still fairly good. Don't wait for an accident.

Clearing a Two-hose Regulator: Take a breath and hold it. Free the mouthpiece and raise it above the regulator. The air will then flow freely. Next, turn the mouthpiece downward to prevent free flow and return it to the mouth. Blow and resume breathing.

Another way to clean a two-hose regulator is to turn the upper half of your body left (exhaust hose) side downward, allowing water to gravitate into the exhalation hose (the left side), where it will be forced out by your exhaled air.

Final method: If the mouthpiece floods along with the area behind the diaphragm, turn your left side downward, seal the mouthpiece tightly, and milk the exhaustion hose. Inhale cautiously. If you cannot hold your breath, roll over on your back. Air will then come through the intake without water. Repeat the procedure of milking the exhalation hose until the water is cleared out.

Clearing the Single-hose Equipped with a Purging Button: Take a breath, remove the mouthpiece, and push the purging button for free flow of air. There is no free flow with a single-hose mouthpiece except when the button is pushed. Release the mouthpiece and exhale; then resume breathing.

Switching from Scuba Mouthpiece to Snorkel: Switch only when surfaced. Before you switch, take a last breath from the apparatus, then remove the mouthpiece. Be sure your snorkel is placed properly in the headband for the mask. Lift your head out of the water. Place the snorkel in your mouth and clear by exhaling. To return to the breathing apparatus, trade mouthpieces, again clear the hose with a good blow, and resume normal breathing.

OCTOPUS RIG (for Buddy Breathing)

The octopus regulator has revolutionized buddy breathing, although techniques on that subject remain a controversial issue. Instead of two divers exchanging one mouthpiece between them to share one air supply, there are two second stages. Physically, the octopus rig can be used in emergency situations in all kinds of diving with scuba. All divers should be trained in its operation.

RESERVE VALVES

When your air supply is nearly finished, the reserve valve furnishes the warning that it's time to ascend.

The Automatic Reserve Valve: This valve permits you to rise from any depth with enough air to reach the surface, but it will not allow you to go deeper. Its purpose is *not* to prolong bottom time. With this valve built into some regulators, an audible reserve device is actuated when your tank pressure drops to 300 psi. Each time you inhale, a noise is produced loud enough to warn you that you are on reserve. Being an expert is no excuse for not wearing a reserve mechanism. Beginners must watch out for dealers who are not familiar enough with equipment to know what an automatic reserve valve is and to see that the tank they get has one.

The Constant Preset Air J-Reserve Valve: "Preset" refers to the spring that is preset at 300 psi on single tanks and 500 psi on twin tanks. You must manually pull the lever in the "up" position. Keep it up when storing the cylinder except when refilling with air. Keep it up while diving, or you risk breathing out all your air without the benefit of the warning for which the J-valve was designed. When you have breathed down to 300 psi of your air supply, a spring valve gradually shuts off the air flow. You will then sense some restriction in your ability to breathe normally. This restriction is your signal or warning that it is time to surface. Pull down the rod to release the valve and reopen the flow of the remaining air. This reserve air will give you enough time to surface safely or even to descend before starting to the surface, but not enough to decompress by stage stops under water should you have made a dive or repetitive dives requiring decompression. *Caution:* The pressure at which this warning takes place is internal cylinder pressure and not the surrounding pressure. Therefore, for example, at a 100-foot depth, about 50-psi water pressure, a 300-psi tank reserve would be only 250 psi more than the water pressure. In your dive plan you should take this arithmetic into account. *Another warning:* Do not depend exclusively on your reserve system to call your attention to your low air supply. Be the kind of safe diver who can predict by his own deductions just when his air will be nearly exhausted.

The K-Valve: The K-valve is not a reserve valve but operates on the residual-air-expansion principle. Tanks featuring this valve are not to be used for dives exceeding 25 feet.

Warning: When using a twin-tank block, an air reserve in one tank contains reserve air in that tank only. The other tank will be nearly empty before you experience breathing difficulty and the need to release the air reserve. When the reserve air is released it will equalize into the two cylinders at half the pressure held in reserve by the reserve valve. At greater depths your supply may be but a few pounds more than the water pressure.

USEFUL TIPS FOR ANNUAL REGULATOR MAINTENANCE

Your regulator should be tested mechanically once a year by a professional repair technician for inhalation resistance, exhalation resistance, and correct intermediate pressure setting. The regulator should work smoothly under stressful conditions under water when breathing may be four times heavier than normal. The airflow from the regulator is directly linked with inhalation effort required to produce the airflow. If the effort required is too great, you will have to work very hard to obtain the air you desperately need. You, therefore, compound the problem of exhaustion with even more fatigue trying to breathe enough to survive.

Here are some of the common causes of poor performance:

1. Salt water corrosion causing regulator to operate sluggishly resulting in increased inhalation resistance.
2. Clogging of the filter on the first stage of the regulator as a result of rust from a tank loaded with internal corrosion. Rust particles also can coat the internal moving parts of the regulator causing sluggish operation.
3. Clogging from ultra-fine dust, which is the consequence of a defective air compressor. This condition is often a result of a slow buildup and can go unnoticed for a prolonged period.
4. A rubber exhalation valve in the second stage can become gummed up with deterioration causing an increase in exhalation resistance and eventually a leakage of water.
5. Dust and dirt can cause first-stage pressure leaks by damaging the high-pressure valve and valve seat.
6. Salt and other foreign materials can corrode the internal O-ring pressure seals resulting in first- or second-stage air pressure leaks.

SAFETY RULES FOR THE USE OF COMPRESSED-AIR CYLINDERS

1. Be careful not to drop cylinders; nicks and scratches can result that will weaken the structure and be a potential source of a violent explosion.
2. Never use a lighting magnet or sling when handling cylinders.
3. Securely close valves before removing, storing, or returning cylinders.
4. Be sure that all cylinders used are approved under Interstate Commerce Commission or Department of Transportation regulations. This means that they should be tested every 5 years.
5. Never use cylinders for rollers, supports, or any purpose other than to carry compressed air.
6. Never drill or enlarge openings.

7. Never weld anything to a cylinder.

8. Do not tamper with the safety devices or valves on cylinders.

9. Never hammer or strike a valve wheel in attempting to open or close valves.

10. Use only wrenches or tools provided and approved for opening or closing valves.

11. Never force connections which do not fit.

12. Do not subject compressed-air cylinders either in storage or service to a temperature in excess of 130°F.

13. Never use oil or grease on any high-pressure fittings. Fumes can cause illness. Use only Dow-Corning silicone lubricant as recommended by the manufacturer.

14. Do not work on any cylinder valve or fitting while it is under pressure.

15. Never place an empty cylinder in water with the valve open or water will flow in, resulting in corrosion, which may weaken the structure.

16. Inspect cylinder harnesses or backpacks to see that all rivets and sewn fittings are secured.

17. The cylinder pressure should never exceed the maximum rated pressure stamped on the tank.

18. High-pressure air cylinders must be filled slowly, preferably while submerged in cold water to prevent overheating.

19. Do not use any cylinder that is improperly marked.

20. All filling tubes, hoses, and fittings must be made for the purpose of filling. Do not use standard fittings or hoses for filling.

21. When filling a cylinder with a reserve valve, pull the lever down to open the reserve-valve mechanism. Pull the lever up before dive.

22. Fill the cylinder until the pressure gauge registers the proper reading.

23. Never fill compressed-air cylinders with any gas or with any mixture of gases other than air.

24. Never leave a cylinder totally empty. Always leave about 50-psi pressure in it and seal the tank valve with masking tape to prevent dirt from entering the tank.

25. Before reusing a cylinder, flush it out with pure air.

Testing Cylinders: All cylinders should be sent to a tank-testing firm for a safety pressure test 5 years after the test date stamped on the tank or when the tank has been scratched, dented, or scored badly enough to warrant an emergency inspection.

A hydrostatic test every 5 years is adequate, provided your tank is given frequent visual internal inspections. Where heavy use and high humidity warrant it, one or two inspections should be made every year. The key to frequency of inspection is moisutre.

Repairing Cylinders: Don't tamper with damaged cylinders or attempt repairs unless you are properly equipped with the required special tools and training.

How to Store Cylinders: Store cylinders in a standing position blocked or tied to prevent their falling or being tipped over. You can buy a hard-rubber cylinder boot, which will keep the cylinder stable. To protect against moisture, condensation, or absorption keep at least 50-psi pressure in the tank at all times. Inspect the insides with a flashlight once a year and look for rust, pits, water vapor, oil deposits, or corrosion.

Transporting Cylinders in an Automobile or Boat: Cylinders in either automobile trunks or station wagons should lie horizontally, with the valve pointing to the rear of the car. They should be tied securely and blocked to prevent shifting and perhaps exploding. Cylinders in transport on a boat should be tied and blocked, especially in rough seas.

RECHARGING CYLINDERS WITH AIR

1. If the date stamped on a cylinder shows it to be more than five years old, have it tested before filling it.

2. A tank should never be charged with any air except that which can and should be certified free of noxious gases and oil par-

ticles. Use compressed air only—no pure gas. The supplier should be told that the air is for breathing purposes and must be filtered, but remember that filtering will not remove carbon monoxide or carbon dioxide. (See pages 222–23.)

3. If the purity of the air supply is suspect, have it analyzed at a local laboratory recommended by a hospital. Oil or oil fumes might have leaked into the compression cylinders used to refill your tank. At surface the small quantity of carbon monoxide may be harmless, but at depth the partial pressure may build up to harmful proportions and become toxic.* The person supplying the air should make sure the air intake is upwind of the exhaust fumes from the compressor engines when a gas-driven compressor is used. Pure air should be odorless and taste like a cool breeze.

Pure breathing air for diving is defined as air that meets the following specifications:

Minimum oxygen—atmospheric air
Maximum carbon monoxide—10 parts per million
Maximum carbon dioxide—300 quarts per million
Absence of odors and vapors
Freedom from oil and impurities by passing 5 meters of air through a #40 Whatman filter.

Consequences of Using Impure Air:
CO_2 will cause a toxic state.
CO can cause fatal poisoning.
An oil deposit or even a smell of oil can cause a marked lung irritation and death.
Dirt will jam valves.

---

* Dalton's Law of Partial Pressures states that the total pressure exerted by a mixture of gases is the sum of the pressures that would be exerted by each of the gases if it alone were present and occupied the total volume.

ASSEMBLING BREATHING APPARATUS FOR DIVES

Attach the backpack to the tank and lock it on.

Inspect all equipment for wear or damage.

Seal off the air intake on the regulator with your thumb or dust cap and inhale through the mouthpiece. If air comes through, you have a leak in the intake hose or where the diaphragm sits on the regulator box.

Exhale through the mouthpiece to free sticky one-way valves.

Before attaching the regulator to the tank, open the tank valves slightly to blow foreign matter out of the valve orifice.

Check the tank pressure with a pressure gauge and plan your diving time accordingly.

Inspect the regulator and intake filter for corrosion.

Place the regulator on the tank valve and tighten the butterfly bolt gently—not too forcibly.

Open the tank valve all the way counterclockwise but gently. When it is open, give it a half-turn clockwise.

Apply the mouthpiece and breathe a few trial breaths.

Turn off the tank valve; don your gear, and tip your head back as far as possible without touching the regulator.

Turn on the tank valve and breathe.

Don your weight belt. Actually, the weight belt can be donned at any time since the new type of backpack has no crotch piece to interfere with emergency release of the belt.

Be certain that the reserve J-valve rod is functioning and in the "up" position before you enter the water.

How to Disassemble:

Take off the harness and gear.

Turn off the tank valve.

Inhale the last breath out of the regulator.

Remove the regulator from the tank. If the butterfly bolt seems jammed, you haven't taken that last breath out of the regulator.

Wipe the regulator dust cap and air inlet to dry them and replace the neoprene dust cap.

Rinse all equipment in fresh water.

Put your gear away neatly wrapped, with no parts left hanging loose.

Tape the high-pressure valve of your tank to keep dirt out of the valve opening while the tank is stored.

PRESSURE GAUGE

Purpose: The pressure gauge is a separate attachment that registers the amount of your tank air supply. To know the amount of air you have in a tank is to know how much time you can spend submerged. A pressure gauge is especially useful if you plan a second dive with the same tank you use in your first dive. Always check your supply prior to any dive. To get a reading of your air supply, clamp a detachable pressure gauge on your tank valve, turn on the air, and take a reading as the gauge registers the air supply in psi. Pressure gauges meant for use out of water should not, under any circumstances, be adapted for use under water.

The submersible pressure gauge (SPG) gives you a visual picture of the amount of air you have in your tank at surface (to see if your tank is full) and at depth during your entire dive. It tells you your air consumption throughout the dive and when to end your dive.

An SPG also tells the diver when and where to turn back on long excursions. If a diver starts his dive with 2200 psi and swims straight out from the beach or boat, he knows that he will have to begin the return swim when the pressure is down to 1200 psi. For cave diving, use ⅓ total pressure going in to the cave, ⅓ total pressure for coming out of the cave, and ⅓ pressure for safety backup.

All single-hose regulators have a high-pressure port for installing the SPG. Never turn on the SPG while looking at it; hold it at arm's length in case of blowout.

The SPG is attached to the cylinder valve and gives you a reading in 500 psi increments. To arrive at the approximate amount of cubic feet left in a tank, multiply the pressure (in psi) by .032. Example: 1000-psi pressure .032 = 32 cubic feet of air left. This calculation is valuable to you especially if you know your depth. If, for example, you are at 33 feet, working hard, having descended with a full 71.2-cubic-foot tank, and your gauge reads 800-psi pressure, multiplication of that figure by .032 will give the result of 25.6 cubic feet of air remaining. This should tell you that you have already used up two-thirds of your supply because of hard work. If you have been down for twenty minutes, this calculation will tell you also that in another ten minutes at the same rate of work, you will be out of air. You can rely on your gauge without the necessity of calculations.

Care and Maintenance: Rinse in fresh water after diving. Be careful not to permit water to enter the high-pressure hose, otherwise contaminants could get into the gauge and tank regulator. Store gear so that the hose is not crimped. Use a rubber cover to protect against banging against objects, coral, or when on board boats. While diving, tuck it securely under a harness strap. If water is visible inside the gauge, then water is probably leaking from the housing, the plastic lens may be cracked, or the O-ring seal is bad. Leaks also occur at the swivel juncture. Remember, the SPG is vulnerable to inaccuracy if water gets in.

After a dive, remove the rubber cover. Soak guage in fresh water, removing salt deposits. Store in cool dry place. Leave rubber covering off until dry. Spray a little silicone over plugs. Let dive store examine at least once annually.

DEPTH GAUGE

Purpose: Especially in deep dives (beyond 33 feet), the depth gauge is useful as an indicator of your exact depth so that you can accurately determine the possible need for decompression according to your depth-time ratio. (See Chapter 6.) It is also an aid in determining the duration of your remaining air supply while submerged.

Put another way, it is used for both planning underwater air consumption and limiting bottom time. Depth-gauge accuracy is crucial as your life depends on it. *Warning:* Increased depth scale raises the possibility of inaccuracy.

Selection: You have a choice of three types: the capillary, the bourdon, and the liquid or gas-filled. The capillary is the simplest and cheapest and quite reliable to about 35 feet. The bourdon type reads well down to 200 feet. The liquid or gas-filled type is the best, but most expensive. The gauge should be built to withstand pressure and to be worn on the wrist and should be so designed that the figures can be clearly read at depth. Of the two general types, the manometer type is reliable for depths up to 50 feet, but the diaphragm type is the best and truest gauge.

Care and Maintenance: Be sure to soak the gauge in fresh water overnight after salt-water dives. Handle the gauge gently or decalibration can result. To determine whether there is a need for recalibration, submerge the gauge to a known depth. Have it checked by dive store ever 6 months or after rough use.

UNDERWATER WATCH

Purpose: The purpose of an underwater timepiece is to keep an accurate computation of your dive time to avoid decompression in the event you plan repetitive dives or deep dives with which decompression problems are likely to arise. (See Chapter 6.) An underwater watch is also used for timing a safe rate of descent and ascent and calculating time-distance rate of swim speeds in connection with submarine navigating.

How to Tell Distance with a Watch: Use the following formula: Speed × Time = Distance. Swim a prescribed course of known distance. Time yourself with the second hand of your watch at your average cruising speed. Divide the distance by the number of seconds it took you to cover it. By this method you will derive your velocity in feet per seconds. Example: Your speed is 3 feet per second or 180 feet per minute. In ten minutes you will have covered 1800 feet. Let's say the distance between buoy A and buoy B is 3600 feet. You are at buoy A; you wish to swim to buoy B. You ought to be able to cover the distance in a well-oriented 20 minutes.

Care and Maintenance: Give your watch a thorough postdive freshwater rinse. Keep it dry and treat it as gently as any fine watch.

Note: If you are swimming at an angle to a crosscurrent, you will soon sense yourself carried downcurrent of your objective. Remember to compensate for this downstream drift by crabbing into the current so that your course is aimed sufficiently upstream of the objective. Make allowances for loss of time created by the crosscurrent and correction. Such is standard navigation practice used by aviators flying through crosswinds and mariners of surface craft crossing known currents.

THE COMPASS AND UNDERWATER NAVIGATION

The problems of navigating under water entail ability to maintain an accurate course, to return to your point of departure, to define the direction of the surface, and to know at all times your approximate depth.

When going down, always follow the golden rule of arriving at the bottom with a fixed reference point established clearly in your mind, be it boat, shore, or some distinct physical feature on the seabed. Just as the airman must often rely on his eyes to identify his position, so it is with the diver. Pick out conspicuous checkpoints and remember them as references in order to establish and maintain your position with respect to your destination and return home.

If while under water you are uncertain of the direction of the surface, watch bubbles: They go *up* only. Look for increased pressure on ears and mask: It means you are going down. Or pick up a nonbuoyant object or nonbuoyant piece of your equipment and let it go momentarily from one hand to the other. As gravity pulls the object, you will see which way is down.

Purpose: Directional orientation begins at the surface and continues throughout your dive. Underwater direction-finding and orientation by means of a compass reduce the chance of getting lost—

especially in prolonged dives. Be aware of time, place, and distance at all times. You are your own navigator. A diver lost is a diver who can panic. A compass is a *must* in ice diving, murky-water diving, searching, exploring, or diving near heavy boat and ship traffic.

Selection: Be sure that the directional numbers of your compass are large and clearly printed. It should be liquid-filled to withstand pressure.

How It Works: Wear the compass on your wrist. The compass needle points to the *magnetic north*. The geographic north is shown on National Ocean Survey charts. Make the necessary adjustment by first checking the compass rose (the two calibrated concentric circles printed at convenient intervals on the chart). The star on the top points to the geographic north. The arrow extending from the inner circle points to the magnetic north for the area charted. In the center of the compass rose is a small cross and a statement of the compass variation; for example, variation 15°3′.

How to Use: Hold the compass so that its center line (the lubber's line) is lying in the same direction your body is moving in the water. (On a boat or ship the lubber's line follows the keel line of the boat.) Sight over the compass, not down at it. The wrist wearing the compass should be up and in front of the eyes. Keep any metallic equipment away from the compass.

Understanding the Compass as Mariner or Diver: To understand the compass, think of the earth as a huge magnetized sphere. A magnetized needle held anywhere on its surface will line up with the magnetic lines of force of the earth. If the north magnetic and south magnetic poles were exactly at the North and South poles, magnetic compasses would indicate true direction. Actually, the magnetic north is more than 1000 miles from the North Pole, located north of Hudson Bay; the south magnetic pole is situated south of Australia. Each government chart has one or more compass roses indicating the local variation. The compass needle will automatically line up with one point toward the north magnetic pole. The correction to true north is then made by allowing for the local variation.

What Is the Variation?: As we have explained, variation exists because the magnetic north pole is located 1000 miles from the true North Pole. Compass variations exist in all areas of the north; charts for each area show the variation. Just as variations change from place to place, so they change from year to year. To obtain a true reading add easterly and subtract westerly variation. Here is a useful rhyme to aid in your calculation:

> With true to compass
> With AWE you SEE *
> From compass to true
> It's SW—AE. †

Another memory aid is the word HAWSER. Dropping the first and last letters you have AWSE, which means Add Westerly, Subtract Easterly errors in converting to compass courses (uncorrecting). When correcting (compass to magnetic to true), reverse the first and third letter as in the last line of the rhyme.

Deviation: Beware of compass deviation caused by the magnetic attraction of nearby metallic objects such as your tank or boat. Determine such deviation when donning your tank. Having compensated for both magnetic variation and deviation, you then have a true reading. Example: The chart may show that the bearing of a reef you wish to reach is 210° from your point of departure. From your point of departure it might also show that your magnetic variation is 23° east. The correct heading for your compass would be 233°. If the variation were 23° west instead of east, the heading would then be 187°.

---

* AWE—Add West; SEE—Subtract East.
† SW—Subtract West; AE—Add East.

Care and Maintenance: As with all equipment, rinse your compass carefully with fresh water and dry it. Avoid dropping your compass. For more information on compasses in connection with navigating your boat, see pages 271–78.

UNDERWATER SLATE

Purpose: A slate is useful when observations are to be recorded or when it is expected that divers may require a means of communicating beyond the limits of hand signals.

Selection: A simple handy slate can be made from a ⅛- or ¼-inch-thick piece of acrylic plastic, lightly sandpapered on both sides and used with an ordinary pencil. The slate should have a loop or lanyard made of sturdy line to prevent its loss.

DIVING LIGHT

Purpose: When diving in the absence of light, a waterproof, pressure-proof light is a must. Major uses include cave diving, night diving, exploring crevices or holes, and ice diving.

Selection: A commercially available, one-piece, plastic-bodied unit with an integral handle, a light, and a sealed-beam headlight will serve. To prolong the life of your light, use best-quality nickel cadmium batteries. To prevent loss, always attach to self with a lanyard.

Care and Maintenance: Wash with warm fresh water after each use. When idle, remove batteries and store apart. Keep spare bulbs and batteries at dive site should they be needed. The O-ring should be lubricated with a silicone grease and checked for any debris which could block a proper seal.

LINE

Purpose: When operating under hazardous conditions, such as when cave, ice, night diving, or when operating in strong currents and you need an ascending line to the surface. Though limited, line is useful as a quick means of communication.

Selection: Lines made of nylon, Dacron, and polypropylene are safe and most commonly used. This material is strong, corrosion-resistant, and of nearly neutral buoyancy.

Care and Maintenance: Inspect and lubricate snaps. Reels and lines for cave diving demand additional maintenance. Replace when any line shows signs of weakness. Reels must be kept corrosion-free, well lubricated, and in perfect working condition.

DECOMPRESSION METER

Selection: There are a number of new meters currently under development which show promise. However, until tests have been completed, these meters must not be relied upon blindly. The decompression meter is only a backup system, therefore, it is not recommended when decompression can be computed using proven tables.

Purpose: The decompression meter automatically computes decompression by simulating nitrogen absorption and elimination in the human body. Despite the complicated function it performs, the decompression meter is relatively simple in construction. It consists of a stainless-steel outer housing, a flexible gas-filled bag, a ceramic gas-flow restricting filter, a rigid housing, a sealed bourdon tube inside the rigid housing, and an indicating meter. The flexible gas-filled bag is attached around the rigid bourdon-tube housing with the ceramic filter connecting the two. Holes in the outer case allow the gas-filled bag to be affected by pressure.

Immediately upon submersion, water enters the outer case through the holes and exerts pressure upon the gas-filled bag. The ceramic filter restricts the flow of gas from the bag into the rigid bourdon-tube housing at a rate approximating that of the absorption of nitrogen by mid-level tissues of the human body. As the diver proceeds deeper or remains longer at a specific depth, more gas is forced from the bag into the bourdon-tube housing, causing a distortion of the bourdon tube and a resultant deflection of the meter needle to which it is connected. When the diver has remained submerged long enough to require decompression, the meter needle will be deflected far enough to indicate such. As the diver's depth decreases during ascent, the pressure differential is reversed and the gas begins to flow from the bourdon-tube housing, through the ceramic filter, back into the gas-filled bag, with a resultant deflection of the decompression needle in the opposite direction. The gas is passed back through the ceramic filter at a rate approximately the same as nitrogen is exhausted from the mid-level body tissues. To decompress, the diver simply follows the needle to the surface, remaining at the depth indicated until the needle moves into the next depth range, and surfacing when the needle moves out of the required decompression zone.

The air trapped in the bourdon-tube housing after surfacing effectively substitutes as residual nitrogen time and allows the meter to be used for repetitive dives for up to 6 hours after the original use. The gas-pressure differential is completely equalized after that period of time and the meter should not be used for repetitive dives with a surface interval of greater than 6 hours. Once the meter has been used by one diver, it cannot accurately be used by another diver until the gas trapped in the bourdon housing has completely equalized with external pressure.

The decompression meter is subject to a gradual deterioration of accuracy, or may be jarred out of calibration if dropped or damaged. A diver will be able to tell if a decompression meter is seriously out of calibration by following the manufacturer's test procedures. Repair or recalibration should not be attempted by the individual, but left up to a qualified technician.

Care and Maintenance: After each use the meter should be rinsed in warm fresh water, dried, and securely stowed. Do not try to disassemble the instrument or clean the holes, as serious damage or decalibration could result.

When using the decompression meter a number of restrictions must be observed. The meter should not be used for repetitive dives if the surface interval exceeds 6 hours. Decompression meters reach saturation after approximately 2 hours of bottom time and should not be used for dives which exceed that limit. Finally, the meter cannot consider the diver's physical condition, the severity of the work the diver is accomplishing, or other factors which affect the nitrogen content of the body. It can only be used when diving with compressed air.

5

DIVING TECHNIQUES

THE BUDDY SYSTEM

"Remember that the greatest single factor in scuba diving is the use of the buddy system."—*U.S. Navy Diving Manual*

The buddy system makes two (or more) divers responsible for each other's safety. When you dive, take the attitude that you and your buddy are diving as a unit. *Never dive alone.*

The buddy system calls for continuous contact with your buddy. Where visibility is good, keep him in sight at short range; where visibility is poor, use a short buddy line to link yourselves together. If you lose contact with your buddy, surface and rejoin before returning to the depths.

Know the standard diving signals so that you can communicate messages to each other. Always watch for any signal from a buddy and acknowledge it promptly. Be alert to help your buddy if he shows any sign of distress. Even if he does not signal, get to him at once if distress is apparent, find out what the trouble is, and take whatever action is necessary. Never separate from a buddy in distress unless he is hopelessly entangled and you must leave him in order to get help.

COMMUNICATION AMONG DIVERS

Sound does not behave the same in water as it does in the air. The speed of sound through the air is about 1090 feet per second, and in water it travels four times that fast. Articulate voice communication is impossible underwater, although a high-pitched shriek can be heard.

To minimize the need for communicating below, accomplish all the communication you can while topside. If necessary, take a slate and crayon down or a plastic card and pencil for written messages between divers under water.

Diving Signals: Before diving, members of the diving unit should master the visual signals or, if the need for them is foreseeable, sound and rope signals for communication between the submerged divers and the surface personnel. Remember to be distinct and clear in your message as well as to whom you are directing your signal. All signals should be acknowledged. Remember that in an extreme emergency a distressed diver may not be sufficiently in control to give a distinct standard signal of his predicament. Therefore, be on the lookout for peculiar behavior at all times.

Distress Signals from a Diver at Surface to Tender: The distress signal for divers on the surface and in trouble is the raised arm meaning "Come and get me"; rotating the arm in a particularly urgent situation means "Come and get me now." Be sure your boat operator knows all hand signals before the dive begins.

Sound Signals Between Divers: When visibility is poor or contact is lost, use the following system of tapping on tanks, knives, or other hard objects:

2 taps: Low on air.

"PICK ME UP NOW"
EMERGENCY

COLD

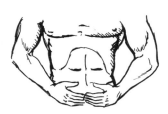

STOMACH CRAMPS
NAUSEA

ATTENTION
STRIKE YOUR TANK

"I AM HAVING
TROUBLE WITH MY EAR"

"HOW DEEP"

"PICK ME UP"

"LET'S GO UP"

66

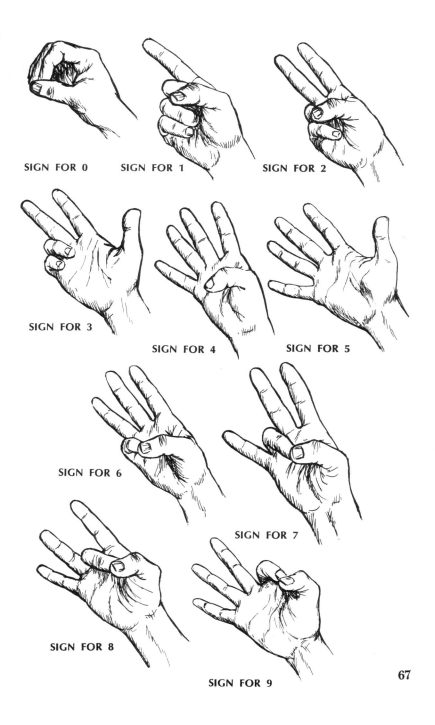

SIGN FOR 0   SIGN FOR 1   SIGN FOR 2

SIGN FOR 3   SIGN FOR 4   SIGN FOR 5

SIGN FOR 6

SIGN FOR 7

SIGN FOR 8

SIGN FOR 9

67

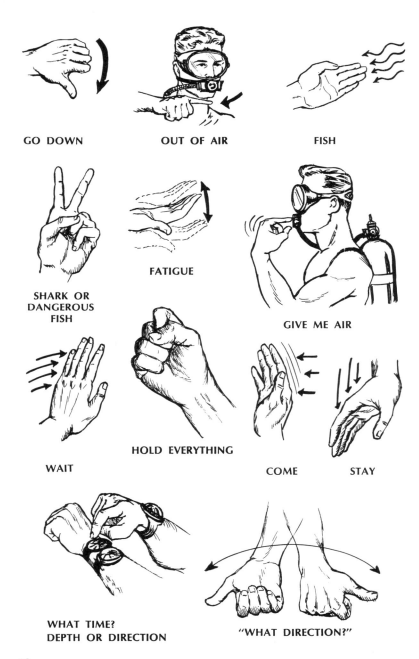

GO DOWN

OUT OF AIR

FISH

SHARK OR
DANGEROUS
FISH

FATIGUE

GIVE ME AIR

WAIT

HOLD EVERYTHING

COME

STAY

WHAT TIME?
DEPTH OR DIRECTION

"WHAT DIRECTION?"

ALL RIGHT

3 taps: Need help.
4 taps: Danger.
5 taps: Going up.
6 taps: Clear the area.

Line Signals: Line signals from Diver A to Diver B or from surface tender to diver:
1 pull: Are you all right? or, when going down, Stop.
2 pulls: Going down.
3 pulls: Stand by to come up.
4 pulls: Come up.
2 pulls,
    Pause,
    1 pull: I understand you.
From Diver B to Diver A in reply or diver to surface tender:
1 pull: I am all right.
2 pulls: Going down or lower me.
3 pulls: Stand by to come up or take up my slack line.
4 pulls: Coming up or haul me up.
2 pulls,
    Pause,
    1 pull: I understand you.

Line Emergency Signals:
To a surface tender or fellow diver attached by a line:
2-2-2 pulls: I am fouled and need your assistance.
3-3-3 pulls: I am fouled but do not need your assistance.
4-4-4 pulls: Take me up.

PLAN YOUR DIVE, DIVE YOUR PLAN

Before embarking on a dive, plan carefully, guided by the following considerations.

Objective: What is the object of the dive? Do all the divers in your party understand the objective? Choose one objective and stick to it. Do not complicate your plans with more than one.

How Much Air Is Needed?: Have enough air for the depth and duration planned. Keep a spare tank available if possible.

Equipment Checklist: Have you selected adequate and safe equipment for this dive? List all diving gear you own and will use this trip. The extent of your equipment will determine what sort of diving you can safely do.

Recompression Chamber: If plans call for a decompression dive, are you equipped for it, trained for it? Have you verified and noted down the location of the nearest recompression chamber? Is it available if needed?

Air Suppliers: Have you verified and noted down the location of the nearest air supplier?

Physician: Have you made provisions to obtain a physician's help in case of emergency?

Briefing on Dive Area: Have you selected a diving location and obtained charts and maps of the area? To be thoroughly briefed, study charts and get acquainted with local divers, fishermen, and boatmen. They can tell you much about weather, shore, and boat conditions, fishing regulations, where to hire a boat, and where to get help if needed.

Weather: Have you checked weather reports in advance? Made your own observations?

Water Condition: Have you determined the condition of the water? Dirty or polluted waters should be avoided. Poor visibility can entail the same dangers as night diving. Contamination can cause infections or otherwise impair your health.

Water Temperature: Have you checked the water temperature to determine what protective clothes to wear?

Selection of Buddies: Have you selected competent and responsible diving companions? Insist that everyone understand the diving objectives and disciplines. Important considerations should be written down by everyone.

Equipment Condition: Do you have all the equipment you will need? Check all equipment before leaving the home base and again at the dive location just before diving.

Estimated Time of Return: Have you notified someone ashore of your plans to dive and of your estimated time of returning home?

Summary: Think of the day's excursion as the dive's PLOT:

P—Person who will accompany you.
L—Location of your dive.
O—Objective of your dive.
T—Time best suited for your dive, time of departure, time of return.

CALCULATING YOUR AIR SUPPLY

How much air do you breathe? What is your rate of air consumption in cubic feet per minute?
How much air do you need?
How long will your compressed-air supply last?
How does your compressed-air supply vary with depth?
How should you breathe and use your air supply properly?
These are questions to which every diver should try to have accurate answers whatever the circumstances.

Effect of Depth on Air Duration: Bear in mind that depth is one of the key factors determining the duration of an open-circuit air dive. At depth each breath requires a greater mass of air than the same breath at sea level. Therefore, the deeper you go, the less air you have. As you descend, the pressure of the water around you is great enough to squeeze the molecules of air closer together, thus reducing your breathing volume. According to Boyle's Law, for example, at 100 feet (4 atm) an air supply will suffice for only one-quarter of the time that the same supply would suffice at sea level.

To compute air time, divide air time at sea level by the total number of atmospheres you plan to descend. For example, if a tank has 60 minutes of air time on land, it will last 15 minutes at 4 atm. This rate is based on a constant rate and volume of breathing at any depth. The endurance of your air supply varies not only with depth but according to such influencing factors as:

Your own individual rate of air consumption.

Your age.

The amount of energy you expend. (Hard work consumes energy quickly.)

Your lung capacity.

The temperature of the water. (Cold water consumes energy, tires you quicker than warm water.)

The duration and depth of the dive.

The breathing technique you use. (Some inexperienced divers tend to breathe rapidly without economizing air.)

It is because of these factors that accurate calculation of endurance of air supply cannot be achieved wholly through mathematics. Each individual will have different requirements according to the way these variables affect him.

HOW TO BREATHE

Adopt a slow, relaxed breathing rhythm. Maintain this controlled pace even when overexerting. *Never hold your breath or skip a breath to conserve air.* Breathe normally.

HOW TO RELAX UNDER WATER

Be sure equipment fits snugly but comfortably.
Move slowly, gently, and carefully under water.
Concentrate on exhaling. The inhaling will take care of itself.
Be weighted correctly.

Effect of Exertion on Your Calculated Remaining Air Supply:
During exertion the diver naturally demands a greater volume of
air, especially with increased depth. The average consumption of air
at surface is 1 cubic foot (28 liters) per minute. Under exertion, this
rate can mount to 3 cubic feet per minute (cfm). At 33 feet, normal
consumption is 2 cfm, while under exertion it can be as much as 6
cfm. At 66 feet, 3 cfm can become 9 cfm. At 99 feet, 4 cfm can
become 12 cfm. Bear this in mind when planning your dives. Remember also that overexertion is characterized by panting and eventually panic. When you sense a shortness of breath or panting, relax,
stop activity, and breathe slowly. If necessary, resurface, float, and
breathe with your snorkel or take a rest on your surface flotation
device. Snorkel breathing in very rough surf can be difficult if not
useless because you may be taking much water into the tube. Alter-
native: Inflate your BC (Buoyancy Compensator) Vest to keep your
head high out of the water.

Another result of overexerting is anoxia, oxygen starvation. To
explain, a hardworking diver uses oxygen faster than a relaxed diver.
As a result, there is a decrease of the sensitivity of the CO_2 break-
point mechanism. The decrease permits the oxygen level to go even
lower. Example: A hard swimmer consumes 1.4 liters, a slow swimmer only about 0.8 liters.

When a diver ascends and the pressure drops, there is a corresponding drop in the partial pressure of oxygen in his lungs. (Remember Dalton's Law, page 33.) The latter drop may be enough to
stop completely any further intake of oxygen. At the same time, the
partial pressure of CO_2 in the lungs also drops, signaling a false
sense of relief from the need to breathe. With these circumstances

the diver deprived of sufficient oxygen supply would probably lose
consciousness and drown.

Increasing Your Breath-holding Capacity in Snorkel Diving:
(*Caution:* Do *not* hold your breath when using an air rig.)

The most popular method is hyperventilation before a dive. Hyperventilation consists of a series of rapid deep inhalations and
strong exhalations or, in other words, deep breaths. The effect is to
purge the bloodstream of excess CO_2 and replace it with a maximum of oxygen. Carbon dioxide is the gas that triggers a nerve in
the brain and then sends a message to the diaphragm mechanism
that it is time to take a breath. If CO_2 does not accumulate rapidly,
the desire to breathe is weakened; yet we sense no great need. *This
is a dangerous stage* because the system can become starved for oxygen (anoxia), and fainting can result. Death can be almost guaran-
teed once a diver has so practiced, so mastered hyperventilation that
his warning mechanism is totally ineffective and he blacks out without warning. Breath-holding competition should therefore be closely
surveyed by one or more monitors. One monitor should be in the
water and one topside. Once the desire to breathe has been eliminated and unconsciousness follows, the victim should be brought to
the surface and given artificial respiration unless he has come to.

Dive Planning and Your Air Supply: The rate of consumption
and the depth and duration of a dive should be determined before
the dive in order to assure yourself of an ample air supply.

The following formulas will tell you approximately how fast in
minutes you consume your air supply with a known tank volume in
cubic feet, how long a full or partially filled tank will last, and how
much air remains after a change of pressure. (If you have neither the
aptitude nor the inclination for working mathematical formulas, you
can refer to the depth-time ratio table. This table gives you at a
glance the depth-time ratio for most air tanks. It also tells you
whether in order to avoid decompression sickness you will need to
use the U.S. Navy Air Decompression Table before you dive.)
Above all, use a submersible pressure gauge and read it at regular
intervals.

A. Approximate consumption of air per minute from a demand unit can be computed by this formula:

$$\left(\frac{D}{33} + 1\right) \times .75 = V \text{ where}$$

D = depth in feet

33 = feet of sea water equal to 1 atm pressure

1 = additional atm to arrive at absolute pressure

.75 = cu. ft. consumption (approx.) of air at sea level from a demand unit during moderate exercise. With hard work this may increase to 1.75 cfm

V = volume (cu. ft.) consumption at depth (D) per minute (As an example compute the consumption of air per minute at a depth of 66 ft.)

$$\left(\frac{66}{33} + 1\right) = 2 + 1 = 3 \times .75 = 2.25 \text{ cfm}$$

B. How long will a tankful last?

To compute the duration (in minutes) of a cylinder of a known volume (see page 76 for another method):

Volume of cylinder

$(D + 1) \times .75 =$ duration of air supply in minutes

Example 1: Compute the duration of a 70-cu.-ft. cylinder at a depth of 66 ft.

$$\frac{70}{\left(\frac{66}{33} + 1\right) \times .75} = 37 \text{ min.}$$

Example 2: Compute the duration for the same cylinder at 50 ft.

$$\frac{70}{\left(\frac{50}{33} + 1\right) \times .75} = 37.5 \text{ min.}$$

C. To obtain the remaining volume with a change of pressure, use this formula:

$$\frac{P^2 \times V^1}{P^1} = V^2 \text{ where}$$

$P^1 =$ pressure of cylinder when filled to rated capacity
$P^2 =$ pressure measured by gauge prior to dive
$V^1 =$ rated volume of cylinder at p^1
$V^2 =$ volume of free air remaining in tank at p^2

Example 1: A 70-cu.-ft. cylinder has a rated working pressure of 2150 psi. How many cu. ft. of air will remain in the tank if the gauge pressure reads 1200 psi?

$$P^1 = 2150$$
$$P^2 = 1200$$
$$V^1 = 70$$
$$V^2 = X$$

$$\frac{1200 \times 70}{2150} = \frac{84000}{2150} = 39.07 \text{ cu. ft. vol.}$$

Example 2: A 70-cu.-ft. cylinder has 1125 psi, and its rated pressure is 2250 psi

$$\frac{1125 \times 70}{2250} = \frac{78750}{2250} = 35 \text{ cu. ft.}$$

To compute how long this same tank will last at, say, 66 ft. with 1125 psi left in it, use formula B as follows:

$$\frac{35}{\left(\frac{66}{33} + 1\right) \times .75} = 15.5 \text{ min.}$$

D. To find out how long (in minutes) one full cylinder of 71.2 cu. ft. will last at 2300 lbs. pressure at a given depth, you must first know three things:

C = capacity of your tank (vol.)
A = pressure of the air in the tank
P = pressure of the water at depth of dive

Formula to use:

$$\frac{C(A - [P + 16])}{4.5 \ (P + 1)} = \text{no. of minutes}$$

where C = capacity of cylinder in cubic feet
    A = pressure of cylinder in absolute atmospheres
    P = pressure of dive in absolute atmospheres

Example:

How long can I stay at 33-ft. depth using a 71.2-cu.-ft. cylinder at a tank pressure of 2300 lbs.?

$$C = 71.2 \text{ cu. ft.}$$
$$A = 171.16 \left(\frac{2300}{14.7} + 14.7 \right)$$
$$P = 29.4 \ (33 \text{ ft. is 2 absolute atm})$$

Answer:

$$\frac{71.2 \ (171.16 - 29.4 + 16)}{4.5 \ (29.4 + 1)} = 65.5 \text{ min.}$$

HINTS FOR DIVING EXPEDITIONS

Whenever embarking on a dive in unfamiliar water, learn all you can from local watermen and fishermen.

Don't attempt to enter the water through heavy surf.

Pick a good entry point with an easy landing from the water.

Avoid rocks and breakwaters.

The anchor makes a good rendezvous point under water.

Beware of barnacles, coral, and sea urchins.

Wear bathing trunks, or coveralls, over a rubber suit when diving close to sharp, jagged submarine terrain—especially when strong currents and swells prevail.

Set up a base near your entry point but out of the tidal level and away from cliffs, where falling rock can be a danger.

Protect your feet over rough or slippery terrain on shore by using rubber booties or sneakers.

Avoid exertion before diving. If winded from topside preparations, relax a few minutes before plunging.

Be alert for tired divers. Help them out of the water and discourage them from continuing.

When diving in fresh water you'll be less buoyant than in seawater. Compensate with weights accordingly.

Beware of obstacles, such as trash, debris, fallen trees, which you may not see until you are virtually on them.

Avoid swift rivers, especially in the vicinities of dams, pipelines, and drain channels.

Old quarries, flooded valleys, dams, and reservoirs are very often favorable for inland diving, but beware of hazardous underwater obstructions and poor visibility.

Be responsible for safe placement of your equipment.

Take care of any accident wounds. (See General First Aid pages 228–41.)

If caught in a tidal flow or rip current, swim across its direction of flow, not against it.

Learn to recognize rip currents by their flattening effect on incoming waves in their path. The waves tend to be larger on either side of the current. Rip-current waters are often muddy or otherwise discolored.

Breaking waves indicate that there are shallow waters or that a bank or reef or other obstruction exists just below the surface.

Make sure if you use a boat that it is appropriate for the number of passengers and the range of your trip.

Stay out of channels and fishing and dredging areas.

Don't disturb fishing nets or lobster pots.

HANDY REFERENCE ON AIR SUPPLY FOR A
71.2-CUBIC-FOOT TANK

Table of Equivalents Between Pounds per Square Inch Cylinder Pressure and Number of Cubic Feet Remaining in a Tank (at Sea Level Pressure of Atmosphere)

Gauge Reading on Cylinder in Pounds per Square Inch	Number of Cubic Feet of Air Remaining in Cylinder	
2200	70.4	To find the approximate number
2150	68.8	of cubic feet of air in the cylinder
1900	60.8	take the pressure gauge reading
1800	57.6	(psi) and multiply by .032.
1700	54.4	
1600	51.2	
1500	48.0	
1400	44.8	
1300	41.6	
1200	38.4	
1100	35.2	
1000	32.0	
900	28.8	
800	25.6	
700	22.4	
600	19.2	
500	16.0	
400	12.8	
300	9.6	

Subsurface Visibility and Dangers: Use extreme caution when diving under conditions of poor visibility or you will face the dangers of collisions, contamination, infection, separation from buddies, disorientation, and/or wounds from marine life. In prolonged dives, buddies should be connected by a length of line.

Appoint someone topside as a lookout to signal surface craft to navigate away from the dive area. The lookout can observe divers and follow them with the boat if they stray too far. If a motor must be used, all divers should be forewarned to stay clear. The tender should keep a record of the divers' time submerged and go to their aid if necessary.

Underwater Depth Orientation: If you experience vertigo and can't tell up from down, just watch your bubbles. The direction they go can only be up. Another indicator is water temperature. If the water gets colder, you are going down, and vice versa. Refer to your depth gauge if you have one. Keep contact with surface-float anchor line.

Underwater Direction Orientation: Look at your anchor lines as a guide. Check against your compass after you complete a pattern of turns. (See more detailed instructions on the use of compass, pages 56–59 and 271–78.)

The best over-all advice for ocean diving is to avoid waters where visibility is poor. Seek clear waters or call off your dive.

Predive Safety Don'ts

Don't dive without anchoring your boat or float securely.

Don't dive without placing a diver's flag on the surface.

Don't dive without a fully experienced topside tender whose clearly understood duty is to observe the diver when down.

Don't dive unless you are physically and mentally fit.

Don't dive if you have been drinking excessively within the twenty-four hours immediately prior to diving.

Don't dive with a cold or with lung congestion.

Don't dive with an unsupervised, foolhardy aim of establishing records or showing off.

Don't dive with faulty equipment.

Don't dive without a fully charged spare compressed-air tank available topside.

Don't dive without a decompression table topside.

Don't dive without experienced divers.

HANDY REFERENCE ON PRESSURE, DEPTH, AND DURATION OF AIR SUPPLY

Depth in Fathoms (1 Fathom = 6 ft.)	Depth in Feet Sea Level	*Absolute Pressure = Atmospheric Pressure 14.7 psi Plus Pressure at Different Depths (Surface 14.7 psi)	Positive (Gauge) Pressure Increase .445 psi per Ft. (Approx. ½ lb. psi) (Surface 0 lb. psi)	Tank Air Volume Decreases with Depth Increase	A Tank Lasting 60 Minutes at Sea Level Would at Normal Breathing Rate Last 30 min.	†A Tank Lasting 90 Minutes at Sea Level Would at Normal Breathing Rate of 1 cfm, Last 45 min.
5½	32	2 atm (29.4 psi)	14.7 psi	1/2	30 min.	45 min.
				(greatest changes occur here. Caution.)		
11	66	3 atm (44.1 psi)	29.4	1/3	20	30
16½	99	4 atm (58.8 psi)	44.0	1/4	15	23
22	132	5 atm (73.5 psi)	58.8	1/5	12	18
Caution: Thoracic squeeze to skin diver without tank						
27½	165	6 atm (88.2 psi)	73.5	1/6	10	15
33	198	7 atm (102.9 psi)	88.2	1/7	8.6	13
38½	231	8 atm (117.6 psi)	102.9	1/8	7.5	11
44	264	9 atm (132.3 psi)	117.6	1/9	6.6	10
49½	297	10 atm (147.0 psi)	132.3	1/10	6	9

*To arrive at *absolute pressure* always add the *atmospheric pressure* (14.7 psi) to the *positive (gauge) pressure*. Ambient pressure is the true pressure on the diver. It equals absolute pressure.

†These figures will vary with individual breathing rates, exertion, etc.

THE SAFE DEPTH LIMIT FOR OPEN-CIRCUIT COMPRESSED-AIR DIVING

The safe depth limit for open-circuit compressed-air diving is 132 feet. The reason is that by the time you reach 132 feet you have built up a nitrogen content in your body that can bring on nitrogen narcosis (rapture of the deep). (See page 223.) The nitrogen buildup has the same effect as too much alcohol—intoxication, giddiness, an exaggerated feeling of well-being, loss of efficiency, irresponsible behavior.

Relief from the intoxicating effects of nitrogen narcosis can be attained by ascending to safer levels. Get up before you have lost your capacity to think clearly. Some divers have been seen to swim deeper, throw away their mouthpiece, and disappear—never to be seen again. The real danger is that you may not realize the trouble you are in.

DIVE SITE EQUIPMENT PREPARATION: GENERAL CHECKLIST

Air Cylinders: Inspect for rust, cracks, dents, or any other evidence of weakness or fault. Pay particular attention to loose or bent valves.

Check cylinder markings and verify suitability for use. Check that the hydrostatic test date has not expired.

Remove masking tape and/or valve cover and inspect O-ring and valve threads.

Verify that the reserve mechanism is in a closed position signifying a filled cylinder ready for use.

Gauge the cylinders according to the following procedure:

1. Attach pressure gauge to the on/off valve.
2. With gauge bleed valve closed and air-reserve mechanism open, slowly open the cylinder on/off valve, keeping a rag over the face of the gauge.

3. Read pressure gauge. If the pressure in the cylinder is not sufficient to complete the planned dive, the cylinder is inadequate and should not be used until it is filled.
4. Close the cylinder on/off valve and open the gauge bleed valve. When the gauge reads "0" remove it from the cylinder. Close the air reserve mechanism. If the pressure in cylinders is too high (50 psi over rating), open the cylinder on/off valve to bleed off excess and regauge cylinder.

Harness Straps and Back Pack: Check for signs of rot or excessive wear. Adjust straps for individual use, and test quick-release mechanisms.

Breathing Hoses: Check the hose(s) for cracks or punctures. Test the connections of each hose to the regulator and mouthpiece assembly by tugging on the hose. Check the clamps for corrosion and damage; replace as necessary.

Regulator: Attach regulator to the cylinder on/off valve, making certain that the O-ring is properly seated. Open the cylinder valve all the way and then back off ¼ turn. Check for any leaks in the regulator by listening for the sound of escaping air.

If a leak is suspected, determine the exact location by submerging the valve assembly and the regulator in a tank of water and looking for bubbles. Frequently the problem can be traced to an improperly seated regulator. This is corrected by closing the valve, bleeding the regulator, detaching and reseating.

If leak is at the O-ring, and reseating does not solve the problem, replace the O-ring.

With either a single-hose or a double-hose unit, the hose supplying air should come over the diver's right shoulder with the exhaust hose on the double-hose unit passing back over his left shoulder. Double-hose regulators are attached so that the inhalation and exhaust ports face up when the tank is standing upright.

Inhale and exhale several times through the mouthpiece, making sure that the demand stage and check valves are working correctly. With a single-hose regulator, depress and release the purge button at the mouthpiece and listen for any sound of leaking air. Breathe in and out several times. Close the cylinder on/off valve.

Flotation Device/Buoyancy Compensator: Inflate orally to check for leaks, and then squeeze all the air out. The final amount of remaining air in the vest should be sucked out so that the preserver is completely empty.

Inspect any CO_2 cartridges to make sure that they have not been used (seals intact) and are the proper size for the vest being used. The cartridges should be weighed upon receipt and every 6 months thereafter and discarded if the weight varies more than 3 grams from the gross weight stamped on the cartridge.

The firing pin should move freely and not be worn.

The firing lanyards and life-preserver straps must be free of any signs of deterioration. When inspection of the Buoyancy Compensator vest is completed, place it where it will not be stepped on or mixed in with other equipment that may damage it. It should never be used as a buffer, cradle, or cushion for other gear.

Face Mask: Check the seal of the mask and the condition of the head strap. Check for cracks in the skirt and faceplate.

Swim-Fins: Check straps and inspect blades for any signs of cracking.

Diving Knife: Test the edge of the knife for sharpness, and make sure that the knife is fastened securely in the scabbard. Verify that the knife can be removed without difficulty.

Snorkel: Inspect the snorkel for obstructions, and check the condition of the mouthpiece.

Weight Belt: Check that the belt is in good condition and that the proper number of weights are in place and secure. Verify that the quick-release buckle is functioning properly.

Wristwatch: Check that the watch is wound and set to the correct time. Inspect the pins and strap of the watch for wear.

Depth Gauge and Compass: Inspect pins and straps on each. Make sure depth gauge is properly calibrated. If possible, check compass against another compass.

General: Inspect any other equipment which will be used on the dive as well as any spare equipment that may be used during the dive. This would include spare regulators, cylinders, and gauges. Also check all protective clothing, lines, tools, flares, and other optional gear. Finally, lay all equipment in a place where it will be out of the way of deck traffic and ready for use.

Diver Preparation: When the diver has completed inspecting and testing his equipment, review the dive plan with all divers involved.
Items which should be covered include:

- dive objectives
- time limits for the dive
- buddy assignments
- route, dive destination
- special signals
- anticipated conditions
- anticipated hazards
- emergency procedures, particularly when to abort the dive, and what will be done in the event of a lost diver.

When the divers are all satisfied that the requirements of the operation are fully understood and that they are in good health and otherwise ready to proceed, they may dress for the dive.

DRESSING FOR THE DIVE

Every scuba diver must be able to put all of his gear on by himself, but assistance of a buddy is encouraged. Dressing sequence is important as the weight belt must be outside all backpack harness straps, or other equipment which could prevent its quick release in the event of an emergency.

1. Protective clothing. For ease in putting on a dry suit or a wet suit, the body and the suit should be sprinkled with talcum powder or cornstarch. If the suit is wet from a previous dive, or if the diver is perspiring heavily, a small quantity of liquid detergent or other dishwashing liquid may be used.
2. Boots and hood.
3. Knife (if worn on the ankle or about the waist).
4. Buoyancy Compensator vest, with inflation tubes in front and the actuating lanyards exposed and accessible.
5. Weight belt.
6. Scuba. Most easily put on with the aid of a tender who can hold the tanks in position while the diver fastens and adjusts the harness. The scuba should be worn centered on the diver's back as high as possible but not so high that his head, when tilted far back, will hit the regulator. All quick-release buckles must be so positioned that they can be reached by either hand. All straps must be pulled snug so that the cylinders are held firmly against the body. The ends of the straps must hang free so that the quick-release feature of the buckles will function. If the straps are too long, they should be cut and the ends whipped with small line or a plastic sealer. At this time, the cylinder on/off valve should be opened fully and then backed off ¼ to ½ turn.
7. Accessory equipment (watch, compass, and depth gauge; snorkel tucked into belt or under a strap; other equipment secure but not in the way).
8. Gloves.
9. Swim Fins.
10. Mask (hold in hand with strap around wrist).

Even if diver is ready, a final check among you should be made to verify that all divers have all minimum required equipment (Scuba, face mask, BC vest, weight belt, knife and scabbard, swim fins).

• verify that at least one diver per diving team is wearing both a wristwatch and a depth gauge.

- verify that the cylinders have been gauged and that the available volume of air is sufficient for the planned duration of the dive.
- ensure that all quick-release buckles and fastenings can be reached by either hand and are properly rigged for quick release.
- verify that the weight belt is outside all other belts, straps, and equipment, and is not likely to become pinched under the bottom edge of the cylinders.
- verify that the BC vest is not constraining nor too loose-fitting, is free to expand, and that all air has been evacuated.
- check position of the knife to ensure that it will remain with the diver (no matter what equipment he may jettison).
- conduct time check and synchronize watches.
- ensure that cylinder valve is open and then backed off ¼ to ½ turn.
- with mouthpiece or face mask in place, have diver breathe in and out for 30 seconds. While doing this, he should be alert for any impurities in the air or for any unusual physiological reactions.
- give the breathing tube(s) and mouthpiece a final check; make sure that none of the connections has been pulled open during the process of dressing.
- check the air-reserve pull-rod to make sure that it has not been bent and is free to move.
- check that the air-reserve mechanism is in the closed position (the pull-rod in the "up" position).
- conduct brief final review of the dive plan.
- ensure that the divers are physically and mentally ready to enter the water.
- verify that the proper diving signals (i.e., flag) are displayed to warn surface vessels.

You are now ready to enter the water, where scuba should be given another brief inspection by a buddy prior to descent.

THE DIVE

Having carried out all preliminary preparations, you are ready for the dive. Besides your minimum equipment, which includes swim trunks, personal flotation device, knife, swim fins, face mask, and breathing apparatus, wear a waterproof wristwatch, depth gauge, BC vest, and weight belt, and possibly an exposure suit and wrist compass. Carry along a buddy line if poor visibility is anticipated.

Immediately After Entering the Water: Put your diver's flag up at the dive site. Keep it with you wherever you dive, towing it as you travel from point of origin. If diving within a radius of 100 feet from a boat or tender that is already flying a diver's flag, another one mounted on your flotation device is superfluous.

The type of entry you make depends on the nature of the dive site, the water, climatic conditions, and shore terrain, and whether you enter from a boat, cliff, or beach. Determine the nature of the waters you will be entering. There are, from the shore, the following possibilities:

1. Gentle shore-lapping waves in protected waters.
2. Waves that break out from the beach and push up to the shore as a welling flood. These waves indicate a gradually sloping but generally even bottom.
3. Waves breaking off shore, rolling in, and breaking again indicate a reef, sandbar, or some sizable obstruction in the area of the first breaker.
4. Violent, smashing breakers of stormy seas.

Surface Check in Water: Remain at the surface to check your own and your buddy's air rig for leaks of any sort before submerging.

Check your face mask for proper seal against flooding.

Check your weight belt for ideal buoyancy. It should be slightly positive near the surface; however, with increasing depth your state of buoyancy will become neutral because of compression. (Main adjustment should already have been made.) Correct any deficiencies discovered. If any deficiency cannot be corrected, discontinue your dive.

Orient yourself with available natural aids (sunlight, current, and landmarks).

If your objective requires swimming to a specific point, check the compass bearing of that point.

When you and your buddy are ready, signal each other and start the dive. If you have a safety man topside, signal him when ready.

Procedure in the Water: Now that you have made your entry into the water, execute a few shallow dives of short duration. Get accustomed to the dive area. Make a mental note of winds, clouds, and weather before descending.

Observe the behavior patterns of currents, the extent of visibility, and the water temperature.

Be alert at all times as a matter of habit.

Hazardous situations may arise during a dive and may be indicated by:

sudden changes in water temperatures;
changes in wind direction and/or velocity;
cloud formations;
pattern of ripples, waves, and breakers;
appearance of storm warnings on vessels or shore installations.

Reminders:
Keep your buddy in sight at all times.
Keep your float and/or boat in sight with periodic checks.
Check your own drift by periodically observing the shore area you have selected for your return.
Take nothing for granted with respect to seeing, hearing, or feeling.
Observe carefully and accurately all curious objects and evaluate and act accordingly. If all procedures are not second nature to you, you shouldn't be diving at all.

Going Down: Make a slow, orderly descent not faster than 75 feet per minute; do not outrun your buddy. Swim down, or if you are using a descending line, pull yourself headfirst down the line to conserve energy.

Be sure that the pressure is equalizing in the ears and sinuses. If pain develops, stop the descent. Level off or ascend slightly until the pressure equalizes.

Discontinue the dive if pressure does not equalize after several tries. Never force the issue.

At Diving Depth: Level off at diving depth, look around, and orient yourself, using any available natural and other aids (sunlight, current, bottom, channel, anchor line, etc.).

Check your compass and depth gauge.

Don't overexert yourself. Breathe normally and continuously as slowly and deeply as possible. At the first sign of breathlessness, slow down; rest if possible. Catch your breath before increasing your physical activity. If a strong current forces abnormal exertion and irremedial fatigue, discontinue the dive.

Beware of entanglement with submerged wreckage, lines, or vegetation. When swimming with poor visibility, keep your hands extended ahead.

Watch the depth and time carefully.

Keep your buddy in sight and look at him frequently. Keep him informed by signal of any change of plan or direction. Be sure that he understands the signal and that he follows or is at least aware of the maneuver.

Line Diving: If, while diving, you tow your surface float by a line of rope, keep it taut but do not pull the float under the surface. Remember that it can snag objects about you. Watch out for entanglements. Fasten the line to your harness beneath the demand valve and against your back. Lead the free rope from this point under your left armpit (if right-handed) down the forearm and give it two turns around the open hand. Do not secure the line by turns around your wrist or forearm.

When using any other lifeline, be sure the surface lookout man keeps it taut. Signal him to slacken or tauten the line if necessary.

Communicate with him occasionally by prescribed line pulls. Keep messages at a minimum and keep them simple.

Remember the risk of entanglement when using a line. Avoid going through small passages or near snags. Use your knife for emergency disentanglements.

Underwater Tending: When you are under water and tending a buddy on a line connected with you, keep him in sight, if possible. If he is out of sight, keep all slack out of the line. Be alert for a distress signal.

Surface Tending as Safety Man: When tending from a surface float or boat, keep the divers in view if circumstances permit. When tending buddies who are using float lines, stay clear but keep floats in sight. Watch them for signals. When tending a diver on a line, keep the line reasonably taut. Communicate with him often by line pulls.

When surface tending free divers (without lines), the tender should stay within short range but not directly above them. If bubbles are coming up very close to the boat, move the boat a safe distance away. Don't turn on the motor. Use a paddle or an oar. In fact, remove the ignition key so that nobody turns on the motor.

Be alert for any signs of trouble or any distress signals.

Observe any diver who surfaces unexpectedly. Before letting him submerge again, make absolutely sure he is not in distress. If he is, help him.

PREDIVE ANXIETY

Mental attitude toward diving will have a great influence on the diver's enjoyment of diving as well as on his or her reaction to stress in unfamiliar surroundings. It is not unnatural to feel apprehensive before a dive, particularly if conditions are not ideal, and a moderate amount of anxiety can be a useful defense against laxity: A diver is more likely to concentrate. However, anxiety escalated to panic is the worst response to an underwater problem one can have. Anyone with a quick tendency to panic should not dive.

Fears and anxieties can bedevil any diver. Here are two of the most common ways. I mention them only because they are to be expected as a purely normal phenomenon even among the most experienced.

FEAR OF SURFACING

A surfacing diver may be seized with anxiety when he first breaks the surface because he cannot immediately orient himself with a landing or cannot locate buddies as surface cover. To relieve that anxiety be sure to provide surface cover, a boat, or flotation devices.

CLAUSTROPHOBIA

Anyone truly fearful about confinement to limited space should not be diving. But under some circumstances a claustrophobic tendency can manifest itself in divers. This can occur when a diver starts to ruminate about the depth and weight of the water over his head; when he considers the difficulty of making it to the surface if his air supply fails or becomes exhausted; or if his exposure suit is tight fitting or very leaky. Usually an experienced diver can reason himself out of this kind of fear before panic takes over. However, if that doesn't work simply signal to your buddies that you wish to surface and do so as calmly and safely as possible.

ENTRIES AND EXITS FROM DIVES

Entry from a Boat: When diving from an anchored boat, plan your dive in a direction upwind, upstream, or upcurrent of the anchored boat. In other words, swim toward the anchor. Set your boat up so that the objective of the dive is in the direction of the anchor; when returning from the dive you can then drift calmly back to the boat, with the least exertion, meeting no resistance from currents, winds, or surf. In short, plan your dive to avoid surfacing downstream or astern of the anchored boat, or you may exhaust yourself, perhaps dangerously, trying to fight against tiring forces on your way back to the boat. Before diving, tie an inner tube or dinghy to the stern for tired divers who may come up downstream or downcurrent of the boat.

In addition, abide by the following safety rules:

Look out for traffic. Designate one side of the boat for entering and another for exiting to prevent one diver from tumbling onto another.

If available, use a boarding ladder.

Climb down the ladder fully rigged except for fins.

Enter water and while still holding the ladder, put on fins.

If entry is from a small boat or raft, don your breathing apparatus, firmly hold your face mask and mouthpiece, and step feetfirst into the water. No jumping or headfirst plunging. Step in. Enter unknown waters cautiously.

Another correct entry from a boat is the roll-back entry. Sit on the rail, back to the water, hold mask firmly, all equipment "go," and simply roll backward as if lying back on your bed. In unknown waters you might elect to slither in slowly, holding the sides of the boat, going in feetfirst.

Return to a Boat: When returning from your dive, remove equipment before boarding your boat and hand it aboard. The lookout man topside should give a hand.

Rough-Water Entry from a Small Boat:
Hold your mask and mouthpiece in place.
Roll gently, as if you were going to lie down.
Use a backfirst entry, falling backward into the water.

Entry from a Sandy Beach: Walk backward to avoid stumbling over your own fins, but look out for sharp objects or stingrays. The latter, when disturbed, can inflict a painful wound in the foot or leg. (See pages 203–204 for a discussion of stingrays.)

Study the wave pattern. Wait until several large waves break. Small waves generally follow. Enter directly after the first small wave, preferably in the wave trough (the area of the wave between crests).

Submerge as soon as you can under the next smaller waves, continuing under water past the line of breakers into deeper and calmer waters. At depth the circular motion in a wave decreases rapidly, becoming negligible at a depth equal to half the wave length. The energy and height of waves is often determined by submarine topography. In submarine valleys adjacent to a straight shoreline, waves are smaller as a result of a loss of energy. Sometimes they do not break at all, while over the ridges they break with energies often ten times greater than over the valleys.

When entering through surf, trail your float and equipment behind you by means of a hand line. Be sure you tie all equipment securely to your float to prevent its disappearance in an upset.

When diving in groups, stay a safe distance from the others until beyond the breaker line in order to avoid collisions; then reassemble in calmer waters.

Return to a Sandy Beach:
Swim as close as you can to the beach under water.

Make your exit from a point similar to that of your entry.

Observe the pattern of waves and when near enough to shore, exit from the water immediately after a breaking wave.

Equipment should be lashed onto your float and pushed ahead of you, secured by a hand line. Swim fins should be removed and held securely or tied down to your float so that at least one hand is free.

Be ready to climb quickly to safety before the next surge.

Pull in your float as you land.

Again, watch out for sharp objects and stingrays.

Entry from a Rocky Shore:
Pick a spot where water is calmest, walking distance is shortest, and rocks are least dangerous. You might lash a rope to a rock and slither into the water. Weight the end of the rope to keep it in place so that you can return to it for your exit.

Watch the wave pattern. Wait for the highest surge and quickly slip into the water by jumping or simply falling in; don't dive in. Entry is made after the wave breaks and you are following the back-surge.

Swim down and away before the next insurge. Stay well beneath the surface because the turbulence is greatest there. Keep an arm extended as protection against unseen obstacles. In this type of entry, bubbles and sand almost always obscure vision.

Note: Before using beaches and rocky shores unfamiliar to you, get as much information as possible about the area from local divers or other watermen.

Return to a Rocky Shore: If because of an emergency situation you must exit through turbulent surf at a rocky shore, ride a large wave and allow yourself to be carried in on its crest.

When at the end of the ride you are deposited on the rocks, hold tight during the wave's backsurge, then make for higher ground before the next surge, otherwise you will be pounded back into the surf.

FRESH WATERS

Lakes, pools, rivers, reservoirs, canals, and quarries are often carpeted with leaves and vegetation and are characterized by thick mud. In fresh water you will require less weight, your buoyancy being much less than in salt water. Visibility will be far less favorable than in tropical or subtropical sea waters.

Rivers: Some rivers with fast rapids often have deep, calm pools (particularly below rapids or waterfalls) that make interesting diving sites. Diving in heavy river currents is hopeless except for daring and experienced divers who are capable of combating currents and avoiding collisions with rocks. Also, because of shallowness, pollution, heavy boat traffic, water skiers, and poor visibility due to high turbidity, river diving is not always safe.

Reservoirs: In most reservoirs diving is forbidden. Bear in mind that in reservoir diving there may be a large outlet valve that can trap a diver. Check with the waterworks authority of the locale.

Small Lakes: Currents are generally nonexistent, except during high winds or in huge bodies of water like the Great Lakes. Visibility varies from one lake to another.

Large Lakes: The behavior of the waters of large lakes is often like that of oceans. Wind and weather can whip them into a fury and generate choppy surface currents or even pounding surf.

TIPS FOR FRESHWATER DIVING

In order to achieve neutral buoyancy in fresh waters subtract 2½ percent of equipment or weights you would use in salt water. When using the U.S. Navy Air Decompression Tables, subtract 3 percent of the depth from the depth. It takes 34 feet of fresh water to equal the pressure of 33 feet of salt water. The Navy tables are based on salt water. Be cautious in your entry: Fresh waters usually have muddy and debris-laden bottoms. If you sink into the mud, you can lose a fin or suffer an injury. Beware of slippery surfaces, fishing lines, hooks, and lures. Watch out for heavy boat traffic. It could be risky near surface. Be sure to tow a diver's flag on a float while staying well under the surface of the water out of harm's way until it's time to quit.

When diving in a river, the strongest current will be encountered on the outside of a bend. Remember that ice diving is something which requires special techniques. All diving rules, plus more, apply; so, attend an ice-diving course or workshop. Altitude diving is special, too. For example, the rate of ascent actually decreases by about 2 feet per minute for each 1000 feet of altitude. In these more hazardous dives, as with cave diving, training is in order. Any of the national certifying agencies can put you in touch with a qualified instructor.

OCEAN WATERS

"The Pacific Ocean is what the United States is between the Atlantic and."—Colonel Stoopnagle

Wind Currents: Wind velocities directly affect the degree of ocean turbulence. A gusty, windy day may indicate dangerous boating and dive conditions ahead.

Swells: Swells result from storms originating far out to sea. They generally reach a height of 2 or 3 feet, following a rhythmic pattern and paralleling the shore. Seasickness can become a problem when larger swells cloud the water.

Along-Shore Swells: Like rip currents, swells along the shore area are a danger to divers. The swells are caused by waves arriving at acute angles to the shore, centering at one or more areas along an irregular shoreline.

Wave Motion: At a depth of 50 feet or more a diver can barely feel the wave motion of surface waves, but wave motion becomes noticeable as the diver moves into shallower waters.

Plunging Waves: Plunging breakers are those that crest over, leaving a hollow, and plunge into a free fall onto the surface below. These are generated by winds or storms identifiable by the appearance of white caps far out, turning into plunging or rolling breakers on shore. They also appear on calm days. Their force erodes the seabed where they break.

Spilling Waves: A spilling wave breaks by cascading down into a trough, causing somewhat less erosion than the former. Visibility will be blocked in these roiled-up waters.

Choppy Waves: Choppy waves indicate dangerous, fast currents, capable of sweeping divers away from their float or craft. Your flotation device can be handy here. Again, seasickness can be a serious hazard. If you are susceptible to seasickness, you should not be diving in turbulent or rhythmic swells.

CHOOSING A DIVE SITE

When choosing a dive site, first check all available nautical charts for information about bottom conditions in your dive area.

Choose a land rendezvous point that is close to your dive site.

Select a site that will not require you or your boat to penetrate dangerous waters or coastlines.

Choose a site that is protected from the violence of the open sea.

Take motion-sickness pills not later than three hours before embarking if you think you might need them to prevent seasickness. Those consistently susceptible to motion sickness while under water should avoid diving in all but calm waters. Also, if calm waters grow turbulent, signal your buddy and get out of the water.

Be particularly careful to guard against cuts and lacerations around coral. Wear gloves and full foot fins or rubber booties.

How to Find the Best Areas by Surface Observation: Clear blue seas and uninterrupted sandy bottoms indicate dull, bland, desert-like seabeds with little appeal.

In the Pacific area, stray kelp on the surface is a sign of nearby dense sea jungles abounding with exciting possibilities for sport.

In the Florida Keys and the Caribbean, darker spotty areas indicate appealing areas to explore. White water is the indirect result of a high rate of sedimentation stirred up after a storm in Florida waters.

Rocky coastlines where there are many coves, bays, tide pools, or inlets indicate good diving locations. Smooth, long coastlines are usually dull and are often subject to ebb tides, which cloud waters, impairing visibility for miles.

Dark-blue waters indicate great depth. Brown areas indicate sandbars. White foamy surfaces indicate a submerged reef—generally interesting for all-around diving.

CORAL REEF DIVING

> "You are about to take a journey into wonderland. It is probable that your state of mind will be one of astonishment—nay, of stupefaction. You will find it hard to remain indifferent to the spectacle unrolling itself before your eyes."—Jules Verne

When Verne wrote the above words in *20,000 Leagues Under the Sea* he had been inspired by reminiscences of coral reefs he had seen.

Diving around coral reefs is great any time of the day, but the best time is in the morning with the sea and weather calm and the neap tide just turning to ebb.

The most prolific and varied growths among coral reefs are to be found on the landward side of the reef in the valleys sheltered from the open sea.

You will find almost all coral reefs resplendent with beauty whether you see them with the eyes of a trained naturalist, with those of a poet, or with those of a curious layman. You will see blue-green pastures with multicolored forests interspersed with formations resembling the columned temples, spires, domes, minarets, and arches of dream cities in colors of every subtle hue and intensity. The reefs of the world are in moderately shallow water, easy to reach in a short dive. Often all you need is a mask, snorkel, and flippers.

How to Locate Good Reef Dive Sites: Look down from your boat. When you see brightness of colors, varied and intensely active coral growth is indicated. Innumerable kinds of small fish, invertebrate life, and coral growth are present.

Visiting the Caverns of a Reef: Caverns are usually shallow, 4 to 5 feet deep and usually less than 2 feet high. Caverns are favored by many small fish and such larger ones as dog snapper, moray eels, and often nurse sharks, so be cautious.

CURRENTS THAT CONCERN THE DIVER

Currents of whatever origin or depth are elements of the sea of which every diver should be aware. Sometimes they can have a velocity and power capable of driving you out to sea or preventing you from returning safely from a dive. Others can drive you against coral, rocks, pilings, and debris with painful results. Therefore, watch out for tidal currents and those caused by jetties, coves, prominences, sandbars, and reefs. Make sure your over-all dive plan takes these into account before you embark. In places where the tidal currents are rapid, try to plan your diving time to periods of slack water, but remember that you will be handicapped by a current of even less than one knot.

Where to Obtain Information About Tidal Currents: Current direction and velocity will vary with place, depth, tide, and bottom configuration. Consult newspapers and marine dealers for the tide tables of the area you intend to visit, as well as U.S. government tide tables for the area and local seafarers. Geodetic tables should be used carefully, since they show only surface conditions, and current velocity normally increases with depth.

What to Do When Caught in Strong Currents: When caught in strong currents, work with them. If possible, don't swim against them or into heavy surf or heavy winds. Do not exhaust yourself; conserve strength. Plan your return swim home *with* the current, if possible. Angle in and out as desired, even if you land at a shore far from your destination. The long walk back is better than drowning. Rescue will be more imminent if, before diving, you warn a friend on shore that if you do not return home at a specified time, you may be in trouble. Be sure to tell your friend where you will be diving.

When it becomes apparent that severe measures of survival must be taken, inflate your life jacket. Then release and drop your weight belt or any other equipment if it really hampers your safety. Relax and stay afloat.

Floating Techniques If You Have No Self-inflatable Safety Float (Which You Should Never Be Without): Float faceup with your head well back, arms extended horizontally. Kick with your fins only enough to keep your face clear of the water. Avoid using unnecessary swim strokes. You will need all your strength. If the sea is heavy and violent, use the bobbing system of floating.

Floating by Bobbing: Hold your breath and let your body sink as far as it will (a pound or two of your body weight will possibly remain out of the water).

When ready to breathe again, push down slightly with the palms of your hands or kick with the fins a few times. This action will raise your head clear out of the water and enable you to inhale.

Then, while holding your breath, relax and submerge again until another breath of air is needed. Retain your mask, fins, snorkel, and protective clothing; they will better your chances of survival.

The Dangerous Rip Current (Known Also as a Sea Puss or by the Misnomer "Rip Tide"): The rip current, if not maneuvered skillfully, is dangerous to divers. In fact, rip currents account for most of the drownings blamed on undertow. Rip currents are the result of water flowing seaward through a gap in a bar or reef, generating a swirling in-shore and leading into a strong current seaward that is capable of washing an unwary swimmer away from the safety of shallow waters. Rips often have a velocity of 2 knots per hour and can extend as far as a half-mile offshore; they rarely exceed a width of 100 feet.

Recognizing the Rip Current: From a shore vantage point (the higher up the better), watch for a gap in the continual line of breakers over a reef. Turbulence is evident in the body of the rip and is accompanied by an interruption of the pattern of waves breaking near shore. The waves are not breaking as actively as they are on either side because of the deeper water. A rip current continues parallel to the reef or bar.

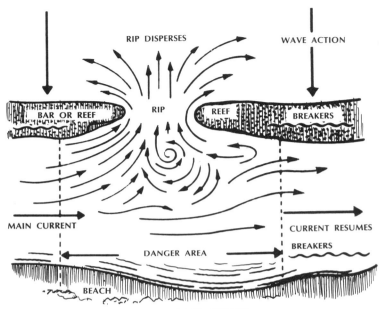

PATTER OF RIP CURRENT

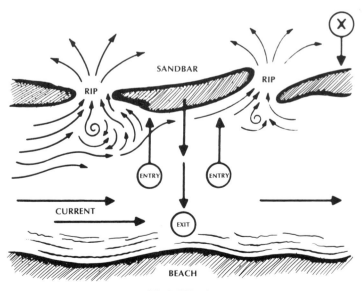

RIP CURRENTS

If you are under water, poor visibility (due to swirling sand and debris) will identify the rip area. The waters of a rip current are agitated by small slapping waves. The water is cleaner on either side of the current.

If caught unaware in a rip current, relax and ride it out. Swim back calmly with the waves on either side of the rip.

Coral Reef Currents: Currents resembling rip currents are found among channels of coral reefs. These currents are very dangerous because they are intermittent and may not exist except when excessive amounts of water flow over the reef into channels inside the reef. The water must eventually escape and so seeks a gap within the reef through which to return to the open sea. The return flow through these gaps may move with great velocity and can brush an unwary diver hard against the sharp coral, severely injuring him.

SURFACING

At the end of time at diving depth, signal all buddies at topside and start for the surface. Breathe continuously and normally during the entire ascent. *Never hold your breath.* Ascend slowly at about 60 feet per minute. By doing so, you allow your body to release nitrogen through the lungs during respiration and you keep the air pressure within the lungs equal to the water pressure.

If making repetitive dives or dives carrying you into depth-time ratios requiring decompression, do not exceed the rate of ascent specified in the decompression table applicable to the dive. If decompression is necessary, follow the appropriate table using proper techniques described in Chapter 6.

Check your weight belt quick-release fit.

Look up and around for obstructions overhead, such as boats. In low-visibility waters, hold one arm over your head to fend off objects in your path.

As you break surface, take a last deep breath from your tank, hold it, and switch to your snorkel if circumstances permit.

Float in a relaxed prone position, keeping afloat with minimum exertion.

Signal the buddies in your topside party on shore or in your boat for pickup.

If exhausted or lost, do not hesitate to jettison your weight belt if it impairs your safety. Inflate your life jacket if a long wait is anticipated. Don't attempt to swim with your tank strapped on. Remove it, but hold it, tugging it along as you go. It can give you added buoyancy.

Buddies and surface members of a group must keep constant vigil at all times until a dive is terminated.

Leaving the Water: Part of your over-all dive plan should include the selection of a spot for your return to shore. Make your selection with the following considerations:

The location of your exit must take into account the amount of equipment you will be carrying back, the terrain over which you will walk once ashore, and your estimated state of fatigue.

The exact location of the exit from the water should take into account the wave pattern at the exact spot chosen for exit.

Aim your landing to coincide with the least amount of breaker action on rocks and beaches.

POSTDIVE INSPECTION

Check yourself for any signs of sickness or injury resulting from a dive.

Dry yourself and dress to avoid chill. In cold weather, drink a hot beverage if one is available.

Check all equipment thoroughly for any signs of damage. Make notes of any unusual observations concerning the dive or the operation of your equipment.

Have all damaged equipment repaired as soon as possible after the dive.

POSTDIVE PROCEDURES

Injuries sustained during a dive—such as cuts or animal bites—may not be noticed at first because of shock or the numbing effect of cold water. Physiological problems may not be evident until some time after a dive. Be alert for the possibility of such problems as decompression sickness and embolism.

If satisfied with your apparent physical condition, check your equipment for damage.

POSTDIVE MAINTENANCE CARE AND STOWAGE

Turn off the cylinder on/off valve and open the air-reserve valve—even if the tank has been only partially used. This will serve as a warning that the tank has been used and must be checked and refilled. It is also a good practice to place it in a specially designated area to avoid any possible mix-up.

Bleed the regulator by inhaling through the mouthpiece, or pressing the purge button, and remove the regulator.

Be sure that the protective cone is clear of water or dirt, check the O-ring, and secure the cone in place over the regulator inlet. This will keep foreign particles out of the regulator and also permit submerging the regulator in fresh water for cleaning without permitting water to enter the first stage of the regulator.

Damaged equipment should be repaired, inspected, and tested as soon as possible unless irreparable.

Wash all equipment with fresh water and be sure to remove all traces of salt. The salt will not only speed corrosion of the materials but may also plug up vent holes in the regulator and the depth gauge. All parts of the equipment which must be free to move—such as diaphragms and check valves, quick-release buckles, the knife in the scabbard, and CO_2 actuators in life vests—should be carefully checked for corrosion, salt, or dirt buildup. The mouthpiece should be rinsed several times in fresh water and an oral disinfectant. Periodically, the breathing hoses of a double-hose regulator should be unclamped and removed from the regulator and mouth-piece and cleaned internally.

When all equipment has been washed and rinsed, it should be hung up to dry and then placed in appropriate stowage. Regulators should be stowed separately and never left mounted on cylinders. When dry, wet suits should be dusted with talcum and carefully folded or hung. The suits should never be hung from a hook or a wire hanger since they will stretch out of shape or be torn. Masks, depth gauges, life vests, and any other equipment which can be damaged or scuffed by rough handling should be individually stored and never dumped collectively in a box or drawer. Batteries should be removed from lights, tested, and stored separately. All lines should be dried, coiled, and properly stowed.

A fully charged cylinder may be stored for months without harm. The quality of the air will not deteriorate. However, it is a good practice to change the air in a cylinder if it has been in storage for over a year. The pressure of each cylinder in storage should be gauged weekly. If a marked drop in pressure is noted, the cylinder should be checked.

PRACTICAL SUGGESTIONS FOR FIELD MAINTENANCE AND REPAIR

Masks: If a mask strap is broken or separated due to a lost buckle (and a new strap is not available), a temporary repair can be accomplished by connecting and whipping the strap ends with waxed linen thread or dental floss.

Swim Fins: Swim-fin straps can be repaired in much the same manner as broken mask straps. If sewing with thread or dental floss is required to repair a strap or hole in the fin, the hard rubber is more easily penetrated if the needle is heated using paraffin candles, or if the holes are prepunched with a heated awl or ice-pick.

Snorkels: Loose mouthpieces or holes in snorkels can be patched with plastic adhesive tape.

Straps and Weight Belt: Ends on straps and weight belts which are made of nylon can be kept from fraying or unraveling by melting them. Nylon line ends can be burned in a similar manner to prevent unraveling. Holes in weight belts can be smoothed by light melting.

Wet-Suit Repair: Tears in wet suits can be repaired using commercial repair kits or tire repair kits. If using glue, instructions on the container should be carefully followed. Torn edges should be trimmed smooth with a knife or razor blade before sewing or gluing. Repair is best accomplished by applying glue and waiting until it is dry to the touch. Edges should be pressed together or clamped if possible. Sewing gives additional strength. Wet-suit zippers and seams should always be both glued and sewn for maximum bonding strength.

All repair and maintenance should be followed by a thorough inspection and testing of the equipment to ensure its full operability and safety. If there is any question about a particular piece of equipment, do not dive with it under any circumstance.

6

DECOMPRESSION
AND DIVING

Many people wonder if there is a difference between a recompression chamber and a decompression chamber. There is no difference. There is a difference, however, in what the chamber is being used for. If a diver is suffering from decompression sickness and is brought to a chamber for treatment, he is first recompressed to the prescribed depth pressure and then decompressed in accordance with the correct treatment. The recompression stage of treatment brings bubbles back into solution. The decompression tables are used for decompressing a person who has been under pressure within the limits of the tables.

You can enjoy a full underwater experience without diving into depth-time ratios that require decompression in a chamber on the surface. Using U.S. Navy tables as a guide and staying inside the safety curve they list, you won't need to make decompression stops. Inside these safety limits, you will find enough opportunity to pursue almost any dive objective without complications. The sea abounds with dazzling marine life and landscapes within 30-foot depths where dives can be made continually (except as limited by your air supply) without the need for decompression. Sunlight provides the energy to keep a whole complicated biological community thriving; therefore, life at this level has its greatest diversity, since it has the most favorable environment for life. Light is always present and dependable. Here also you will find a special exuberance, a kind of rapture of the shallows. If you stay above 33 feet, when one tank runs out of air, you can keep strapping tank after tank on your back and dive all day long, and you cannot get decompression sickness regardless of the length of time or amount of compressed air breathed. In tropical waters you can dive continually and comfortably at such depths without chilling.

To repeat, diving beyond the safety curve, or beyond the No-Decompression limit, offers no improvement over the pleasures of diving at lesser depths; it offers only greater risks. The safest dive is a no-decompression dive. If, on the other hand, you are compulsively adventurous, fearless of deep diving and its dangers, or if you must, under certain circumstances, exceed depth-time ratios and then require decompression, follow the instructions set forth in this section.

NO-DECOMPRESSION LIMIT

(Depth-Time Limits for Air Dives Not Requiring
Decompression on Ascent)

The times you can spend in dives at progressively increasing depths without the need of making decompression stops during ascent are shown on page 110.

Do not go beyond these time and depth limits, or you must resort to decompression in the water prior to surfacing. This means you must follow U.S. Navy Air Decompression Tables accurately and make whatever stops they indicate. The U.S. Navy Standard Air Decompression Table (see page 313 in the Appendix) indicates at what level and for how long a diver must stop in his ascent to prevent decompression sickness.

A word of precaution concerning the psychological effects of deep diving: Generally speaking the well-practiced diver can overcome the anxieties related to diving. Nevertheless, any diving beyond normal limits will impose nervous strains unknown in mod-

Depth (ft.)	No-Decompression Limits (Min.)
10	—
15	—
20	—
25	—
30	—
35	310
40	200
50	100
60	60
70	50
80	40
90	30
100	25
110	20
120	15
130	10
140	10
150–190	5

Recommended sport-diving depth — 60

Maximum sport-diving depth — 130

Rate of Ascent: 60 fpm

Remember: The safest dive is a no-decompression dive.

erate depths, whatever the experience. Remoteness from base, the cold, darkness, increased physical effort of movement and of breathing—all will tend to bring nearer the onset of panic while making its control more problematical. Perhaps more to be feared than panic is the sense of euphoria and cockiness which can mislead more advanced divers into poorly judged decisions, and possible catastrophe.

SINGLE DIVES

A single dive is the first dive of the day. It is denoted by an exposure to a specific depth in feet for a specific time in minutes. An example would be 134 feet for 14 minutes. The depth is the maximum depth attained. The time is the actual bottom time. Bottom time is the time between leaving the surface in descent and leaving the deepest depth in ascent. A combination of depth and time listed in the decompression tables is called a *dive schedule*. All dives are included and covered in the next deeper and next longer schedule. Do not interpolate.

REPETITIVE DIVES

Even though you dive within No-Decompression limits, you will have some residual nitrogen in your body. You must take this into consideration if you make a second dive within a 12-hour period after the first dive. Follow the U.S. Navy tables (pages 313–18) in the Appendix—The No-Decompression Limits and Repetitive Group Designation Table and the Residual Nitrogen Timetable for Repetitive Air Dives give instructions and examples.

EXAMPLE OF A TYPICAL REPETITIVE DIVE SITUATION

Let's say you plan two dives on the same day. You descend at 9:00 A.M. to a maximum depth of 83 feet and make your way slowly to an objective at about 65 feet. You then ascend as planned, making a note of the time. Your ascent brings you to the surface at 9:22 A.M. After a light lunch, you begin another descent, this time at 11:07 A.M. You dive and explore at a depth of 65 feet for half an hour. Your ascent from 65 feet to the surface begins at 11:37 A.M.

To understand and use the tables effectively, you must master the following important terms:

Bottom time refers to the total elapsed time, starting from the time you begin your descent until you begin a direct ascent to the surface.

Depth is the deepest point reached during a dive.

Surface interval time is the time you spend on the surface between dives.

Repetitive dives refers to any dive that begins within 12 hours of surfacing from a previous dive. If the surface interval between dives is 10 minutes or less, consider both dives as one long dive with a bottom time equal to the total bottom times of both dives.

HOW TO USE A DIVE PROFILE

A dive profile is an easily sketched diagram by which you can plan and analyze the repetitive dives; with it you record time, depth, and information from the decompression tables. Sample of dive profile for the aforementioned dive is given below:

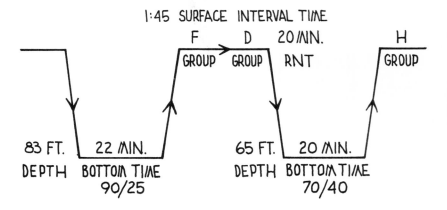

To stay within the No-Decompression limits, you consult the No-Decompression Limits and Repetitive Group Designation Table (pages 318–22). Looking at the first two columns, you find that any dive between 80 and 90 feet is considered a dive to 90 feet with a maximum bottom time of 30 minutes. In other words, you would have to ascend within 40 minutes. You decide to end the first dive well before this time limit is up. The actual depth and bottom time of the first dive is 83 feet for 22 minutes. Enter this information on the dive profile. Returning to the No-Decompression Table for the 90-foot depth, you find that the exact or next greater time, over 22 minutes, is 25 minutes. You then enter this information in the profile: "90/25."

According to the No-Decompression Table, a dive to 90 feet for 25 minutes puts you in the repetitive group F. Then enter this information in the dive profile. The repetitive groups A through O systematically reflect how much residual nitrogen is in a diver's body after a No-Decompression dive. An A diver has the least, while an O diver has the most nitrogen.

In your typical dive, the surface interval time between your dives is 1 hour, 45 minutes. Enter this time on the dive profile. While on the surface, you are constantly giving off nitrogen. When you begin the repetitive dive, your body will therefore contain less residual nitrogen than it did at the end of the first dive. For credit based on this decrease in residual nitrogen, turn to the second table, The Residual Nitrogen Timetable for Repetitive Air Dives.

Since you terminated your first dive as an F diver, you enter the Residual Nitrogen Timetable at F on the left-hand side of the table. The numbers printed in pairs over to the right refer to maximum and minimum surface interval times.

Reading from left to right, you discover that your time: 1 hour, 45 minutes, puts you in the fourth column from the right side of the table, i.e., the box containing 1:30 (minimum time in that designation) and 2:28 (maximum time). Trace the column downward to discover that the decrease of residual nitrogen moves you from the F group diver-designation to the D group diver-designation.

Even though you have less nitrogen in your body, you still have some that must be taken into consideration for the second dive. Add your new group designation D to the dive profile. Now turn to the lower half of the Residual Nitrogen Timetable. In this part of the table, convert the group letter and the depth and the next repetitive dive into minutes of residual nitrogen time that you must consider having already spent on the bottom before you begin the next repetitive dive. The far left-hand column contains the list of depths for the next dive.

The Residual Nitrogen Timetable shows that a D diver going to a repetitive dive depth of 70 feet will have a residual nitrogen time of 20 minutes. The residual nitrogen time (RNT) is added to the dive profile. This indicates that you must start the second dive at 65 feet as though you had already been at this depth for 20 minutes.

To be certain that you don't exceed the No-Decompression limits, refer back to the No-Decompression Limits Table. There you will see that a dive to 70 feet (65 actual feet) will have a maximum bottom time of 50 minutes.

In order to stay well within the No-Decompression limits, you elect to limit your actual bottom time to 20 minutes. Since you are beginning the repetitive dive with a residual nitrogen time of 20 minutes, your total bottom time will be 20 plus 20 minutes, or 40 minutes—10 minutes less than the 50 minute No-Decompression limit.

When the repetitive dive is terminated, refer to the No-Decompression Limits Table to find your repetitive group designation. This is H. The table shows that your second dive of the day was 70 feet for 40 minutes (65 actual feet and 40 actual minutes), which makes you an H diver. The H repetitive group designation is to be entered on your profile as shown for use when another repetitive dive is decided.

Good Planning When Decompression Is Anticipated or Fore-seeable: Know the location and phone number of the nearest decompression chamber. Make sure it is operating. Plan a way to get there. You can probably count on the Coast Guard for transportation. Be sure the dive is well planned and organized.

Use only the depth-time combination on the newest U.S. Navy Standard Air Decompression Table.

Estimate your diving time for the descent, the time on the bottom, and the time of ascent, and compute the amount of air necessary, allowing an adequate safety factor. Wear your underwater watch.

Maintain a 75-feet-per-minute rate of descent.

Maintain a 60-feet-per-minute rate of ascent for two vital reasons:

1. to allow time to release nitrogen through the lungs during respiration; and
2. to prevent air pressure in the lungs from being unequal with the surrounding water pressure, causing air embolism.

Incidentally, the rule governing the rate of ascent applies to any dive.

If diving 130 feet down or more, be on the alert for signs and symptoms of nitrogen narcosis (rapture of the deep), and don't hesitate to move to a lesser depth if you or your buddy show evidence of it. Your prime symptom will be a feeling of well-being, of feeling "high" (see page 223 for detailed discussion). For prolonged dives, wear an exposure suit even in warm-water areas. "Long Johns" should be worn under a dry suit in extremely cold waters. Water temperatures drop drastically as you move deeper. Most divers have found that a wet suit worn under a dry suit makes the best cold-water diving combination.

Be sure that you and your buddies agree on and understand the signals of communication (see pages 64–69 for underwater signaling).

Use the best equipment thoroughly checked before each dive. If a decompression dive is preplanned, use a fully charged twin tank. Maintain your proposed depth, but if you should change your planned depth, refigure the change in your decompression stages.

Use a shot line of the bottom marked with knots tied at 10- and 20-foot levels to mark decompression stops. Take into account tidal changes affecting true depth of the markers. The line should be bright in color, preferably nylon, and no less than $3/16$ inch in diameter. It will serve to guide you back to your boat, as a device for signaling to the surface and as a reference for decompression stops. Before diving, you can attach a spare tank to this line or hang it over the side of your boat ready for use when your own tank supply is insufficient to see you through decompression stops. To save energy, use enough extra weight to pull you down to desired depths. Always have a timekeeper to keep an accurate log of dive time and one or more fully geared standby divers watching lifelines and ready to help any diver in trouble on instant notice.

SYMPTOMS OF THE BENDS*

Symptoms may not appear for several hours after surfacing. Get to a recompression center at once. Don't wait for symptoms if decompression sickness is expected. If transportation is needed, call the Coast Guard or police. (See page 244 for phone numbers to locate 24-hour decompression facilities.)

Those who make dives requiring decompression should keep a log for future reference with the following data:

1. Name
2. Date
3. Type of work underwater
4. Wearing suit   Wet___   Dry___
5. Depth of dive (in feet)
6. Time at surface
7. Time at bottom
8. Time left bottom
9. Decompression schedule of time and length of stops in minutes
10. Time reached surface
11. Comments on any remarkable experiences or events

* Also see Decompression Sickness (page 226).

7

SPECIAL DIVING ACTIVITIES

"Maybe the simple fact that one finds happiness in diving is enough excuse for doing it. Whether such an occupation is useful or idle matters little. Must we forever be seeking the warm glow of satisfaction doing useful things like boy scouts getting a kick out of doing a daily deed? Diving not only involves the human body but the human spirit as well."— *Philippe Diolé*

One diver is happy just to submerge and cruise around, do some souvenir hunting, and go home. Another might achieve near Nirvana contemplating such undersea trivia as a peppermint shrimp fearlessly laundering the fangs of its client, a green moray eel. For still another, diving, if repeatedly uninformative, can grow monotonous and eventually extinguish interest altogether. Keep a weather eye out for the unusual, make a mental note of what you see, and pursue the subject later with books to fuel your interest and satisfy your curiosity. Sooner or later you'll find serious inquiry so irresistible that you may dive no longer only for the pure sport but for scientific or professional reasons as well. The underwater laboratory of serious research and study in geology, biology, physiology, photography, archeology, and so on, started for many divers as a mere playground.

FISH WATCHING

If you are not inclined to fish killing or fish trapping, there is the fun of fish watching. As a fish-watching diver you need not confine your study of fish to aquariums or dead bottle specimens. You can observe the behavior of living fish as they go about their daily routines undisturbed by your presence right in their native habitat.

Fish-Watching Hints: Be especially alert in the vicinity of dead or wounded fish. They usually attract whatever sharks or barracuda might be in their vicinity. The best fish-watching grounds are around shores, reefs, wrecks, and seaweed. To get a close look at fish, bait them to you with a broken-up sea urchin, crayfish, or lobster. Then watch them come to feed. (Don't use a blood fish for bait; it may draw predators.) Collect a few good books on ichthyology to help you identify what you see.

Fish watching as a hobby would hardly be complete without photography. Shoot what you watch. Whenever you snap the shutter you'll capture aquatic animals in action for future study of their feeding, spawning, courting, and defensive habits. (For more on photography, see Chapter 9.)

Bird watchers have their Audubon Society. Fish watchers can join the American Littoral Society, Sandy Hook Marine Laboratory, Highlands, New Jersey. The A.L.S. publishes illustrated reports by fish watchers in its excellent quarterly publication, *The Aquatic Reporter and Underwater Naturalist.* Don't overlook reporting your observations to other scientific publications. Science is always interested in contributions by amateur naturalists.

SYMBIOSIS

The alert fish watcher will marvel at community life of the animal kingdom under the sea. He will learn of war and coexistence.

Coexistence of dissimilar organisms is scientifically termed "symbiosis." Symbiosis is divided into three categories: parasitism, commensalism, and mutualism.

Parasitism: A parasite animal lives in or on the host animal and feeds on the tissue of the host. For example, deep-sea angelfish have males that are parasitic to the female. The male attaches itself to the body of the female at an early stage of growth and receives all food from her. The male consequently degenerates to a small animal consisting of reproductive organs only.

Commensalism: A relationship in which one of the participants receives benefits from the other without harming the other—such as food, transportation, protection, or support. This type of symbiosis is practiced by the conch fish, which hides in the shell of the living conch to protect itself against predators. Pilot fish adopt large sharks as protective companions and scavenge scraps from the sharks' meals.

Mutualism: A cooperative association in which each of the participants shares in the benefits of the relationship. The diver-biologist is in a uniquely privileged position to study these relationships and perhaps uncover new ones. Did you know, for example, that more than twenty species of small fish and shrimp are now known to clean other fish of parasite fungi and infected tissue, particularly in tropical waters? Some cleaner-fish have even set up shop in fish communities, where they are visited regularly by a clientele of fish dependent on their services.

TRAPPING LIVE TROPICAL FISH

A step beyond watching fish is trapping them for your aquarium. Some divers prefer using the slurp gun (a hand-operated vacuum gun that sucks fish into its container) for trapping. Others may find the hand net equally effective or better. The hand net should be at least 1 foot in diameter and have a depth of 15 inches. Nylon or plastic screening serves well as a netting. The serious ichthyologist ought to have several types of device in his kit for diverse conditions and bottoms.

Slurp Gun: The slurp gun is an excellent tool designed specifically for catching small fish alive. The quarry, when caught, is visible through the plastic tube of the gun. The gun operates manually on the simple principle of the vacuum cleaner with a suction powerful enough to suck the fish right into its tube. To use the gun, you slowly move its muzzle within inches of your quarry. Seek out a crevice or hole into which fish scurry to hide. Aim the muzzle of the slurp gun at the mouth of the hole and pull the plunger to suction your catch right into the tube. Quick action is a necessity because fish may dart out of the tube as rapidly as they are drawn in. Give the tube a twist and let the fish swim into the holding chamber. Twist the tube back and you are ready to continue hunting.

Hand Net: Allow fish to become accustomed to your presence. Be slow and graceful, never jerky. Once you spot a desirable specimen, approach gently and slowly and coax the fish into the net. Once the quarry is well inside the net, scoop suddenly, forcing the fish to the net's bottom. Close the net swiftly with a quick twist of the handle. Keep a sharp eye out for predators, as small fry in distress attract them.

Throw Net: The throw net is circular with lead weights at its periphery. As it is thrown, the operator tries to spread it so that it strikes the water fully expanded. This takes practice. One such net is about 3 feet in diameter and has a hole in the center just big enough for your arm. The net is laid down over a small coral head or coral rubble bottom on which desirable fish are hiding. One arm is inserted into the net to move the coral and rock while the other is pressed down upon the net to catch the fish. The fish are removed by the hand inside the net.

Push Net: The push net is a simple net on a frame which is shoved ahead of the operator over grass beds, picking up fish that have concealed themselves among the fronds of attached vegetation.

Lift or Blanket Net: Fish are attracted to a position over this net by bait, or at night by a light, and the net is brought up suddenly to capture them. The net may be broad and flat and lifted from the periphery by multiple lines.

Hook Net: The hook net is commonly used to catch crabs and hence is often called a crab net. With a deeper net bag you can catch small fish that come to the bait tied in the middle of the net. In clear water, with a face mask or with a glass-bottom viewing bucket, you can observe the net and pull it up rapidly when the desired fish is in the position to be caught.

Dip Net: The dip net is in universal use in various operations. A long-handled dip net is used to catch fish at the surface or at poison stations or during night-light operations. A short-handled dip net is used in underwater collecting. Two small dip nets, one in each hand, can be an effective means of taking small fish underwater if the collector is experienced in their use.

Once a small, bottom-dwelling fish is trapped in a net, it can be brought to the surface with the mouth of the net held upward. When a fish has moved away from the bottom it expends all its energy fighting to go downward, and there is no need to cover the net. As soon as possible after sweeping for a fish, the mouth of the net should be directed upward. A piece of wire is often useful for poking into holes and crevices to induce fish to leave their hiding places.

Some divers prefer to use a glass jar with a dip net. The jar may be set on the bottom at some vantage point, such as an escape route next to a rock. The net is then used to frighten the fish into the jar, which is not readily detected because of its transparency. The jar may be baited with crushed sea urchins or other attractive bait. Small fish, particularly wrasses, enter the jar to feed and can be captured by flipping a lid in place or by covering the opening with a net.

Hook and Line: Angling with a relatively harmless hook can be effective without harming or killing the quarry.

HANDLING FISH

Minimize touching fish, especially with dry hands, or you may rub off the protective slime that shields fish against parasites.

SUGGESTIONS ON SHIPPING TROPICAL FISH

Fish need oxygen to survive. For short trips of no more than 8 hours, place your catch in a bait bucket or ice bucket full of water native to the fish. The sloshing around of the water should generate sufficient oxygen content to keep the fish alive in transport. For long-range destinations, air-freight shipping is recommended. Place fish in heavy-duty, water-filled plastic bags available from commercial dealers in tropical fish. Don't crowd the bag with more than 8 fish per gallon of water. There is no need to feed them except upon an expert's advice to the contrary; they'll manage on the various minute organisms in the water. See that the bag is tightly closed with all air squeezed out, and then fill with pure oxygen (available at any welding supply shop). Seal the bag, enclose it in a box, then ship immediately. The oxygen should keep the fish alive for 48 hours. Transport of larger fish may require such complicated facilities as a battery-operated air pump, which you can buy from any local aquarium supplier. If there is no air-freight service and if ground transportation takes more than two days, don't bother. Return the captives to the sea.

WHERE TO SELL TROPICAL FISH

Aquariums, pet shops, and big distributors are some of the possible outlets for live tropical fish. Check laws of the state governing the collecting of fish for resale by consulting your local conservation department officer.

What Deal to Make: Survey retail prices. Subtract 60 percent as your wholesale price to a dealer-retailer. Insist on a clear-cut contract stipulating who pays the freight, when payment is to be made, and so on.

SPEARFISHING

Active fish hunters need to be in excellent physical condition. Study the behavior of fish and try to determine how they are apt to react under different circumstances. Stay alert to dangers. Practice and develop a good breath-holding capacity.

The Law and Spearfishing: In most countries, spearfishing with the aid of a breathing apparatus is strictly prohibited by laws. Laws or no laws, it simply isn't sportsmanlike to use a breathing apparatus when hunting fish. The use of a breathing apparatus is warranted only when the goal is to find food or kill dangerous fish. Obey all laws and get a fishing license if required locally.

Rules of Safe Spearfishing:
Don't cock or load a spear out of water.

Don't use carbon-dioxide-powered guns except under the supervision or after expert instruction. Keep carbon-dioxide cylinders out of the sun; heat can cause an explosion which could send your spear into someone—fatally.

Don't spear fish too big for you to handle.

Don't tie a spear line onto yourself or your buddy. A big fish just speared can pull you down to great depths, or smash you into coral reefs painfully or mortally. Use a fall-away spearhead for big game.

Be extra alert and sure of your target in water of poor visibility. In such waters shorten the line that attaches the spear to the gun.

Don't tow speared game in the water or you may attract such dangerous fish as sharks and barracuda. Place the game in a game sack attached to your surface float.

If the game you have just speared is attacked by a shark or other predatory fish, let it go.

Respect spears as you would firearms.

Beware of fish equipped with poisonous fins. Wear cotton gloves to protect your hands against injury by fish spines and gill rakers.

Types of Speargun: There are four types of speargun: sling, spring, CO_2 gas, and pneumatic. Start with a simple hand spear and work up to more complicated weapons. There are any number of varieties. A long, tapered hand spear with a fixed or a detachable spearhead and propelled by surgical rubber is quite adequate for beginners. Almost as simple to use as the hand spear is the Hawaiian sling made of a small tube with a small piece of surgical rubber tubing attached to one end. The procedure is the same as in hand spearing except that the diver holds the tube with one hand, draws back the spear with the rubber band (as with a slingshot), points, and releases the spear at the fish. It is suitable for fish up to 25 pounds. No line is attached to the spear, so be close to the fish before releasing the spear.

Spearfishing Techniques: Check local navigational charts to find the best fishing bottoms. Warm, clear, tropical waters among reefs are best. Dress according to water temperature.

While seeking your prey, keep a sharp eye around rocks, undersea obstructions, or shipwrecks, which are favorite hiding places for fish. Look in all directions.

Dive quietly, gracefully. Try keeping the sun behind you to prevent fish from spotting you. Know the range. Make it close. Long shots usually miss or lack the penetration needed to kill. Before submerging, swim slowly just below the surface, breathing quietly through your snorkel. If while stalking a fish you can't get him in range, turn off in another direction and he may stop running and turn toward you.

When you spot a fish, to attack, start your dive and be careful not to kick up a splash. Get into position broadside or topside of the fish and as close as possible. If using a hand spear (pole gun with a fixed or detachable head) point just behind the gill plate and thrust hard, swimming against the spear while gripping it firmly to push it completely through the fish. Don't aim below the fish's lateral line (a belly shot) where the flesh is soft; the fish can pull itself off a spear there. Try placing the spear along the fish's backbone.

Once the fish is impaled, grab it with your free hand to prevent it from escaping. Resurface for air. Get the fish out of the water so that its blood does not attract sharks or barracuda.

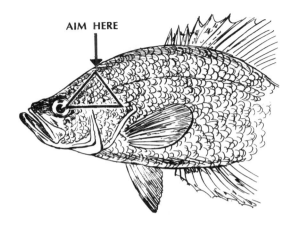

AIM HERE

Avoid game that is inherently dangerous because of extreme size. Also, avoid game that you know has poisonous fins, for penetration can cause painful injury. These fish include the freshwater catfish, the grouper, the weeverfish, and the scorpionfish. (See Chapter 11 for further discussion.)

What to Do with Speared Fish: Get it off the spear and line quickly. Hang it on a stringer only if in waters uninhabited by such dangerous fish as sharks; otherwise get it onto your float.

The best float for spearfishing is a neoprene or canvas-covered surfmat, a fiberglass or balsa paddleboard, or an inflatable life raft.

Poor Spearfishing Areas:
Sandy bottoms with little vegetation.
Unprotected beaches with polluted, cloudy surf.
Muddy bottoms.
Note: In freshwater lakes, larger game live near the bottom—20 or 30 feet beyond where the line of submarine vegetation ends.

Finding Fish by Timing: Some times of day are better than others for spearfishing. Some fish don't like strong light and during daytime inhabit greater depths to avoid light.

More fish are found near the shore at high tide than at low tide. More are found at flood tide than at ebb tide.

What Game Is Safe to Eat: Make a point of learning to identify fish unsafe to eat. Some species are naturally poisonous, while others, not normally poisonous, can be contaminated by having eaten a normally poisonous variety. (See Fish Poisoning, pages 238–41 and Epicurean Splendors, Chapter 10.)

Fish hunting with the objective of feeding yourself and family has its justification. So aim your spear at the edible varieties. Do not spear with no other objective than wanton killing. There are many exotic and beautiful specimens that should be spared.

How To Keep Fish from Spoiling: Clean the fish, keep it out of the sun, and refrigerate it as soon as possible. If refrigeration is not immediately available, keep your catch moist and in the shade.

SHELL HUNTING AND COLLECTING

Some of the most beautiful specimens of seashells can be found along the shallow littorals and on the beaches of the world, but the aqualung offers the collector the added access to rarer specimens farther afield and deeper down. To anyone with a sensitive eye for beauty, seashells, especially the rare varieties, have a peculiar esthetic of their own. Even the names given shells have a poetic ring to them. Here are just a few of them: the angel wing, shark's eye, old maid's curl, kitten's paw, bubble, star pagoda, superb gaza, regal tegula, glory of the seas, trumpet triton, tapestry turban, imbricate cup and saucer, blood and mouth conch, dragon head, cowrie, king's helmet, tuscan helmet, eye of Judas, pontifical miter, noble volute, elephant's snout volute, half-heart cockle.

What Is a Shell?: Shells are actually external skeletons of the soft creatures belonging to the phylum Mollusca, a zoological classification of invertebrates (animals lacking a backbone). The shell is a calcareous covering that protects the body of the mollusk. This covering is built up by a rapidly hardening secretion produced by a modified part of the body wall, the mantle, parts of which form the ridges, ribs, flanges, knobs, and spines that adorn many species. The mantle also produces color patterns and an outer coat, the periostracum, which may appear like varnish, fur, or fiber. There are almost fifty thousand varieties of marine mollusks in the world, about six thousand of which are found along American shores. Shells or mollusks are divided into 5 classes, represented by the octopus, snail, bivalve, tooth, and chiton.

Where to Hunt Shells: Lots of shells are only a tankful of air away in lagoons or bays or on gently sloping shores protected by promontories, outer reefs, or kelp forests. Ideal bottoms for shell hunts are mud, sand, seaweed, loose rocks, broad shelves pitted with pockets, and tide pools where shells often camouflage themselves in the color of surrounding algae. Coral reefs shelter cone shells, cowries, and snails.

Some shells move about by day, others by night or as the tide ebbs, or, conversely, as the tide turns. Watch for trails left in the sand. Place all specimens in a fine mesh bag. Watch out for predators and beware of currents.

Cleaning of shells: To remove the fleshy part, soak the entire shell in a solution of alcohol and water or boil it for 10 minutes or so, then remove the soft part with a pin or an ice pick. Flush thoroughly to prevent foul odor. Further cleaning of the outer coat of the shell is optional. Some collectors prefer shells in their natural state. Others want shells cleaned of the marine growths that encrust them. To clean a shell, brush its exterior with a fine wire brush or polishing wheel. Acid should be avoided. Shells with a highly glossed or enamel finish should not be tossed into boiling water or they will crack. Start them in warm water, bring them to a boil slowly, and then let them cool gradually. Save the horny operculum or trapdoor of those species that have them. When the shell is dry, a block of cotton will hold the operculum in the aperture. After cleaning shells, label each specimen with its scientific name. The contributions of amateur collectors account for a large percentage of museum shell collections.

How to Trade Shells: You may not want to limit shell hunting to making your own collection. You may prefer being a trader in a very active world market. When you offer a specimen for examination, give all pertinent details. Describe accurately the locality of the find and its date. The self-taught conchologist can eventually be an expert.

Many American shells bring good prices; but the greatest shell of them all is the glory-of-the-seas cone from the East Indies. There are less than two dozen known specimens on record, and they bring prices between $600 and $1200.

COLLECTING CORAL SPECIMENS—DON'T

The master builders of the great and beautiful coral reefs—the coral polyps—are so small they can hardly be seen by the naked eye. These tiny creatures build the spectacular jeweled fairy-cities called coral reefs. Coral thrives abundantly in warm waters with temperatures in the 70s F.

Species are numerous and diversified and tempt the souvenir hunter in some of us to take home a specimen or two. Please resist the temptation. If you feel you must take coral where it is legal to do so, do not indiscriminately destroy more than you collect. Pick up pieces already detached from the coral bed. Remember that the coral reef is an ecological community which took years and years of gradual development, gaining only an inch or two a year. Note too that it is illegal in most waters to remove marine growth without express permission from authorities. Fines can be pretty severe: up to $20,000 and/or one year imprisonment for violations.

DIVE FOR HIRE AND POLICE VOLUNTEER DIVING

Divers can offer their skills to recover lost articles for clients. The work pays from $6 to $25 per hour depending on your experience. You can offer your services as a volunteer with city police, state police, and fire departments. Often a police department has its own paid divers, but volunteers are called upon in big search or salvage jobs.

UNDERWATER GOLD PROSPECTING

Americans are gold consumers now that it is legal again to own and trade gold. A diver with gold fever has the edge on dry-land prospectors. He is willing to get wet and knows how to dive for the stuff. If you are rough-and-ready enough for the great outdoors, as well as for the hardship and tedium associated with prospecting, this activity offers rewards in who knows how many ways. You'll have to educate yourself about basic geology, gold hideouts in rivers and streams, and equipment. You'll certainly have to be equipped and trained to camp out and hike long treks into the wilderness. Information on where to find gold is available at the Division of Mines in each state. Licenses and permits can be obtained from the Division of Mines where these are required by law.

California, Nevada, southwestern Montana, Idaho, Colorado, New Mexico are still productive. Don't overlook this diving activity, but I can't offer lessons in gold mining. Get a book and write to the Bureau of Mines, Department of Interior; the U.S. Mint; and the Geological Surveys of Canada, Department of Mines and Technical Surveys, Ottawa, Ontario, Canada.

CAVE DIVING

Every year thousands of divers are lured to caves, springs, and sinkholes, and with good reason. The visibility is usually crystal clear, the settings spectacular, and one can see very curious life forms such as fish that swim upside-down, sightless crustaceans, and other fauna. Caves include springs, sumps, sinkholes, and siphons. Be very careful of siphons! Water flows downward into the earth and divers must exit against the current. A sinkhole is a cavern formed as a result of the collapse of the roof of an underground cave, exposing the water within the cave. A sump is a water-filled passage in a normally dry cave. Submerged caves can usually only be entered safely in slack tide.

A point to remember about fluid (hydrostatic) pressure in cave diving: Although an underwater cave is largely covered with rocks, not water, the pressure inside will exactly equal that of the open sea at the same depth (the pressure, you will remember, is transmitted horizontally). Therefore, the general theory of pressure and its physical effects will apply as in open-water diving.

The danger associated with cave diving is compounded by the possibility of not being able to make a free vertical ascent in an emergency. Instead, you may be forced to weave your way through winding passageways before an ascent is possible. Darkness and silt pose problems, even with lighting. Darkness and the threat of claustrophobia are factors which demand of the diver psychological stability and preparedness.

Remember that cave diving is highly specialized and should not be attempted without sufficient precave-dive training and practice. There are clubs devoted to cave diving which are probably your best bet the first time out. See your local dive shop or contact diving instructors where you live for advice. It is a good idea to practice and train in small nondangerous coral caves or on night dives before attempting a real cave dive. You might also try a land cave hike to familiarize yourself with the look of a cave. You might discover then and there whether you are psychologically fit for the close quarters of cave diving.

Rehearse emergency situations which might occur such as running out of air, losing a buddy, failure of lights, enfoulment, breaking of a safety line, and calming a panic-stricken diver.

In cave diving, special emphasis should be given to dive planning, life-support, and special techniques.

Planning includes selection of equipment, determination of the physical and physiological limits of the least-experienced diver of the group and establishing a feasible plan for emergencies.

Divers should plan to use one-third of their air supply for entering the cave and one-third for leaving; the remaining third is in reserve for emergencies.

A life-support system must include a compass, a light, safety reel and line. The reel should be neutrally buoyant, compact, rugged. Large reels and lines create too much extra drag and exertion on the diver.

In cave diving, manual buddy breathing may be impractical and occasionally impossible due to distance and cave configuration. The octopus rig is therefore recommended. Special attention should be given to buoyancy control and lighting. Carry at least two lights.

Overhead ceilings, darkness, visibility, current, and the physical peculiarities of the cave are the specific hazards of cave diving, but perhaps the greatest specific hazard is that of silt and every effort should be made to avoid stirring it up.

When running a safety line, the reel man should maintain tension at the reel drum so the line remains taut. The line should be tied within surface light and two wraps made every 50 feet. The line should be centered in the cave. The reel man is first in and last out. Physical contact with the line should be avoided.

Make sure that you can see what's ahead before you swim into it.

NIGHT DIVING

Night diving is not recommended for amateur divers. All the risks and dangers of ordinary diving by day are of course increased at night, even with artificial lighting. Predators are all the more dangerous at night not only because of total darkness but because they hunt food with greater voracity.

For those to whom lobster hunting is appealing, night diving is unavoidable. The lobster hides in dark crevices and holes during the daytime and saunters forth at night.

Familiarize yourself with the conditions at the dive site. Check weather, water, and visibility in the daytime before the dive. Avoid entry from a beach or diving into heavy vegetable growth. It is safest to dive from a boat or the protected side of a breakwater. Begin adapting your eyes to the dark at least two hours before a night dive. Without light, color vision is lost at night. It takes between 20 and 30 minutes for eyes adapted to bright light to achieve maximum efficiency in the dim light of dark water at night. To hasten adaptation insert a transparent red visor into your facemask and wear it for 30 minutes before you dive; do not remove it until you are in the water. (Night-flying pilots use red cockpit lights so that bright lights do not impair their night vision.) The effect of the red-vision technique provides at least 30 percent greater working vision when no artificial light is used.

You will have to rely on navigation skills in night diving. Weightlessness and restricted vision can lead to disorientation and vertigo. You may not even know which way is up. A line should be used for ascending and descending.

A boat is a satisfactory base of operations. Extra equipment is readily available, entries and exits are quick and safe, and the boat is easy to locate for return. Be sure the boat is left well-lighted and is identifiable by divers from a distance. Always dive against any current to avoid an overexerting struggle when returning. A flashing light is an ideal reference for all divers to home in on.

It is easy to become separated from a buddy at night. Use a buddy line, hold hands, or hold onto a diver's harness to maintain buddy contact. Have a plan to reestablish contact if you should become separated. Provide some means of illumination on each other's equipment. Sharp-beamed waterproof flashlights with three or more cells are recommended. Secure one to your wrist by a strong rubber band or a strap so that both hands will be free, because you will have to rely heavily on your sense of touch.

To get the attention of a buddy diver, wiggle your light around several times, but do not blind anyone by shining your light in his eyes. Aim at the chest when you want someone's attention.

When making an ascent at night, observe your gauges. Proceed slowly and beware of overhead obstructions.

ICE DIVING

This is an activity for advanced divers only and requires proper supervision. For maximum visibility, pick a sunny day to dive under snow-free ice.

If a wet suit is worn, bring a large flask of warm water with you and pour it into the suit before you get into the water. Wear warm gloves before diving. If your hands are cold before you submerge they will not warm up again.

Each diver must have a tender standing on the surface holding his lifeline with attentive care.

Cutting hole: Use a chain saw. Hole should be big enough for at least two divers to fit in. Chunk should be removed as is or slid under the ice to adhere to the underside and stay in place. Sprinkle sand or gravel around the hole to prevent slipping.

Ice Dive Signals:

	FROM TENDER	FROM DIVER
1 pull	Are you all right?	I'm OK.
2 pulls	Go down.	Give me more line.
3 pulls	Get ready to come up.	Take up my slack.
4 pulls	Come up.	I'm coming up, pull in the line.

	EMERGENCY SIGNALS
2-2-2	I am fouled and need assistance.
3-3-3	I am fouled but OK and can get out alone.
4-4-4	Emergency, emergency, haul me up fast.

Never attach lifeline to wrist, weight belt, or tank strap. Anchor man, the first diver on the end of the line, should have rope secured around his waist. Best knot for this is a close-fitting bowline because it does not come loose or tighten when pulling. Be sure the lifeline does not interfere with quick-release buckles on your gear. The long end of the line is paid out and retrieved by the tender, who must keep enough drag on the line to allow for clear signals in both directions.

Regulators should be kept warm to prevent freeze-up, which can happen in two ways. Moisture from breath freezes valves into an open position, which would cause a constant free flow of air. This is correctable, for as soon as the regulator is immersed in ice-cold water, the valves will free themselves. The other cause of freeze-up is more difficult to correct because it occurs in the water. In very cold water, the sudden cooling of the air can sometimes result in ice forming in the regulator.

Be sure you are neutrally buoyant to avoid being pressed against the ice, but buoyant enough not to kick up silt.

When entering, all divers should be tied to the line before the first man goes in. Sit on edge of hole, turn around so you rest on both hands, and slide in.

Terminate your dive before going on reserve. When ready to ascend, last man on the line signals the tender to pull in the slack as group ascends.

At the edge of the ice-hole entry point, give a strong scissors kick and pull up by arms vigorously. Replace block of ice. Mark hole with barriers for protection of snowmobiles, ice boats, and skaters.

TIPS ON ICE DIVING

Ice dives should take place in areas you have explored prior to the onset of the ice cover. The ice should be thick enough to support several people and equipment.

Safety lines should be limited to 150-foot radius from the hole. More would be too much to handle. Yellow line is more clearly visible. The lines for stand-by divers are 250 feet in length. The free end of the safety line must be secured to something which will not move and cannot fall through the hole. Long ice-fishing chisels driven into the ice have proven best for this purpose. As a further precaution, tie a float onto the end of the safety line.

If you become separated from the safety line, ascend to the ice and remain stationary. Safety divers will soon begin a circular-sweep search pattern at the surface with a floating line when you fail to respond to line signals.

If you get lost under thin ice, chip a hole for your snorkel and push it through. The lookout should be able to see the red tip of the snorkel poking through and take instant action to guide you to safety.

At least one diver, suited, geared, and ready to dive in, should stand by. If a diver is separated from his lifeline, his first step toward being found is to ascend to the ice and remain there. The standby diver should then enter the water, run out his lifeline just under the ice, and make a 360-degree sweep, keeping his lifeline snug and close to the surface of the ice. The line eventually will touch the lost diver in its sweep. When contact is made, the lost diver should grasp the lifeline and be towed back. To avoid confusion and interference, all other divers should leave the water during this phase of the rescue operation.

KELP DIVING

Kelp is found in dense beds along much of the colder and temperate coasts of the Americas. Attaching to practically any solid substrate (i.e., rock, concrete, steel, etc.), it forms a tree-like structure, the trunk of which is composed of a few to perhaps several hundred intertwining stipes. A pneumatocyst (float) is found at the base of each blade which causes the frond to be buoyed upward resulting in part of it floating on the surface. This may form a dense canopy which will have numbers of thin spots or openings scattered throughout. Entries or exits are easily made through these openings or by swimming in under the edge of the canopy.

When working from a boat, it is best to anchor in an opening so that the wind or current will drift the boat back on the anchor line to a second opening. Divers may also anchor outside the bed and swim in. Disengaging an anchor from kelp is difficult.

The feetfirst, legs-together water entry is preferable to the headfirst roll, or back entry, which can result in entanglement. Once through the surface canopy, you will find yourself in a forest-like area. When you approach the surface, you should raise your arms over your head unless there is a convenient opening. As you enter the canopy, you should use your arms to move the kelp fronds aside and surface through the hole. Once on the surface, you should stay in the vertical position so you can either exhale and sink, or submerge by raising your arms from your sides back over your head, thus forcing the body under water. Excessive movement may cause entanglement.

Kelp can easily be broken with a fingernail or pulled off. It is unwise to remove kelp from the regulator with a knife if the kelp is thick and the regulator hose cannot be seen or felt.

If you run out of air and are forced to return to shore or a boat through a kelp bed, you have several choices. You may simply skin dive from opening to opening and if you need a breath between openings, you can come up through the main canopy. This is done easily with a little practice. You may also do a variation of the "dog paddle" in which the body is parallel to the surface and the swim fins used in a very close flutter kick. The arms reach across the kelp to an extended position, then grasp the kelp and press down, with elbows close to the body to keep as streamlined a shape as possible. The regulator second stage should not trail behind the diver or it will become entangled in the kelp. Swim fins with adjustable heel straps may also pose a problem as the kelp fronds can become caught in the strap-adjusting buckle and strap end. This may be eliminated by taping the strap end to the main strap. Knives worn on the belt or on the outside of the calf of the leg will also act as kelp catchers. Consequently, knives should be worn inside the calf. Inflating buoyancy compensators while under a kelp canopy may also increase the chance of entanglement. Deflate cautiously if entangled.

Egergia (ribbon kelp) grows from the intertidal to perhaps 45 feet in depth, and although quite thick, it seldom forms the thick canopy associated with *Macrocystis.* "Elk kelp" (*Pelagophycus porra*), is a deeper-growing plant found usually in 45-60 feet to 150 feet of water. It consists of a single stipe, ½ inch across, growing from a small holdfast. The stipe enlarges 3 to 6 feet from the float and is spherical and hollow in structure. The top of this ball gives rise to antler-like protrusions, each with several blades, which may be 3 feet wide and 15 feet long. Elk kelp seldom reaches the surface in a healthy state but forms a bed 15 to 30 feet down. Often when the diver penetrates a large kelp bed in 60 to 90 feet of water, he will find a second canopy of elk kelp below the first, with a resulting drop in already low light levels.

All kelp beds are influenced by currents and surge, and major beds may disappear in a swift current as a result of being held down on perhaps a 45° angle. This has its advantages, as the kelp streams in the direction of the current and may be used for navigation.

DIVING WITH NO BOTTOM REFERENCE

Special precautions are required when diving in water that allows no reference to the bottom. These conditions may be found when diving in deep-ocean water, extremely dirty water, or when diving at night. A lack of reference points can be disturbing and create a form of vertigo.

Deep-water diving makes depth and distance estimates difficult. When possible, a weighted line suspended from a surface buoy should be used at the dive site. When working from a large vessel, a small boat should be used to tend the divers directly. Wind and surface currents often carry the vessel away from the dive site. Buoys that have been deployed for over a day attract sharks, therefore no garbage should be dumped at the dive site. A useful aid in marking a dive site is a small open jar of fluorescent dye dropped into the water. The vertical column of dye left behind as the jar drops through the water will be distorted by currents, giving a visual display of the current pattern in the water column.

Dirty water, where visibility may be reduced to zero even at high noon, presents similar problems of orientation. When possible, divers should be tended from the surface or a descent line used.

A WORD ABOUT HIGH ALTITUDE DIVING

Diving at high altitudes (1000 feet or more), such as in mountain lakes, creates a new set of problems compared to dives begun at sea level. The possibility of bends is increased because when you ascend from a dive, the atmospheric pressure is lower than at sea level. The difference between water pressure at depth and air pressure at surface is widened. Therefore, decompression computers and depth gauges are inaccurate above sea level. So are the U.S. Navy Air Decompression Tables. In order to use the latter at altitude, convert the apparent depth at altitude to the equivalent depth at sea level by adding 3 percent of the depth to compensate for the difference in density in fresh water. The rate of ascent in altitude diving decreases as altitude increases. With a lower surface atmospheric pressure, less depth is required to equal the pressure. For example, if the surface pressure were only one-half an atmosphere, the pressure would be doubled at a depth of only 17 feet. The rate of ascent to the surface would be only 30 feet per minute. On surfacing, you can lose consciousness because of oxygen hunger; atmospheric air has less oxygen. Under water there is no problem, thanks to increased total pressure, but an out-of-breath diver surfacing at altitude could experience air starvation. Avoid exertion in altitude diving.

Some of the problems of altitude diving: Rate of ascent decreases with altitude. Narcosis occurs at shallower depths than at sea level. Depth gauges read inaccurately, increasing chances of bends. If you drove up to the dive site via an elevated mountain route and dived right away, you would be placed in a repetitive dive category. If you drove from sea level to a mountain lake and dived immediately, you would be saturated with high nitrogen content. Nitrogen in your system at sea level needs 12 hours to reach equilibrium at altitude.

Consider yourself:

A Group D diver (see Appendix "Residual Nitrogen Timetable for Repetitive Dives" for group definitions) for your first dive up to 6000 ft. altitude.
A Group F diver from 7000 to 8000 ft. altitude.
A Group H diver from 9000 to 12,000 ft. altitude.

Refer to these groups in U.S. Navy Air Decompression Tables in Appendix for group designations.

Rule of Thumb to Figure Rate of Ascent at Elevation:
Subtract 2 feet per minute for each 1000 feet of altitude. Examples:

At 7000 ft.: $7 \times 2 = 14$ feet per minute (fpm) slower ascent
   $60 \text{ fpm} - 14 = 46 \text{ fpm}$

At 6000 ft.: $6 \times 2 = 12$ fpm slower ascent
   $60 \text{ fpm} - 12 = 48 \text{ fpm}$

At 5000 ft.: $5 \times 2 = 10$ ft. per minute slower ascent
   $60 \text{ fpm} - 10 = 50 \text{ fpm}$

RECOMMENDATION: Don't mix sea-level dives with elevation dives the same day.

To determine the equivalent depth at sea level for your altitude dive, use the following formula:

4 Percent Rule

Add 4 percent of the depth to the depth for every 1000 feet of elevation above sea level. Example:
A 60-ft. dive at 5000 ft. is expressed
$ED^* = 5(.04 \times 60) + 60 = 72$ ft.

This rule is effective to 8000 feet and to depths of less than 130 feet. Warning: No Decompression time alters at altitudes. In our example, that 60-foot dive at sea level allows 60 minutes' time you can spend without decompression stops. But at 5000 feet it allows only 40 minutes.
Another way of expressing this is:

Altitude	Adjustment to Get Dive Depth
300 to 900 ft.	Add ¼ of measured depth
900 to 6000 ft.	Add ⅓ of measured depth
6000 to 9000+ ft.	Add ½ of measured depth

EXAMPLE: A 90-foot dive of 22 minutes bottom time is made in a lake 1800 feet above sea level. Adjustment increment—add ⅓ of measured depth; i.e., decompress for a 120-foot dive of 22 minutes bottom time.

DIVE HOLIDAYS

In North America, where 80 percent of the continent is too cold 75 percent of the time for diving, over half the diving population travel out of state to take the plunge. About a quarter of them go abroad, particularly to the Caribbean, the Gulf of Mexico, and the Pacific.

* ED = Equivalent Depth.

Travel then involves time ranging from an overnight trip to a full holiday of a week or more. A holiday for diving can be a major undertaking. It must be carefully timed, placed, supplied, and financed if it is to be a success. That success depends on locale, weather, air supply stations, transportation, and the availability of spare parts for equipment. If you destination is to be far from civilization and commerce, investigate the availability of spare parts. If they will be a problem, supply yourself in advance and include extra filled tanks. Make a checklist of equipment. Review it several times before starting out. Nothing can be more disappointing than discovering long after leaving home that you have forgotten some basic hardware.

A word of caution to the less experienced diver-camper: Until you have the know-how, curb the urge to pioneer into remote diving areas where modern conveniences are out of reach. Stick to known areas where there are plenty of expert diver-guides well supplied with equipment, a boat, plenty of air, and fully packaged underwater trips, gear included. Guides know a variety of underseascapes in their vicinity, the sunken wrecks, the best reefs and hunting waters. For the lazier vacationer, expertly supervised package tours are plentiful. In addition, they provide companionship.

For the holiday-bound diver or would-be beginner many seaside resorts have complete dive services and facilities at your disposal. A thoroughgoing resort dive center usually offers a full range of equipment, dive-guides, instruction, certification, air, repairs, sales, and rentals. Those who don't bring their own gear can rent everything including photographic equipment. Guides can be relied on for knowing where the best diving can be found in their area. It is true that some of the best sites are also closely guarded secrets, however. For those who have neither the time nor the inclination to strike out on their own the dive center offering tours and professional introductory lessons is the answer. Many get their first taste of the underwater experience this way—and they are hooked.

Whatever type of diving holiday you take, choose your companions for their expertness in diving as well as for social compatibility. Should you be manning a boat without a hired crew, see to it that one or more of your party is a competent sailor or skipper.

Take first-aid equipment, and don't forget to bring along this book, as it may come in handy. Watch out for sunburn, a great nemesis of vacationers. Snorkelers are the greatest sufferers with their backs exposed to the sun and sea. Build up a slow tan. Wear a T-shirt when sorkeling.

A diving holiday need not be expensive. If real economy and real fun are what you want, the best arrangement is overnight camping. Basic needs: blankets, cooking stove, lamps, a base camp, and a shelter. Since a full coverage of camping is beyond this handbook's scope, supply yourself with a book or two on the subject.

8

UNDERWATER ARCHAEOLOGY AND WRECK DIVING

Because of the enormous riches still held by the sea, underwater archaeology is one of the most promising branches of the sciences. The amateur diver drawn to the sea by dreams of finding objects of archaeological value and with a flair for archaeological research would be well advised to bolster his interest with readings in history, archaeology, and epigraphy. To the enlightened amateur archaeologist the humblest chunk of marble, a clay pot, or any homely utensil of daily life in some remote century adds to the thrill of discovery and recovery. A proficient diver who picks up a fragment of the past from one dive to the next does not make an archaeologist, even an amateur archaeologist. One does not enter underwater archaeology or any ocean-related science by way of diving, any more than one enters civil engineering by way of plumbing, but proficient free diving is sooner or later indispensable to the sea-bound archaeologist.

A great deal more is involved in underwater archaeology than the mechanics of diving and seeing, finding, and recovering things. In the first place, archaeology is a science of which underwater work is a relatively new branch. Undergraduate and graduate preparation is just the beginning. A long and arduous apprenticeship follows far from the seabed. Archaeological diving is exhausting, drudging work requiring inventiveness, stamina, a strong sense of responsibility, and great experience at underwater work.

Also, the naked efforts of even the most imaginative diving archaeologist must be supplemented by sophisticated machines and contrivances designed especially for underwater work. Often there will be great difficulty in distinguishing the evidence of what you are seeking in the tangle of marine vegetation. Silt, sand, coral, and mud also impair ability to see what might be awaiting discovery. The seabed has a very uniform appearance—uniform to the degree that a sunken ship, historical relic, or artifact is often indistinguishable from living coral growths, sponges, mosses, mollusks, and seaweed. In some areas of the Mediterranean, for example, carrara marble relics such as fluted columns are so deeply eaten into and eroded by clumps of lithodomi (date mussels) that it is only with great diffiulty that the eye can pick them out from the rock among which they lie. In the coastal deeps off Brittany, seaweed covers everything with an impenetrable marine fleece that makes accurate examination of evidence virtually impossible.

In other areas you will be defeated as a searcher by the luxuriant growth of posidonia, a flowering plant. There is ample evidence that the sea is unreceptive to those who lack the ability to separate and sort what it possesses. Even with complex tools of salvage, the chances of recovering a real find are slim. For the present the amateur will have to be contented with a modest beginning, not much more than souvenir hunting, but even that can be very exciting.

Thousands of years of naval and maritime adventure, war, storm, and a host of other perils have sent hundreds, perhaps thousands, of ships to the bottom of the Mediterranean. Few are found except by chance, and it is a cunning or lucky research worker who locates a classical wreck or can find the man who actually knows the exact location of one.

Ships that sank in a shallow harbor were generally salvaged immediately or destroyed to prevent danger to other ships. A ship driven onto the shore by a gale was soon pounded to pieces by the crashing surf. Only those ships that struck isolated rocks or were swamped and sunk in deep water were preserved from the strong forces dominating the surface of the sea. If by chance a ship settled into very soft mud and was quickly covered over with sea-bottom deposits, the wood would be permanently protected, but few such wrecks are found because they are so difficult to detect. Early mariners limited their voyages to the summer seasons and nearly always hugged the coast. They preferred a rugged coast, with its easily identifiable landmarks, to a flat one with few points of reference. It is for this reason that many of the conspicuous headlands and islands of the Mediterranean are mentioned in Homer's *Odyssey.*

It seems to follow that the greatest dangers to classical mariners were submerged rocks rising from the sea floor to within only a few feet of the surface. These rocks, called *secs* by the French and *secci* by the Italians, are fatally common off the steep coasts of the Mediterranean. Although not often marked on charts, they are visible from the air or from high ground and can be found with an echo sounder. If a diver searches around these submerged *secs* or *secci* on a known ancient trade route, he has a chance of finding not one but several wrecks. Some local fishermen and sponge divers are helpful to the diver investigating a small area in detail, but others are close mouthed and cagey about what they know unless you give them a good payoff. Your success will depend on your experience with the Mediterranean business mentality.

From 3000 B.C. to the fall of the Roman Empire more than three hundred major coastal ports and cities were constructed along the Mediterranean shores. Between these cities were thousands of fishing villages, trading ports, and seaside villas. As a result of a rise in sea level and geological evolution, about half the original cities and associated minor ports and villas are now under water. Many have been explored; many more await discovery and exploration. Because of the high cost of uncovering larger cities of record, there is little likelihood that they will be excavated in the near future, if ever. On the other hand, amateur divers are encouraged to look to the possibility of locating minor cities farther afield and off the beaten paths of research. For his sources an archaeologist-diver must refer to such ancient historians and geographers as Herodotus, Thucydides, Strabo, and the itineraries of Antoninus and Peutinger. He should consult the classical atlases and the Admiralty charts that show coastal ruins, and whenever possible, he should make full use of local informants. The real problem is to find clues and to establish a site's relationship to the present coast. It would be sensible to research archaeological journals containing details of past work done on a site. The next steps are to determine the precise nature of the excavating problem, to obtain permissions from local governments, and to decide if and how to finance and supply a major undertaking. Through resourcefulness and a certain amount of sociability you ought to meet people who share your archaeological inquisitiveness and have access to the means required for costly research and recovery projects.

WRECK DIVING EXPEDITIONS

Wreck exploration is one of the most exciting adventures in diving, rather specialized and not without hazards. Expeditions should therefore be planned with great caution and only by divers who feel at home in the water. Find and join a club or group of divers active in wreck diving. With membership you have a built-in training course that is practically a must, especially where the objective is to find treasure of archaeological artifacts. Often serious, well-financed wreck expeditions welcome volunteers willing to work long, hard hours under water. Wreck diving involving complex recovery techniques with the aid of sophisticated electronic tools should be left only to well-financed professional expeditions. Remember also that an irresponsible attack on a wreck site may do great harm to valuable antiques.

The history of wreck discovery shows that almost always amateur divers have been involved. Some divers have hit pay dirt, but wreck diving for treasure can be fruitlessly hard work and financially ruinous for those infected by the fever of treasure hunting.

The Legal Aspects of Salvage: Before embarking on an expedition or making a serious effort at salvage which might involve much time and large sums of money, seek the advice of a lawyer on the legal aspects of your rights of salvage, recovery, and possession. The laws are complex, requiring a more authoritative discussion than I can offer here.

WHERE THE WRECKS ARE

The littoral zones of the United States, the Great Lakes, the Caribbean, the Gulf of Mexico, Bermuda, and the shores of some of our large rivers are dotted with sunken vessels of all descriptions. Not all wrecks are as exotic as the galleons that sailed the Spanish Main, and the circumstances surrounding their sinkings are not as romantic. Once you have located the general area of the wreck, you must find it by visual observation. Assign several divers to scout in the general area or use a glass-bottom boat. If you are part of a well-financed expedition you might hire an airplane or helicopter on a clear day to reconnoiter from aloft. From the air the outline of a wreck may be distinctly visible in calm waters.

The nautical charts you will need in connection with wreck research give considerable detail of the topographical conditions of the seabed and indicate the approximate location of wrecks. Do not count on the charts for pinpoint accuracy. Treasure maps and literature on known wrecks and maritime disasters can be obtained from a local dealer, dive shop, or marine supplier, or write to any of the following:

Merchant Vessels of the U.S.A.
Bureau of Customs, Government Printing Office
Washington, D.C. 20402

Chief of Public Information
U.S. Coast Guard Headquarters
400 Seventh Street S.W.
Washington, D.C. 20590

Treasure Maps in the Library of Congress
Research Department, Map Division
Washington, D.C. 20401

Marine Disasters North of San Francisco
Treasury Section, National Archives
Wasington, D.C. 20408

List of Wrecks and Casualties
Coast of Rhode Island and Fishers Island
Treasury Section, National Archives
Washington, D.C. 20408

Shipwrecks and the Florida Coast
Treasury Section, National Archives
Washington, D.C. 20408

Wreck Reports of the Great Lakes
Treasury Section, National Archives
Washington, D.C. 20408

Marine Casualties of the Great Lakes
Treasury Section, National Archives
Washington, D.C. 20408

U.S. Department of Commerce
National Oceanic and Atmospheric Administration
Rockville, Maryland 20852

Navy Department
Supervisor of Diving
Washington, D.C. 20362

Other sources of information for locating wrecks are insurance companies; historical societies; court records; the U.S. Naval Academy Museum at Annapolis; records and papers of the Vice-Admiralty Courts of Boston, Philadelphia, and Charleston, South Carolina.

Plotting the Position of a Wreck: Whenever you find a record of a wreck, your first steps are to seek the latitude and longitude of its site and then to determine the appropriate National Ocean Survey charts on which to fix or plot the position. The chart itself may or may not have a symbol indicating a wreck.

Let's say you want to locate a wreck reported in records to have sunk at a latitude 40-25.5 N and longitude 69-40.0 W. To plot the wreck, draw a horizontal line from 40-25.5 on the right-hand scale of the appropriate chart and a vertical line from 69-40.0 from the bottom scale. The point of intersection of the two lines is the reported position of the sinking.

If you make a chance discovery of a wreck or some interesting artifact while on the water, take cross bearings to locate its position and plot the position on the appropriate chart. Drop a buoy to mark the spot for your return trip if you contemplate salvage or even merely a second look.

TIPS ON WRECK DIVING

1. Wrecks are usually found in deep dark cold waters where apprehension adds difficulty to the dive.
2. Get the name, depth and dimensions, water depth, and maximum information of planned wreck.
3. Be sure to obtain permits necessary from the local government, insurance company, or owner before salvaging.
4. Beware of spiny fish, moray eels, and sea urchins, all of which are attracted to wrecks in East Coast U.S. waters.
5. Currents should be accounted for. Check the tide tables. Dive to the lee side of a wreck whenever possible and use caution where current will be encountered. Remember to trail a stern line from the surface vessel to assist divers downcurrent of boat when returning from below.
6. When diving within a wreck, attach a penetration line to the outside of the wreck. Use a safety line to ensure safe exit out of the passageways and chambers of the interior of a sunken vessel.
7. Use two underwater lights in case of failure of one.
8. Don't stir up silt. Avoid contact with sharp edges and dangerous cargo.

9. Watch surroundings for proper orientation. Interiors of wrecks can deceive, disorient.
10. Don't remove your mouthpiece in air pockets. The air may be totally depleted of oxygen content through oxidation; the air could contain toxic or corrosive gases.
11. Air bubbles from your exhaust can be caught and trapped inside wreckage. The lift brought about by trapped air can cause the wreck to shift or even break up, creating a hazardous situation. Decayed wood and corroded metal can collapse. Watch out for fishing nets, lines, and hooks.
12. Techniques of wreck diving vary with region. Check with local divers first.
13. Remember, the only known way out is the way in.

SEARCH METHODS

Accurate underwater navigation is paramount in search missions. Do not undertake a search unless you are properly equipped, accompanied by trained companions, and under the supervision of a qualified leader. In murky water cover every inch of the search area by sight or touch. Work out all your preparations prior to entry and determine the details of depth, visibility, bottom topography, tides, and currents. Set up marker buoys to guide boats and divers to the search area. Search expeditions require intense concentration and hard work, so be sure that the safety, health, and experience of the team are taken into account.

The two main search methods are either visual or electronic. With the visual you use your own gift of sight to make observations from a glass-bottom boat, with a mask, or even from an aircraft. The electronic methods include the use of detectors operated from a boat or by divers. Bear in mind that wreck detection for amateurs unaided by electronic tools may prove hopeless in most cases. And there is the unlikelihood that an amateur diver can afford the high cost of a major detection job with mechanical or electronic aids.

Grid-Pattern Method: Lay out a square with anchors at four corners connected by a rope grid. Additional ropes or wires within the square will make up a gridwork. The diver makes a careful search in each of the smaller interior squares of the grid.

Tow-Sled Search Method: Another method is for the diver to search the bottom while being towed on a diving sled pulled by a motorboat. Be sure to operate the motorboat slowly. Speed can rip off a diver's mask, perhaps even his bathing trunks.

Anchor-Tow Method: The ocean floor can also be scanned by a diver who is lowered on an anchor and towed at a very slow rate while hanging or sitting on the partially suspended anchor.

SEARCH LINE

SEARCH DIVER'S PATCH

SEARCH DIVER

ANCHOR MAN

SURFACE

ANCHOR LINE

SEARCH DRIVER

ANCHOR MAN

SEARCH LINE

SEARCH AND RECOVERY

Circular-Sweep Search Pattern: For searches in clearer waters, not overly affected by currents, use the circular-sweep search pattern. Lower a weighted line tied at its base with a distance line. The latter line will be towed by the diver making the circular sweeps. The length of the distance line depends on the size of the area to be searched. The distance line should be marked every foot or yard.

Submerge holding onto the shot line. Swim to the end of the distance line, hold it taut, and mark your position with a stake or rock. Start swimming and search in a circular span around the shot line until you are back to your point of departure. Remove the marker. Move toward the next position closer in on the distance line. Mark the new point of departure for the next circular sweep. Start to swim. Repeat the process until you reach the hub of the search wheel at the shot line. If you have not found the object you are searching for, lift the base of the shot line and reposition it about halfway between the old base and the last sweep. Repeat the search from the new location.

TIPS ON SEARCH AND RECOVERY

A diver, a tender, and a stand-by diver are the minimum required number of people to search safely in dark, swift water. A tended diver on a safety line is safer than a diver with a buddy in these conditions.

When the object sought is found, mark its location. It is not uncommon for divers to lose an object after finding it and then have to search for it again, so be sure to mark the object with a buoy before doing anything else.

In river searches, do not swim against a current, but use the current to aid the search instead. Line should be let out a small amount at a time to a diver working slowly downstream while facing upstream. Do not pull a submerged diver against the current since entanglement and injury are possible. Have divers surface prior to pulling them against the current.

A hazard exists when lifting an object under water, for the air inside a partially inflated lifting device will expand during ascent causing acceleration and a potential hazard. The object may get out of control, rocket to the surface, lose buoyancy, and sink rapidly back down on the submerged divers.

Keep silt from covering the object. Search and recovery operations frequently take place in dark or dirty water where visibility is poor or nonexistent, so the silting would not seriously affect visibility. Settling silt can obscure an object and prevent recovery.

Lift bags should be equipped with a dump line attached to the highest point. This line allows divers to control a lift by tipping the bag to vent excess air. Control of the lift makes recovery operations much safer.

Most useful knots: The bowline is an excellent underwater knot with many uses as is two half-hitches. A sheet bend is useful for tying two lines together. A square knot slips under water and a sheepshank has little application.

A good grid pattern of search is useful when the object sought is small in size. When a meticulous, careful search needs to be conducted for objects such as watches or rings, a grid of ropes or pipes is usually placed over the area to assure thorough coverage.

CONDITION OF UNDERWATER WRECK SITES

A wreck is usually so greatly altered and camouflaged by nature that visual detection is impossible. The organic, mechanical, and electrolytic forces of nature, especially in tropical waters of the Western Hemisphere, substantially, if not totally, damage the remains of wooden vessels; it is therefore possible to swim over a wreck site of a once proud wooden galleon and never detect its presence at all. There are, however, certain marks that identify the location of a disintegrated ship.

RECOGNIZING THE WRECK OF A WOODEN SHIP (GALLEON)

Wooden ships, especially those dating back hundreds of years, virtually defy recognition in tropical waters because the teredo worm has long since devoured all the wood in the ship. Two identifying marks of a wreck site are cannon, whose elongated iron barrels survive time and encrustation, and prominent mounds of round, smooth rocks (usually baseball or volleyball size) carried on board as ballast. Some wrecks are evidenced by ingots of pig iron, a type of ballast used by English men-of-war. In some instances, a pile of ballast does not necessarily identify the site as that of a wreck. In plying the trade routes, ships often dumped ballast as a matter of routine procedure and sailed on, especially when heaving to an anchorage or harbor. Wrecks are usually found in shallow waters mainly because sinkings were often the result of running aground or ramming coral reefs.

In tropical waters, look along beaches and areas known to have wrecks in the vicinity. Sometimes after a tropical storm the beaches are awash with flotsam and jetsam (including coins tossed ashore by waves), which means a wreck is nearby. Modern-day wrecks, such as merchantmen, are more distinguishable on the sea bottom because their steel structure survives the almost total disappearance suffered by the early wooden galleons. Most latter-day wrecks are well catalogued.

Chains and anchors are good indicators of the existence of a wreck. Since a wreck is almost always encrusted with coral, check and test every clump of coral with a hammer. Tap gently: The coral may be hiding a valuable find.

TYPES OF WRECKS AND HOW THEY HAPPENED

The circumstances under which a ship might have gone down are numerous. Some of the major types of sinkings commonly encountered several hundred years ago in the Western Hemisphere explain why wrecks and debris are found the way they are.

Scattered Wreck, Delayed Sinking: The ship strikes a reef, skips over it with great destruction to its hull, and sails on for several hundred yards, then goes down far from where it first hit. In many cases, guns, rigging, and other heavy objects fall from the ship or they are tossed over by the crew in a desperate attempt to lighten the ship after impact.

Fixed Wreck, Fast Sinking: A ship strikes and then sinks between reefs. Frequently, the ship settles to the bottom and is wedged between coral reefs, which protect it from wave action. Sand drifts over the bilge portion of the hull and protects the wood from the teredo worm. This is particularly characteristic of shipwrecks in the Bermuda reefs.

Ship Rams Reef, Tossing Cargo, Sails On, Sinks Later: The ship strikes a reef, tossing equipment and cargo overboard, then floats on to sink in another reef. This is a type of wreck especially prevalent in the widespread Bermuda shallow reef flats.

There are two factors that seem to be common to all wreck sites: First, the hull of the wooden ship, except at the turn of the bilge, is seldom preserved; second, the area along the sides of the wreck are littered with a jumble of scattered cargo and equipment dropped in the paroxysm of the ship's final minutes and in its subsequent disintegration in its resting place.

RECOVERY TOOLS

Three basic types of tools are available to the serious underwater explorer for use in removing the overburden of a site: the airlift, the water jet, and various hand tools such as a hammer, crowbar, and wire basket.

The Airlift: This is an open metal tube into which is blown a jet of air from the bottom upward to the surface of the water. This rush of air exerts a strong sucking effect, which sweeps up sand, mud, and small objects. The top of the airlift usually is fed into a floating screen to catch any objects that might have escaped the diver operating it. An airlift should be very carefully selected and very carefully used because it can cause great damage to valuable specimens. For use in layers beneath the overburden, there is a small airlift that extends upward some 8 to 10 feet above the operator and does not reach the surface. This small airlift (called by some a sand gun) is valuable in slowly removing sand or mud when working in pay dirt.

The Water Jet: This is nothing more than a high-pressure water hose with a special nozzle feeding part of the water backward to neutralize the jet action of the water stream which would otherwise make the instrument difficult to handle. It must be used with great caution since specimens can be swept from their original location and lost. One great disadvantage of the water jet is that it merely moves mud or sand around on a site and does not remove it as does the large airlift.

Hand Tools: Hand tools vary. Where visibility is good, small digging tools such as the hoe or trench shovel may be used with care. When very small objects are being found, a small, weighted wooden paddle should be used. This is the equivalent of the archaeologist's brush and is used to remove gently small quantities of sand by fanning.

EFFECTS OF SALT WATER ON ARTIFACTS

Silver, such as coins, is usually blackened, because of conversion to silver sulfide and chloride. Silver coins are often found attached to spikes, cannon, sword blades, and the like. (A silver coin in contact with other metal will survive in good condition without conversion if it has had cathodic protection.) A silver coin that has been converted beyond recovery will appear as a rough, black shape two or three times its original thickness. Sometimes it may carry a light tan to white sand crust, and in many cases it will be apparent from the shape of the mass that the coin is touching another metal. Sometimes in hard-clay sea bottoms, silver coins remain undamaged because the clay has insulated the coin from electrolytic action.

Gold rarely suffers any radical alteration by salt water, but there may be some scratching because of friction generated by movement in sand and coral. Gold remains shiny, bright, and clean. When surrounded by coral, it may acquire a thin brown crust, which is easily wiped off with a cloth. Possession of gold bullion is illegal, and it is subject to seizure by federal authorities. Whenever you find gold in antique coin, keep it that way; it has more value.

Wrought iron and *cast iron* suffer varying degrees of corrosion and are usually encrusted by a layer of black material. In extreme cases, the iron is completely destroyed and only powdered oxide remains. When the crust of a slightly corroded object is scraped away the object appears shiny and bright.

Copper and *brass* objects in thick forms and masses suffer only superficial corrosion and take on a light green surface tinge. Thinner forms will convert to its salts. Note: Metal objects covered by sand or mud will accumulate a crust but by virtue of the protection given by burial will not furnish a ground for living coral. Once fanned away, the sand will yield a readily identifiable artifact whose shape has been preserved.

Wood stays intact whenever there is an absence of the teredo worm. In cold waters or buried sand, wood usually escapes the teredo worm, which thrives in water of tropical temperatures.

Pewter behaves irregularly; it may be found either completely intact or extensively corroded.

Lead suffers little from immersion in seawater except for a superficial coating of white corrosion.

Glass survives intact, although some metallic lead deposits or superficial erosions may form on its surface.

Gems: Pearls, being organic, suffer from exposure to sea water by losing their nacre and luster. Emeralds, aquamarines, rubies, sapphires, and members of the quartz family survive chemical effects from immersion but do suffer superficial scrapes from sea action in the sand.

Stones and *minerals* such as marble or limestone survive except for erosion and damage by sea life such as worms, which exude a calcium-destroying substance.

For a detailed treatment of the entire subject of underwater exploration I urge you read *History Under the Sea* by Mendel Peterson, published by The Smithsonian Institution, 1965.

THE CARE AND PRESERVATION OF ARTIFACTS

Finding and salvaging artifacts, especially from the remote past, is thrilling, but the experience can be enhanced if you know the history behind them. Take your finds to a museum or university to identify them and their link with the past. Your education will soon point out that treasure consists not only of precious metals or gems but of such homely objects as pots, pans, tankards, bottles, and eating utensils. All have value (often very great value) by historical, as well as economic, standards.

The effect of nature's destructive forces on the objects remaining on a wreck site is extremely detrimental, and one of the great problems of underwater exploration is the preservation of such objects— especially those that have been extensively damaged or changed in chemical composition by these forces.

Some materials that have suffered little alteration in their submergence require only cleaning and possibly a coat of wax or lacquer to preserve them. Others of more marked change may require application of chemical preservatives.

General Rule: When preparing materials in the field, keep them wet until they are packed for shipping. Objects encrusted with coral should be stored in salt water. Organic materials, such as animal or plant life, should be soaked in a solution of 10 percent formaldehyde, then wrapped and packed in an air-tight plastic bag. Packing cases should be added to prevent breakage.

Basic Preservation Techniques: The principal steps of preservation are cleaning, desalting, drying, reduction of corrosion, and sealing and hardening. These steps apply to all materials: inorganic materials such as metals, ceramics, glass, minerals, and gems; and organic materials of animal or vegetable origin such as wood, hemp, ivory, bone, leather, horn, tortoiseshell, and seashells.

Organic materials can be brought out of the water in varying conditions of survival. For example, ivory survives but can disintegrate through decalcification. Leather usually survives in fragile condition if long buried in sand or mud. Organic materials will sometimes be preserved from the deleterious effect of fungi and rot by the salt of metals with which they may have become permeated—for example, wood or hemp that has been saturated with iron oxide. Like metal, very highly mineralized wood will survive inside a sand crust.

Here are the 5 basic steps:

1. *Cleaning:* To clean the encrustation from surfaces, soak ferrous metals in Rustoline to remove all traces of rust; scrub and apply silver polish to silver; soak and clean bronze and brass (nonferrous) in a solution of Rochell Salt.
2. *Desalting:* The destruction of harmful sea salts that have permeated metal is ordinarily accomplished by boiling the object in a sodium hydroxide bath.
3. *Drying:* To dry out an artifact, remove it from the bath after desalting. Iron, steel, and other metals may be oven dried at 105° C. or 220° F. Wood, pottery, and bones may be dried naturally in the shade.

   All ceramic materials may have calcereous sea growths on their surfaces and stains from metal salts such as iron oxide. Well-fired ware, such as terra cotta, may survive intact, but porrly fired native ware sometimes erodes badly or will crack or fall apart in drying out. Keep pottery out of the sun, or vapor entering the object's pores might cause a crack. Woods behave differently. Soft wood, if buried, will survive a long immersion though in very fragile condition. Hard wood, if buried, will do better, and heavy tropical wood will often survive in a strong condition. Some wood not affected while submerged will deteriorate rapidly when removed from water.
4. *Reduction of Corrosion:* To reduce the metal corrosion to the metallic form of an object, coat the object with a plastic or wax to seal the surface from air and prevent further damage through corrosion.
5. *Sealing and Hardening:* Ferrous metals may be sprayed with Krylon. Wood objects may be simmered in solution of alum for two to three hours or soaked in Alvar. Bone, unless very fragile,

may be treated like wood. If wood artifacts are fragile, soak them in a solution of cellulose acetate dissolved in acetone. Use Duco cement to mend breaks.

REPORTING A WRECK SITE

Wreck diving is not limited exclusively to treasure or artifact hunting. Underwater naturalists will be attracted to wrecks because of the high concentration of animal populations in and around them. The naturalist can report his observations to the American Littoral Society, and his report should contain the following information (see Fish Watching, page 118):

1. Exact location:
   a. Land ranges
   b. Dead-reckoning bearings
   c. Longitude and latitude coordinates
2. Historical data, if available, about the sinking of the ship
3. Present status of ownership, if known
4. Present condition of the wreck and how it lies on the bottom. Is the ship intact or in pieces? How many pieces? How are they situated?
5. The depth of the water in which the ship rests and the depth to the uppermost part of the ship
6. As much information as possible on the abundance and types of marine growth on the ship
7. Estimates of the quantities of all different species of fish or other animals on the wreck at various times of the year
8. Estimated number of divers using the wreck during the year and, if possible, the estimated number of anglers fishing the wreck during the year
9. Information pertaining to any past, present, or intended salvage operations on the wreck about which you may be aware
10. Any reference sources available about the wreck—newspaper accounts, books, etc.
11. Any information on the temperature of the water at the surface, around the ship, and on the bottom
12. Visibility conditions on the wreck at various times of the year.

9

MASK AND LENS: UNDERWATER PHOTOGRAPHY

The underwater world is uncommonly photogenic, a fact which, along with its accessibility, accounts for the high popularity of photography among the skin divers whether for fun or for art or in connection with underwater research.

To understand underwater photography the novice should first acquire a reading knowledge of general photographic theory and practice.

VISUAL EFFECTS OF DEPTH

The Nature of Light Under Water: An understanding of light at depth is a prerequisite to effective photography under water. The intensity of light decreases with depth: at fifteen feet it is one-eighth that at surface; at 130 feet it is one-thirtieth. Color intensity, since it is filtered out by water, rapidly weakens with depth. In pure water, deep seas, and some lakes, color disappears in the following approximate order:

Red begins to dull at 15 ft.
Red is considerably reduced at 20 ft.
Red vanishes at 30 ft.
Orange is reduced at 25 ft.
Orange vanishes at 30–35 ft.
Green vanishes at 80 ft.
Only blue-green remains at 90 ft.
Gray-blue remains at 100 ft. and deeper.

Colors can be restored with artificial light. Reds can be partially restored by means of red filters provided you open your lens one or two stops larger or as specified by directions from your filter package.

Visual Distortion of Objects Under Water: To the eye as well as to the camera lens, underwater objects will appear one-third larger and one-fourth closer than they really are. The camera lens sees just as the eye does. Therefore, if an object looks to be, say, two feet away from your camera, focus your lens for two feet.

WHAT EQUIPMENT TO ACQUIRE

The complexity and cost of equipment vary widely. Your cnoice is personal, depending on your requirements, objectives, experience, and pocketbook. Beginners should start with a wholly automatic camera. There are several submersible, self-contained cameras on the market that do not need a custom-built housing. Underwater cameras today are so automated that they defy error. They can be used on dry land too. If you already own a land camera, you may consider purchasing an inexpensive housing for it to begin with. Don't use a plastic bag as a temporary housing.

Light Meter: Once you decide that a subject is worth shooting, shoot it right. If you do not already have a light meter on your camera, obtain one. If your budget permits, buy one of the specially housed submersible meters; otherwise, a standard land light meter can be sealed in an ordinary jar in order to take it underwater with you. Always shoot according to exposures recommended by your meter. If in doubt about correct settings, the best insurance against failure is to take a series of different exposures bracketed around a meter reading most likely to be correct. If shooting at f 5.6, try shooting one stop down at f 4 and one stop up at f 8 but maintain a constant shutter speed. For finer variations change your settings by a half-stop. Another method of bracketing is to reverse the procedure that is to maintain a constant f stop and shoot at different shutter speeds. Whenever the meter is used for color its reading should normally be based on the lighter (not the lightest) parts of the subject. For black and white film the reading should be based generally on the darker parts of the subject. Whenever possible take your readings at close range (from a distance of about one foot) being certain that your own shadow does not fall on the meter or the subject. Bear in mind that readings must often be modified in accordance with the requirements of filters and unusual subject color.

Artificial Lighting: Most underwater cameras now available can be bought with a flash attachment that uses the same bulbs used in topside photography. Standard flashbulbs can be used effectively underwater, and these include Press-5, No. 25, M5, M3, M2, and AG-1. The flash unit should be attached to extend forward and aside so that light will not illuminate suspended sediment in the water just in front of the camera and spoil shots with flashback (light reflected back from suspended sediment). Side lighting produces good constrasting tones. Use an indoor type of color bulb when shooting with color film: No. 5 (blue bulb) for close-ups to 3 feet distance in clear water and Nos. 25 or M3 to cover distances from 10 to 15 feet. The guide number for underwater flash exposure is approximately one-third of the rating specified on the flashbulb carton. Example for obtaining an f-stop setting: Carton guide number is 160; subject is 10 feet from the camera. Take one-third of 160 to get 5.3. The setting nearest that on most cameras would be 5.6. Set it there.

Carry bulbs in a nylon mesh sack hooked to your belt. When carrying bulbs to depths of 30 feet or more of water, beware of the possibility of implosion caused by pressure. Small bulbs such as the

M3 are less likely to implode than larger bulbs. Don't touch burned-out bulbs bare-handed until they are cooled. Wear a glove for protection. Underwater flash should be used sparingly and mainly in conjunction with available (natural) light.

While flashbulbs give satisfactory results, electronic flash gives more natural results and it can be used repetitively without losing time to change flashbulbs.

HOW TO USE STROBE LIGHTING

For best results, camera and strobe should be separated. Aim the strobe downward and inward, from your upper left, at an angle of about 45° to the subject. Avoid illuminating the snow-like particles between the camera and the subject. As you gain experience, try shifting the strobe to get different effects.

RULES FOR BEST RESULTS

Exposure settings for underwater photography depend on the amount of sun, the clarity of the water, the distance of the subject below the surface and from the camera, the color of the bottom or background, and the movement and color of the subject. You can rely on your automatic system to give you the proper settings. In selecting a subject, look for its simplicity, order, clarity, pattern, and rhythm. Sharply outlined silhouettes are good; so are highly textured and detailed forms that are especially plentiful in coral reefs.

For maximum available light, shoot in fair, sunny weather between 10 A.M. *and* 2 P.M. in clear, shallow waters. In color work, early morning or later afternoon light produces marked deviations from color "norms," color casts being markedly false on the film. However, falsity of color cast does not disqualify a photograph. It can still be a prize shot. Color pictures taken under overcast skies appear almost monochromatically bluish throughout. Get in close to your subject, hold your camera as steady as possible, and focus your lens with exactness. Set your focal length for the distance the subject appears to be away from your eye. Use a shutter speed of $^{1}/_{125}$ of a second. Increase the shutter speed to as much as $^{1}/_{500}$ of a second as the light becomes brighter.

If you must shoot at a slower speed, brace the camera against the slightest movement or the shot will be blurred. In some instances, shooting effectively at slow speeds calls for a tripod, or you can operate comfortably with a good foothold on the bottom by tying a 5-pound lead weight to each foot, enabling you to stand or even plod along the bottom like a helmet driver.

Depth of Field: With smaller lens openings you will increase your depth of field so that not only your subject but more background and foreground are in focus. This is recommended only if visibility is exceptionally good. Without such visibility (100 feet or more) there would be no point in trying to increase your depth of field, as the background would be hardly visible in your results.

COLOR CORRECTION FILTERS

Underwater path length of the light (feet)	Filter	Exposure increase in stops
1	CC 05R	1/3
2	CC 10R	1/3
5	CC 20R	1/3
8	CC 30R	2/3
12	CC 40R	2/3
15	CC 50R	1

For distances of greater than 15 feet a composite filter with the appropriate number of filter units can be used.

UNDERWATER PHOTOGRAPHIC LIGHT SOURCES

Type of Lighting	Depth Limit (ft)	Factors Limiting Visibility	Accuracy of Color Rendition	Ability to Light Subject for the Human Eye as Camera Will See It	Control of Effects From Light Scattering	Duration (sec)	Intensity	Means of Determining Exposure	Power Requirement	Extent of Use	Remarks
Natural	50 to 100	absorptivity, scattering	poor (predominantly green)	very good	fair to good	continuous	good at surface, but decreases with depth	meter	none	general	–
Flood	none	absorptivity, scattering	fairly good	very good	very good	continuous	relatively low	guide number determined by experiment	high (1/2 to 2 kw)	general, especially at greater depths	–
Flash bulbs	none	absorptivity, scattering	fairly good	poor	fair	1/50 to 1/100	high	guide numbers	self-contained battery	general	Diver must replace bulbs
Electronic flash	none	absorptivity, scattering	fairly good	poor	fair	1/1,000 to 1/2,000 or faster	very high	guide numbers	self-contained battery	general	Electronic flash is probably better than regular flash for use under water.

SUGGESTED EXPOSURE GUIDE FOR NARROW BEAM ELECTRONIC FLASH

Distance to subject (feet)	ASA rating		
	25	64	160
1	f16	f22	f32
2	f8	f16	f22
3	f5.6	f8	f11–16
4	f4	f5.6	f11
5	f2.5	f4.5	f8
6	–	f3.5	f5.6
7	–	f2.5	f4
8	–	–	f3.5

FILM FOR UNDERWATER WORK

Black and White Underwater Photography: Every film has what is known as an ASA (American Standards Association) rating. The higher the rating, the more sensitive the film to light, meaning that less light is required to make a picture. For underwater work, the faster the film, the better, because you can use faster shutter speeds to catch the swift movements of fish and for clarity and sharpness of focus. Although there is no special underwater film, the best all-around black and white film for underwater work is Kodak Tri-X, a fast film with an ASA rating of 400. Tri-X is ideally fast yet gives fine grain prints. Perfectionists seeking less graininess in prints might prefer using Kodak Panotomic-X for close-up work under very bright conditions (100 feet or more visibility), but even then Tri-X will accomplish just about the same results. If there is any difference in graininess between these two films, I have to date found it hard to detect.

APPROXIMATE EXPOSURES FOR UNDERWATER PHOTOGRAPHY

KODAK Film Bright Sunlight–Light Bottom*	Depth	
	2 to 5 feet	10 to 20 feet
VERICHROME Pan and PLUS–X Pan Stills at 1/50 or 1/60 sec...............	f/8	f/2.8
TRI–X Pan Stills at 1/50 or 1/60 sec.................	f/16	f/5.6
TRI–X Reversal Movie Film at 16 or 18 F.P.S	f/11	f/4
KODACHROME II for Daylight Stills at 1/25 or 1/30 sec Movies at 16 or 18 F.P.S	f/8	f/2.8
KODACHROME–X, EKTACHROME–X, or KODACOLOR–X Stills at 1/25 or 1/30 sec.................	f/8	f/4
High Speed EKTACHROME, Daylight Type Stills at 1/50 or 1/60 sec.................	f/11	f/5.6

*A dark bottom may require one or two more lens openings; even so, it may cause poorly lighted subjects. Hazy sunlight will usually require at least 1/2 a lens opening larger.

Types of Color Film for Underwater Work: Use outdoor daylight film only. One of the marvels of the underwater world is its color, and there is every reason to encourage wet photographers to start right in with color film. Recommended for use are:

Kodachrome X (ASA 64) intense, grainless
Ektachrome X (ASA 64)
Hi-Speed Ektachrome (ASA 160)
Kodacolor X (ASA 64)—for prints only

ASA rating of Ektachrome films can be "sped up" (through chemical variations in the developing process) and exposed as if they had a rating as high as 640. Films you wish to process this way should be clearly marked accordingly when sent to the processing laboratory.

MOVIE MAKING

There are several good moderate to high-priced motion picture cameras on the market. For the amateur an 8-mm or Super-8-mm camera is practical. For black and white work, use Tri-X. For color, high-speed Ektachrome or Kodachrome II (ASA XX). As in still photography, use a light meter. Floodlights, available in a variety of models, will enhance your results.

Rule of Thumb for Moving Making: With visibilities of 15 feet or more, for any depth up to 20 feet, open your lens 3 f-stops more than you would on the surface. Open it an additional f-stop for every additional 10 feet of depth. When aiming your camera upward for silhouette shots, switch to "manual" operation if your camera is on "automatic." Close the lens 2 f-stops to account for glare from above. Shoot close to your subject. Jot down settings for future reference.

CARE OF YOUR CAMERA

After all submersions of your camera, soak it in a tub of fresh water and wipe it dry. Never let a camera stand in the air or sun after using it in salt water. The O-ring seal on the lid should be loosened when the camera is not in use for a long period. Rub the camera with a film of silicone grease lubricant.

In underwater work, condensation will form on the lens and window of the housing because of lower temperatures and damage the camera. Condensation can be reduced by keeping the equipment out of the sun while topside. As an added precaution include a bag of silica gel or dessicant in the housing. If the interior of the camera should ever become flooded, rinse and dry it thoroughly and take it to a camera shop for an overhaul.

WHERE TO GET FILM DEVELOPED

Your black and white film can be developed and printed through mass production commercial channels if you are satisfied with corner-drugstore quality. For high-quality processing, send your film to a custom processing house rather than to a mass production service. Dyed-in-the-wool shutterbugs can, of course, do their own black and white processing. As to color: Even pros send their work to commercial processors.

FINAL OBSERVATIONS ON UNDERWATER PHOTOGRAPHY

The light conditions of day are such that no two hours between dawn and dusk are alike. By the same token, no two bodies of water are alike; no two areas of water have the same color cast, and the conditions of even the same body of water may vary from season to season, from day to day, and from hour to hour because of weather and other influences or disturbances, natural and man-made. There is therefore no system of universally applicable formulas for camera settings. Exposure formulas are a comfort only to those who want to be led by the hand. Rigid application of formulas inhibits creativity, which, to my mind, makes any craft, art, or even a casual hobby worthwhile. I'm for experimentation, which is the basis for creative expression. A good cameraman, therefore, has to be a flexible tactician with his eyes and his equipment and must meet each challenge as it comes. This is the fun of it—and the responsibility if you seek the highest degree of personal gratification from top results.

10

EPICUREAN SPLENDORS

Epicurean sportsman, having laid aside your mask, fins, and snorkel for the night and taken up the casserole, think now of all the exquisite morsels, delicious chowders, stews, tangy game, and other tasty provender of nature awaiting your voracious appetite. So venture forth to the libraries and kitchens and by campfires. Beg, borrow, or steal every recipe you can. Here are but a few.

Diving and catching fish are not only adventures in themselves but also the prelude to a special kind of adventure—that of gastronomy.

EDIBLE FISH

The tastiest fish come from fresh water. The best fish for good eating are whitefish fried, broiled or au gratin, pompano, shad, speckled or brook trout, and, of course, fillet of sole.

Mackerel: Fish of the mackerel family are great for broiling; they include the tuna, mackerel, and kingfish.

Flat Fish: Flat fish are another family and include the flounder, sole, and halibut. They can be cooked in the form of a fillet in deep fat or sautéed with equal culinary success.

Wall-eyed Pike: An American freshwater food fish having large, prominent eyes.

Sunfish: Another family of fish whose species are numerous and widely distributed is that of the sunfish. The most important members are the bass and the black crappies.

Pan Fish (Small): There are many pan fish; the bluegill, sunfish, and yellow perch are examples.

Pike: Pikes include the pickerel, the Great Lakes pike, and the muskellunge.

Eels: To Europeans, eels are a delicacy. The eel for the most part has escaped the "uncivilized" American.

Catfish: Catfish come from warm waters. Their species are many and far-flung.

Shellfish: The shellfish include prawns, scallops, oysters, crabs, mussels, terrapin, turtles, abalone, crayfish, shrimp, lobsters, conchs, and clams.

Coral feeders: Porgies, black seabass, jewfish, snapper, jack, parrot fish, and grouper are edible.

Warning: although there are 30 varieties of parrot fish considered edible, some may be poisonous in some areas. Large groupers may be poisonous due to eating poisonous species directly or indirectly down the food chain. For this reason do not eat large groupers and do not make stews with large fish. Freshwater clams and mussels are not edible.

DIET TIPS

Fresh-caught fish makes delicious eating. What is more, there is hardly a protein food that lends itself to more varied and delectable treatment than fish. Wherever you get your fish—on the point of a spear, from a pier, or at the market—here are some helpful guides and recipes for camp and kitchen.

Fish is lower in calories than meat, acceptable on low-cholesterol diets, and a welcome item for all those watching their waistlines. Olive oil, too, is approved for low-cholesterol diets, being pure vegetable oil very high in unsaturated fatty acids.

TIPS FOR CATCHING DINNER

Coral rocks, along beaches or extending out into deeper water as reefs, provide the greatest amount of food. The more exposed surface of the reef bears clinging shellfish. Be sure that all the shellfish you take are healthy. Do not select them from colonies where some are dead or dying.

Fish, crabs, lobsters, crayfish, sea urchins, and small octopi can be poked out of holes, crevices, or rock pools. Be ready to snare, catch, or spear them before they move off into deep water. If they are in deeper water, tease them shoreward with a baited hook, piece of string, or stick.

A small heap of empty oyster shells near a hole may indicate an octopus. Drop a baited hook into the hole and wait until the octopus has entirely surrounded the hook and line; then lift it up quickly. To kill, pierce it with your fish spear. Octopi are not scavengers, like sharks, but hunters, fond of spiny lobster and other cráb-like fish. At night, they come into shallow water and can then be easily seen and speared.

Snails and limpets cling to rocks and seaweed from the low water mark up. Large snails called chitons adhere tightly to rocks just above the surf line. Mussels usually form dense colonies in rock pools, on logs, or at the base of boulders. *Black mussels are poison-*

ous in tropical zones during the summer, especially when seas are highly phosphorescent.

The safest fish to eat are those from the open sea or deep water beyond the reef. Silvery fishes, river eels, butterfly fishes, and flounders from bays and rivers are good to eat. Remember that fish caught in the tropics spoil quickly.

WARNING (see pages 238–41)

Fish with Poisonous Flesh: There are no simple rules for telling undesirable fish from the desirable ones. Often those considered edible in one locality may be unwholesome elsewhere, depending on the place, their food, or even the season of the year. Cooking does not destroy the poison.

Large barracudas can cause serious digestive illness; yet those less than 3 feet long have been eaten with safety. The oilfish has a white, flaky, rather tasty flesh which is very poisonous. The fish of the Southwest Pacific and all great sea eels should be carefully avoided. *Never eat entrails or eggs of any tropical fish.*

Undesirable fish have certain characteristics. Almost all live in shallow waters of lagoons or reefs.

Almost all have round or box-like bodies with hard, shell-like skins covered with bony plates or spines. They have small, parrot-like mouths, small gill openings; and the belly fins are small or absent. Their names suggest their shapes—puffer fish, file fish, globe fish, trigger fish, trunk fish.

Fish and Shellfish With Venomous Spines: Reefs are no place for bare feet. Coral, dead or alive, can cause painful cuts. Seemingly harmless sponges and sea urchins can slip fine needles of lime or silica into your skin, and they will break off and fester. Don't dig them out; use lime juice, if available, to dissolve them. The almost invisible stonefish will not move from your path. It has poison spines that will cause you agony and death. Treat as for snakebite.

Don't probe with your hands into dark holes; use a stick. Don't step freely over muddy or sandy bottoms of rivers and seashores;

slide your feet along the bottom. In this way, you will avoid stepping on stingrays or other sharp-spined animals. If you step on a stingray, you push its body down, giving it leverage to throw its tail up and stab you with its stinging spine. A stingray's broken-off spine can be removed only by cutting it out.

Cone shell snails and long, slender, pointed terebra snails have poison teeth and can bite. Cone snails have smooth, colorful, mottled shells with elongated, narrow openings. They live under rocks, in crevices of coral reefs, and along rocky shores of protected bays. They are shy and are most active at night. They have a long mouth and a snout or proboscis which is used to jab or inject their teeth. These teeth are actually tiny hypodermic needles, with a tiny poison gland on the back end of each. This action is swift, producing acute pain, swelling, paralysis, blindness, and possible death in 4 hours. Avoid handling all cone snails.

Handle the big conches with caution. These snails have razor-sharp trapdoors, which they may suddenly jab out, puncturing your skin in their effort to get away. Don't use your hands to gather large abalones and clams. Pry them loose with bars or wedges; they will hold you if they clamp down on your fingers.

HUNTING LOBSTER

Lobster must be hunted down where they hide: under rocks, sunken trees, crevices, quarries, lakes, pilings, dams. A certain degree of trial-and-error goes into capturing a lobster live without incident. One way is to coax the lobster out of its hideout by using a hook. Wear gloves. When it is out, grab it behind the large claws, over the back, and hold firmly. Place in a goodie bag. (The upper claw of an 8- to 10-pound lobster can bruise a diver's finger, but do no damage to a gloved hand.) If a frontal approach is required, grab it by the ripper claw, not the larger crusher claw, and hold for a second so as not to give the lobster time to put his crusher claw into action.

Another approach is to grab both claws. Hold them firmly and pull the lobster from its hideaway. Then, transfer your grip to the body, holding its back. With free hand, open goodie bag and deposit lobster within.

When out of water, rubberband or tape the claws, as they are dangerous, even to other lobsters. A lobster will suffocate if left in fresh water. Keep lobsters on ice until ready for cooking. The capture of females with eggs, and smaller lobsters, is prohibited. The eggs are a highly visible red, carried under the tail.

Recommendation: Check local lobster laws. It is totally unsportsperson-like, and in some areas illegal, to spear, hook, impale, or otherwise puncture any lobster; they may only be taken by hand, snare, pot, or trap. Possession of a lobster with a hole in it is prima facie evidence of a violation (penalty: up to one year in prison and/or $600 fine). In many jurisdictions no egg-bearing lobsters may be taken, possessed, or sold at any time; egg-stripping is illegal (same penalty as above). Spiny lobsters (*Panulirus argus*) must have a carapace length of at least three inches (taking, having, or selling "short" lobsters carries the same penalty as above). Removal of lobster tails prior to landing on shore is often illegal.

TURTLES

In some areas and territorial waters it is illegal to take, possess, sell, molest, etc.:

any sea turtle nest or eggs at *any* time
any sea turtle on the territorial beaches at *any* time

Leatherback, hawksbill, and ridley turtles (and all parts thereof, dead or alive) are totally protected under federal law, as endangered species.

Although there is a local legal season on the depleted green and loggerhead turtles, in territorial waters, from October 1 to April 30, both species have been proposed for inclusion on the federal endangered species list; they are expected to be included in the very near future. Good conservation practices dictate that *all* turtles be left undisturbed at all times and places.

Note: Local penalties for violating turtle regulations: up to $600 and/or one year in jail. Federal penalties: up to $20,000 and/or one year in jail.

MARINE MAMMALS

All whales, porpoises, and dolphins (not the fish) are protected by federal law; this includes territorial waters. Violations can bring penalties up to $20,000 and/or one year imprisonment.

Recommendation: Check endangered species lists as well as area laws.

FEATURES THAT IDENTIFY FRESH FISH

The eyes should be full, bright, clear, and moist.

The gills should be reddish pink and free of slime and odor.

The scales should retain their bright sheen and cling strongly to the skin.

The meat should cling close to the bones and be firm to the touch and springy enough so that when pressed it returns to its original shape. Aside from the characteristic odor of fish a fresh fish has not objectionable odor.

Shellfish should be closed tight. Crustaceans should be cooked alive.

Warning: Fish in highly polluted waters are often inedible.

HANDLING, PREPARING, AND STORING FISH

How to Handle Fish You Plan to Eat: Don't leave fish on a stringer. Kill them as quickly as possible. Draw them, remove the gills, and wipe the fish thoroughly dry. Keep your fish separated and loosely packed in paper in a well-ventilated container or a creel with dry grass. Don't place fish in water to keep them fresh. Don't leave them in the sun; they will soften rapidly and lose much of their savoriness. Do not keep them on ice if they can be kept fresh without ice. Allow all frozen fish to defrost in a refrigerator just before the fish is to be cooked.

How to Pan-dress Fish:
Wash the fish in cold salted water.
Lay it on a wooden surface.
Grasp its head with one hand.
Remove scales with a sharp knife. Work from the tail toward the head.
Split the full length of the belly from the vent to the head. Remove the entrails.
Remove the pelvic fins. Remove the head, including the pectoral fin, by cutting above the collarbone and through the backbone. Cut off the tail.
Dip the fish quickly in salted fresh water to remove any blood or remaining membranes.

How to Fillet Fish:
Cut down through the flesh along the back from tail to head.
Cut down the backbone just above the collarbone. Turn the knife flat and cut the flesh along the backbone, slithering the knife along the rib bones to the tail so that the fillet comes off in one piece. Turn the fish over. Repeat the filleting process on the other side.

How to skin Fillets:
Lay the fillet flat, skin side down.
Grasp the tail end with the fingers and cut through the flesh to the skin.
Flatten the knife on the skin and cut the flesh away by pushing the knife forward toward the fish's head. The fillet is then skinned. Always hold the free end of the skin firmly with fingers and thumb. Wipe the fish with a damp cloth. The fish can be dressed in a number of forms.
Small fish may be drawn but should be left whole, dressed and pan dressed. Some varieties can be filleted in either single or butterfly forms, and larger fish may be chopped into steaks or sticks. If

you fillet fish of a pound or less, leave the skin on but remove the scales and bones.

The "Cuts" of Fin Fish:

Whole or round: Fish totally intact, usually very small fish.

Drawn: Only entrails are removed. Fish are left intact. All small fish should be drawn and cooked whole.

Dressed: Head, tail, entrails, and fins removed.

Pan dressed: Smaller varieties of fish—entrails, head, tail, and fins removed. Sometimes the fish is split along the belly or back and the backbone is removed.

Steaks: Steaks are usually cross-section slices of large-size dressed fish. The cut is not lengthwise along the fish but across it, usually an inch or more thick. The backbone is the only bone left in the steak.

Single fillets: The sides of the fish are cut lengthwise and removed from the backbone.

Butterfly fillets: The fillets are held together by the uncut belly skin of the fish. The bones are removed from most fillets.

Sticks: After the head, fins, and entrails have been removed, sticks are cut crosswise or lengthwise in uniform portions with the backbone left in.

Storing Fish by Refrigeration: Clean the fish before storing it, first removing all the blood and entrails. Wrap it in waxed paper and place it in the freezer. The fish will keep until defrosted. If the fish is to be kept fresh for no more than several days, place it in a glass dish tightly covered and leave it in the refrigerator.

Removing Fish Odors from Hands and Pans: Do not use soap at first. Rub hands well with moistened salt, then rinse them with hot water. Rub them with natural lemon juice, then use soap.

COOKING FISH INDOORS

There are many ways to cook fish, indoors or out. Fish can be baked, broiled, steamed, fried, oven-fried, smoked, sautéed, or cooked in any number of sauces: sweet and pungent, creole, meu-nière, etc.

Baking: A quick easy wasy way to cook fish is to bake it. Be sure that the fish is cleaned, dressed, and wiped dry and that all the blood is removed. Removal of the head is optional. If the fish is to be stuffed, never fill more than two thirds of it. To hold the stuffing in fish, skewer or lace up the opening with thread. Place the fish in a shallow baking pan over a layer of butter or waxed paper. Preheat oven to 400° F. Don't overbake. Baste occasionally with fat. Remove skewers. Serve the fish immediately upon removing it from the oven.

Broiling: Serve broiled fish sizzling hot; do not overcook. An ideal cut of fish for broiling is a steak cut to preferred thickness, but a good average thickness is one inch. Keep the fish on a rack, sandwiched between two halves of a folded grate to simplify basting, two to five inches under flame of broiler, preferably a double broiler. When broiling a split fish, leave in the backbone for juiciest results. Prepare a whole dressed fish for broiling as you would for baking. Preheat the oven and pan to broiling heat, over 500° F. Wash fish in salted water. Douse with flour. Brush fish with butter. Season as desired. Place the fish below a medium flame. Don't turn fillets and split fish during broiling period. Baste often so that the liquid permeates the fish. Add more seasoning if desired when broiling is done. Fish sticks and whole fish are broiled on one side, turned and broiled on the other. Baste after turning. Serve at once, sizzling hot.

Deep Frying: Fillets of fish are more suitable for deep frying than other cuts of fish. The steps in deep frying are:

1. Wipe fish with damp cloth.
2. Dip fish in milk and then in cracker crumbs.
3. Place one layer of fish in wire frying basket.
4. Heat butter or fat in a deep dish to 385°. Fry until golden brown. Three to 5 minutes will do. Serve immediately. See that care is taken not to allow butter or fat to smoke.

COOKING FISH OUTDOORS

For cooking outdoors, a grill is absolutely essential. You can build them in just about any size and price range you desire.

For a grill type of fire, the best fuels are charcoal lumps or briquets. You may want to use a hardwood or fruitwood such as apple or hickory chips to give added flavor to meat. Pine and similar soft woods do not give a satisfactory bed of coals and give foods a sooty coating.

Building a Good Charcoal Cooking Fire: Start with a bed of charcoal several inches deep, enough to last for several hours. Spray a charcoal lighter fluid over the bed and ignite. When coals burn to a gray ash covering over a ruddy, smoldering glow underneath, you will have a cooking fire that gives an effective, glowing heat. It should take at least thirty minutes to get your fire to this stage of readiness for cooking.

Another way to start a fire is to begin with a small amount of kindling, paper, and a few charcoal lumps. Add more lumps as the coals begin to glow. Cooking time will depend on the type of grill, its size, the degree of heat, and the wind velocity. When flare-ups occur during cooking as a result, for example, of fat dripping on the coals, douse the flames with a little bit of water. A toy water gun is handy for this purpose.

Pan-frying Fish: Many varieties of fish may be pan fried. Frying seals in the juices of a fish. The fish is dropped quickly into very hot butter or vegetable fat and heated in a frying pan or, for large specimens, a skillet. Whatever kind of cut you use, trim it down to serving size. Do not fry large pieces of fish at a time, for the outside dries up and the inside may well remain uncooked. Follow these stages:

1. Wipe fish with damp cloth.
2. Dip fish in milk, then in cracker crumbs or flour.
3. Melt enough vegetable fat or drawn (clarified) butter to fill the

bottom of the pan to a depth of about ½ inch. Don't let the fat or butter smoke or scorch.

4. Fry over a moderate flame 3 to 5 minutes or until brown. Brown both sides. Garnish and serve.

FISH FRY

2 lbs. ocean perch fillets	½ cup flour
¼ cup evaporated milk	¼ cup yellow cornmeal
1½ tsps. salt	Butter or other fat
Dash pepper	Lemon wedges

Cut large fillets into strips, 1½ to 2 inches wide. Combine milk, salt, and pepper. Combine flour and cornmeal and dip fish in the milk mixture, then roll it in the flour mixture. Place fat or butter in a heavy iron frying pan. Place on a barbecue grill about 4 inches from the source of heat. Add fish and fry for 4 minutes. Turn carefully and fry for 4 minutes longer. Drain on absorbent paper. Serve with lemon wedges. Serves 6.

BUTTERED FRIED FISH

¼ cup (½ stick) butter	1 lb. fresh perch fillets
2 tbsps. lemon juice	or
½ tsp. salt	1 pkg. (1 lb.) frozen perch fil-
¼ tsp. dill weed	lets, thawed

Use a skillet or form a pan by using a double thickness of aluminum foil and turning up its edge 1 inch all the way around. Miter the corners. Melt butter in skillet; add lemon juice, salt, and dill weed. Add fish skin side down. Place skillet on grill 4 to 5 inches from coals. Cook 10 minutes, basting frequently with sauce. Turn fish; cook, basting with sauce, for an additional 10 minutes or until fish flakes. Serves 4.

Boiling Fish: To boil, or more accurately, to poach, fish over an open flame, the fish should be sliced and the slices wrapped in cheesecloth or thin muslin and the cooking begun in a cold salted fish broth. Bring the liquid to a boil, reduce the heat, and let the fish simmer until it is well done, allowing about 6 to 8 minutes for each pound. The slices should be thick and the liquid barely enough to cover them, otherwise the fish will lose its flavor and the flesh will disintegrate.

Never puncture or skewer a fish to test it because this permits the juices and flavor to drain off.

To poach fish in the open, lay fillets or whole fish in a buttered shallow pan and cover them with a court bouillon, wine, milk, or any desired liquid except water. Cover the pan with a second pan and put in a moderate oven, 300° to 350° F. Baste the fish frequently, and use whatever liquid remains to make a sauce.

Steaming Fish: To steam a fish, lay it on a rack where only the steam from the boiling liquid in the bottom of the kettle will touch it. The liquid itself can be a broth prepared from the head and tail and bits of the fish.

Campsite Steamed Fish: Clean fish, removing the vital organs, leaving the head and fins on. Season. Roll each fish separately in waxed or buttered paper. Wrap the whole bundle inside a sheet of plain paper. Finally wrap all in thick newspaper and soak long enough to get the outside thoroughly wet. Bury the whole bundle in the hot ashes or coals. The outside of the paper may char, put it will not burn through to the fish. The moisture inside the bundle does the steaming. The fish should be done in about 20 minutes.

Open-Fire Broiling: Take a fish weighing from 2 to 5 pounds. Remove the entrails and head, wash the body carefully, but do not scale or remove the fins and tail. Cut and sharpen a green stick about the width of your thumb and a yard long. Insert the point of the stick in the back behind the head just above the backbone, running it through lengthwise until it comes out at the tail. Season the inside of the fish with salt and pepper and place it before the fire with the spit supported at two ends on rocks or other convenient objects. When the skin is well blackened on the fire side, turn it over and cook the other side. Just before it is about to fall off the spit, the cooking is done. Skin, bones, and fins can now be pulled off easily, leaving a clean, flaky meat.

Planked Fish Oregon Style: Spread open a firm-fleshed fish, clean it, and nail it to a water-soaked wood plank. Then prop the plank upright into a bed of charcoal. Fat from bacon tacked to the board across the spread fish will melt down on the fish. Great for beach cookouts.

Another Method of Planking Fish: Tack a spread fish to a plank. Stand the plank up before the fire where it will get good heat but not burn. Baste with bacon tied to end of a twig, or tack the bacon across the fish. The plank should be turned end for end several times during the process for even cooking. When the fish flakes to the touch of a fork, it is done. Serve it on the plank. Season to taste, adding lemon.

Grilling Fish Sticks: Cut any good edible fish into four or five sticks of about ¾ of an inch thick, one per guest. Combine in a shallow dish ½ cup of cooking oil and ¼ cup of lemon juice. Place the fish sticks in the dish. Cover with waxed paper and let stand about one-half hour, turning and basting each steak frequently. Then drain the fish and place it in a greased steak broiler. Grill the fish 3 minutes, 5 inches from coals, brushing lemon juice mixture or melted butter on both sides. Season with salt and pepper and one teaspoon of monosodium glutamate. A slice of any vegetable such as an onion, tomato, or eggplant or a combination of vegetables may be wrapped with this fish steak in tinfoil and grilled about 10 minutes, 3 inches from the coals.

Grilling Fish Steaks: Brush the fish with pure vegetable oil and soy sauce as they grill for added flavor and to avoid excessive drying. And be sure the grill is well greased to prevent sticking.

The fish is done when it loses its translucent appearance and flakes easily with a fork. Do not overcook or the fish will become dry. Small fish grilled over medium coals take three to six minutes on each side. Fish steaks that are about 1 inch thick take about 3 to 5 minutes per side.

For a special treat, accompany the fish with a sauce warmed on the grill. Canned tomato sauce with green onion and the slightest hint of sweet and sour flavoring makes this sauce intriguing.

DIVERS' BARBECUE

1 small whole fish or	1 tbsp. lemon juice
2 fish steaks	1 tsp. sugar
Pure vegetable oil	¼ cup water
Soy sauce	1 (8-oz.) can tomato sauce
1 green onion, thinly sliced	

If a whole fish is used, clean it, removing scales. Brush fish or fish steaks with vegetable oil and soy sauce. Place over bed of hot coals. Cook, turning and basting with oil and soy sauce until fish is done. Meanwhile, combine onion, lemon juice, sugar, water, and tomato sauce and heat. Serve with fish. Serves 2.

Grilling Halibut: Halibut steaks lend themselves perfectly to grilling at a favorite beach spot after diving or other water activity. (Fish, as well as corn on the cob and watermelon, keep appetizingly cold and safe for hours in insulated containers or on ice during an afternoon of diving. Perishable foods wrapped in newspapers will even stay cold one to two hours.) Six halibut steaks, weighing about 2 pounds, are cut 1 inch thick to cook over coals. Barbecuing fish steaks in an oiled hinged broiler facilitates turning fish without breaking them. Or grease the grill well and turn carefully with a wide spatula.

A basting sauce combining canned tomato sauce with horse-radish and garlic salt is easily mixed on the spot. Sour cream and chives are added to remaining basting sauce for a special accompaniment to the fish.

BARBECUED HALIBUT STEAKS

6 halibut steaks, 1 in. thick	½ tsp. salt
⅓ cup lemon juice	½ tsp. garlic salt
Pure vegetable oil	1 cup sour cream
1 8-oz. can tomato sauce	1 tbsp. chopped chives
1 tsp. horseradish	

Sprinkle lemon juice on halibut steaks and brush with vegetable oil. Combine canned tomato sauce, horseradish, salt, and garlic salt. Place fish on barbecue grill and brush with sauce mixture. Cook and turn until done, about 20 minutes. Just before serving, add sour cream and chives to remaining barbecue sauce.

Salmon Sour: Eaten particularly in the Pacific Northwest, a salmon is cut into fist-sized chunks and cooked in a quart of water, seasoned with a cup of cider vinegar, salt, pepper, sugar, and bay leaves.

From the Mediterranean—The Greek Way: In Greece, fresh-caught fish is grilled over charcoal and brushed with olive oil to keep the flesh moist and the skin crisp. Instead of a barbecue brush, half a lemon on the end of a long fork is dipped in a bowl of olive oil and rubbed continually over the browning fish, giving the fish a lovely lemony flavor, as you do it. When grilled to perfection, the fish is then served with a sauce made simply of olive oil and lemon juice.

Thoroughly clean and scale fresh-caught fish. Place in a colander, sprinkle with salt and pepper, leave for 15 minutes. Place a sprig of parsley in the cavity of each. Stick half a lemon in the olive oil, rub the fish all over with the lemon-scented oil. To prevent the fish from sticking, do the same with the grid before placing it over the charcoal. When the fire is ready, the charcoal well-coated with ash, arrange the fish on the grid, 3 or 4 inches from the heat, and cook until delicately browned on both sides, brushing frequently with the lemon dipped in the olive oil. Serve with the following sauce: Blend together ¼ cup of olive oil, the juice of ½ a lemon,

¼ teaspoon of salt, freshly ground black pepper, and a little finely minced fresh parsley or dill.

And Italian Style: The Italians enclose fish in parchment, "papil-lote" (aluminum foil can be used for the same purpose), adding an olive oil sauce to the fish before it is wrapped up to be placed in the oven. When foil-wrapped, the fish can be baked right in the ashes of the charcoal fire for extra-delicious flavor.

BASS OR PERCH EN PAPILLOTE

Clean and scale the fish (if it is fresh-caught), allowing one small fish for each person. If purchased at the market, figure on one half pound of whole fish per serving. (For fillets, 3 servings to a pound.) Place each fish in a large sheet of heavy-duty aluminum foil. Cover each with some of the following marinade:

½ cup of olive oil	¼ cup minced parsley
1 or 2 garlic cloves, crushed or ⅛ tsp. instant minced garlic	1 tbsp. instant minced onion
	1 tbsp. minced fresh tarragon or ½ tsp. dried tarragon
½ tsp. salt	Few drops lemon juice

Wrap the fish securely in the foil and bake in a 350° oven; or place the foil package right in the coals of a charcoal fire. As an added precaution, when baking the latter way, wrap the fish in a second sheet of foil to prevent leakage. Bake for approximately ½ hour until the outside of the fish is firm to the touch and the flesh flakes easily.

SHELLFISH COOKERY

Clams:

CLAMS ON THE HALF SHELL

½ doz. clams per person Lemon wedges	Cocktail sauce

Wash the clams, then open them. Serve them chilled or on cracked ice with lemon wedges and cocktail sauce.

CLAMBAKE ROAST

Lay out a circle of flat stones on which to build a hot wood fire. Let the fire burn 2 to 3 hours; rake away the ashes. Cover hot stones with fresh seaweed. Place scrubbed clams on top of the seaweed. You can place potatoes and unhusked corn as required on the seaweed as well, but they should cook for only an hour. Cover with a second layer of seaweed. Then cover everything with a piece of canvas. Weigh the edges down with stones. Let the clams bake 1 to 2 hours until they open. Serve them picnic style with the potatoes and corn.

STEAMED CLAMS

Take several quarts of large live clams. Scrub the shells and rinse them several times in cold water. Place the clams in a large kettle with one cup of hot water and cover tightly. Let the clams steam until the shells open partially, otherwise overcooking will make them tough and rubbery. Serve the clams in the shells. Season them with individual dishes of melted butter, seasoned with a little lemon juice and tarragon vinegar.

Mussels: Mussels cling to rocks, wharves, and mud by means of masses of byssus threads. Therefore, when you pull up or dig out a mussel, be sure there is some resistance and some of the thread is still visible, otherwise the mussel may be dead. Dead mussels that fill with mud or sand are plentiful and should be avoided. Live mussels are often, as in New England salt waters, clustered together by the dozen entangled in the beard-like stuff. If a dead one slips by and ends up in your pot by mistake, it will not open when steamed. It should, of course, be thrown out. Once caught, give mussels a thorough scrubbing with a wire brush and pull off the threads.

How to Open Mussels: Steam them in a large pot with a ¼ cup of water. Any that remain closed after steaming should be tossed out.

They were dead in the first place. Mussels may be eaten raw like oysters and clams but are tastiest when cooked.

STEAMED MUSSELS

Put about 4 quarts of mussels in cold water and scrape them thoroughly with a knife to remove dirt and seaweed. Rinse them in cold water several times. Throw away any with open shells. Place the mussels in a large kettle with one finely chopped onion, one small bunch of parsley, a bit of thyme, a bay leaf, and crushed peppercorns. Add one wine glass of dry white wine and cover and seal the kettle. Let steam for a minute or two until shells open. Remove meat from the shells and put it into a bowl. Strain the cooking liquor and pour it over the meat.

FRENCH MUSSELS

1 doz. mussels per person	⅛ tsp. ground pepper
1 chopped shallot	2 tbsps. chopped fresh parsley
¼ cup Chablis	Butter
Pinch thyme	2 tbsps. flour

Scrub the mussels thoroughly. Place them in a pot with wine, herbs, and seasoning and steam them until the shells open. Then remove the top shells and place the mussels on a large platter. In another pan, melt the butter and add the flour; make into a paste. Slowly add the stock from the mussels, stirring constantly until the sauce is the consistency of a thin gravy. Pour the results over the mussels. Serve with French bread to sop up this wonderful Gallic gravy.

MUSSELS ITALIAN STYLE

Brush and clean 4 dozen tightly closed mussels. Combine in a kettle ¾ cup of dry white wine, ¾ tablespoon of imported Italian olive oil, 3 tablespoons of chopped shallots, and white pepper. Boil for one minute. When the mixture has reached a racing boil, add the mussels and cover the pot. Cook until the shells open. Then place the mussels in a soup dish with the top shells removed. To the remaining liquid add 4 tablespoons of chopped parsley, stir, and pour immediately over the mussels. Serve immediately.

Scallops: Some people consider scallops among the finest seafood delicacies whether eaten raw or in a salad, broiled, deviled, baked in a shell with crumbs and butter, simmered in cream, grilled, and even scalloped.

SAUTÉED SCALLOPS

Dry the scallops carefully. Dust them lightly with flour in a paper bag and fry only a handful at a time, scattered so that they won't stick. The butter should be brown and sizzling in a heavy iron skillet. Brown the scallops on each side. Serve at once with a garnish of lemon and parsley.

Lobsters: Lobster is an incomparable dish with a rich and delicate flavor. Use only live lobsters. When a lobster is removed from the water, its color is a dark bluish green; after cooking it becomes brilliant red. Lobsters must be alive and kicking at the time of cooking. The tail should curl under the body and not hang when the lobster is picked up. The tail of a cooked lobster should spring back to its curl after it has been straightened.

Cleaning the Lobster: When splitting halves, remove the stomach and the small sack that lie in the head, and the spongy lungs, which lie between the meat and the shell. Also remove the intestinal line running through the center of the body. Save the tomalley (the liver) and the coral roe; they are delicious.

GRILLED LOBSTER

One live 1½-pound lobster per person. Place the shell side down on the grill, 4 to 5 inches from the coals. Grill 20 minutes or until the shell is charred brown. Baste or brush the lobster frequently with butter sauce. Serve in the shell. Crack the claws.

MAINE BOILED LOBSTER

Plunge the lobster headfirst into boiling, salted water. Cover. Simmer for twenty minuters. Place the lobster on its back and cut it in half lengthwise. Crack the claws. Serve with butter.

BROILED LOBSTER

Two or more 1-lb. lobsters	A dash of paprika
1 tbsp. of melted butter	¼ cup of butter, melted
1 tsp. of salt	1 tbsp. lemon juice
A dash of pepper	

Place the lobster on its back. Insert a knife between the body shell and the tail segment. Cut down to sever the spinal cord. Cut in half lengthwise. Crack the claws. Lay the lobster open as flat as possible on a broiler pan, flesh side down. Brush the lobster with one layer of melted butter. Add salt, pepper, and paprika. Broil the lobster about 4 inches from the source of heat for 10 to 15 minutes or until slightly browned. Mix the melted butter and the lemon juice and serve with the lobster.

CHARCOAL-BROILED LOBSTER

A 1- to 2-lb. lobster per person   1 cup lemon juice
Quantities of melted butter

Place split and cleaned lobster, shell side down, on grill over fire. Brush the flesh with the melted butter and lemon juice. Broil for 10 minutes. Turn and broil the shell side about 6 minutes. Turn the lobster over and brush with melted butter. Test lobster with a fork; if the flesh separates easily and is tender and white, it is done.

Abalone Steaks: Native to Pacific waters just off California, abalones are a shellfish that can be pryed from rocks and reefs. After tenderizing the flesh with a mallet, dip steaks in flour, then egg, then cracker meal. Deep fry or pan fry in butter without overcooking. Fry 1½ minutes on each side after seasoning. Correct the seasoning and serve with tartar sauce.

Petit Point Oysters: In the Pacific Northwest, oysters can be grilled on a bed of rock salt. When you open them, anoint them with a sauce made of lemon juice, a few dashes of Worcestershire, Tabasco, shallot, vinegar, and chopped parsley.

Conch Salad: Take raw conch from the conch shell and grind with onions. Add chopped green pepper, pimento, and lime juice. Marinate the ingredients in the lime juice. Season with salt and pepper and, if desired, Tabasco sauce. Incidentally, raw conch, like the oyster and clam, is delicious right from the shell but must be fresh out of the sea.

BATTER, BUTTER, AND SAUCE

Batter for Frying Fish: Following are recipes for four variations of batter:

1. Mix 1 cup of sifted flour with ⅔ cup of cold milk and add a few grains of cayenne and ½ teaspoon of salt.
2. Mix 1 cup of flour with 1 teaspoon of sugar and ½ teaspoon of salt. Add ⅔ cup of cold water and beat the mixture well. Then stir in ½ teaspoon of olive oil and 1 egg white, whipped to a froth.
3. Sift 1⅓ cups of flour with 2 teaspoons of baking powder and ¼ teaspoon of salt. Gradually add ⅔ cup of cold milk, beating constantly.
4. To batter No. 3 add 1 well-beaten egg white and 1 tablespoon of olive oil.

Compounded Butters:

LOBSTER BUTTER

Pound 1 tablespoon of cooked lobster meat with 2 tablespoons of butter. The coral roe or tomalley may be used for this butter.

CRAY FISH BUTTER

Pound together in a mortar 1 tablespoon of finely shredded crayfish and 1 tablespoon of butter.

MEUNIERE BUTTER

Brown as much butter as is required. Pour it on the food, sprinkled with lemon juice and a pinch of finely chopped parsley.

CLARIFIED BUTTER

Clarified butter is the result of clearing butter (also known as drawn butter). Place the required amount of butter in a cup. Stand the cup in hot water, and when the butter is melted, pour it off, leaving the whitish sediment in the cup.

Sauces:

LEMON BUTTER SAUCE

Cream ¼ pound of butter with 1 tablespoon of strained lemon juice. If the sauce is to be used for boiled fish, soften it a little on a very low fire.

MAÎTRE D'HOTEL BUTTER SAUCE FOR BROILED FISH

Soften slightly 5 tablespoons of butter and mix with a teaspoon of finely chopped paprika. Season with salt and pepper to taste and add 1 teaspoon of strained lemon juice.

BERCY SAUCE

Sauté 1 tablespoon of finely chopped shallot and 1 tablespoon of butter until the shallot begins to brown. Add 1 wine glass of white wine with ½ cup of fish stock made from trimmings of the fish and ½ cup of rich cream sauce. Bring the mixture to a boil and let it simmer very slowly for a few minutes, stirring frequently. When ready to serve off the fire, add 1 generous tablespoon of butter and a little finely chopped parsley.

BON APPETIT!

11

DIVING HAZARDS, PREVENTION, REMEDIES

For man, a landbound creature by nature, armed with his wits and an artificial atmosphere strapped on his back, a descent into an alien, watery environment that nullifies the best part of his senses is inherently hazardous. The probability of calamity below depends on the skill, prudence, and health of the man coupled with the soundness of his equipment. The accident rate is almost negligible in terms of the estimated three to five million amateurs now actively diving, but accidents do happen. This chapter is written for instant reference in case of an emergency. I first list the hazard, then tell you how to recognize it, how to avoid or prevent it, and, should it become necessary, how to treat the consequences.

Note: Any diving accidents or illnesses should be reported to the National Underwater Data Center, University of Rhode Island, P. O. Box 68, Kingston, RI 02881. The Center will send you a copy of their Underwater Accident Report form to be filled out. The information you report is analyzed and becomes part of a continuing national study to reduce scuba accidents and thereby improve the overall safety of scuba diving.

POTENTIALLY DANGEROUS MARINE LIFE

All creatures are concerned primarily with food and self-defense and they are built for both. Almost all living creatures have a means of defending themselves, some effectively enough to finish off an assailant permanently. Except for sharks, nothing beneath the sea can be said to be guilty of outright aggressive behavior toward man except in performing an instinctive act of self-preservation; to wit, defending itself when it thinks its life is threatened or eating when it is hungry. The voracious appetites of sea creatures are directed almost exclusively at other marine life, not at man. Attacks on man are usually cases of mistaken identity or of fright. Again, sharks excepted, all marine animals in authentic encounters with man have not picked the fight; the man has. To safeguard against trouble, use your power of observation, forbear against a sudden move, which may provoke an attack, and keep a healthy distance between you and those splendid but unpredictable instinct-motivated inhabitants of the deep.

SHARKS

General Comment: Only about 10 percent of the 225 species of sharks in the world are believed to attack man. They are flesh-eaters; feeding on seals, turtles, fish, crabs, lobsters, shellfish, other sharks, and you, if you are in the wrong place at the wrong time and confronted by the wrong shark. Perhaps the main characteristic of attacks on human beings in coastal waters, particularly those involving skin divers, is that the attacking shark is rarely seen before it strikes.

Appearance: See the descriptions given in this chapter.

Behavior: Sharks are attracted by the smell of blood, carrion, the sight of brightly colored materials, and by thrashing or unusual noises. They pick up vibrations of distressed creatures through their lateral line. When they are in packs, their eating habits are com-

WHITE SHARK

HAMMERHEAD SHARK

MAKO SHARK

pletely unpredictable. They are curious but not always prone to unprovoked attack unless hungry or excited. Behavior depends on the stimuli of the moment, health, and age of the shark and your behavior. You cannot count on any sure formula for predicting any shark's behavior. Even though researchers have been successful in establishing general patterns of behavior there is always the exception to the rule, the one shark, the rogue, that will completely reverse the expected trend.

Where Found: Most sharks are found in tropical, subtropical, and warm-temperate oceans, from shores to mid-ocean.

195

Name of Shark	Maximum Size in Feet	Appearance	Behavior	Where Found
White	30	Slaty brown to black on back	Savage, aggressive	Oceanic; tropical, subtropical, warm temperate belts, especially in Australian waters
Mako	30	Slender form, deep blue gray on back	Savage	Oceanic, tropical, and warm temperate belts
Porbeagle	12	Dark bluish gray on back	Sluggish except when pursuing prey	Continental waters of Northern Atlantic; allied species in North Pacific, Australia, and New Zealand
Tiger	30	Short snout, sharply pointed tail	Can be vigorous and powerful	Tropical and subtropical belts of all oceans, inshore and offshore
Lemon	11	Yellowish brown on back, broadly rounded snout	Savage, aggressive	Found in salt water creeks, bays, and sounds. Inshore western Atlantic, northern Brazil to North Carolina, tropical West Africa

Lake Nicaragua	10	Dark gray on back	Savage, aggressive	Found in shallow water. Fresh water species of Lake Nicaragua
Dusky	14	Bluish or leaden gray on back	Bottom feeder, very fast swimmer	Found in shallow water. Tropical and warm temperate waters on both sides of Atlantic
White-tipped	13	Light gray to slaty blue on back	Indifferent, fearless	Tropical and subtropical Atlantic and Mediterranean; deep off-shore waters
Sand	10	Bright gray-brown on back	Stays close to bottom	Indo-Pacific, Mediterranean, tropical West Africa, South Africa, Gulf of Maine to Florida, Brazil, Argentina
Gray nurse	10	Pale gray on back	Swift and savage	Australia
Ganges River	7	Gray on back	Ferocious, attacks bathers	Indian Ocean to Japan, ascends fresh water rivers
Hammerhead	15	Ashy-gray on back, flat, wide head	Powerful swimmer	Warm temperate zone of all oceans including Mediterranean Sea, out at sea or close inshore

Courtesy U.S. Navy

How to Avoid Attacks: Do not carry speared game under water. Do not remain in water contaminated with blood from injuries or wounded fish. Wear dark-colored clothing, no jewelry or bright objects. If cruising over shark- or barracuda-inhabited waters, do not dangle feet or hands in water. Be especially alert in murky water: You may not see an approaching predator. Sharks, said to have a sense of security in murky waters, may press an attack more quickly than in clear waters and at night.

Sight does play an important role in the feeding behavior of a shark, but only where the clarity of the water enables the animal to employ its visual apparatus. With a suitable current moving from the souce of the stimulus, a shark can detect an odor such as blood or fish oil from over a quarter of a mile away.

The hearing system of the lateralis, commonly known as the lateral line, is extremely well developed, running the entire length of the body. Vibrations or sound waves act upon this system, transferring the vibrations into nerve impulses which are instantly communicated to the brain. The results of experiments and studies have established conclusively that any swimmer who behaves in an excited, unusual, or panic-stricken manner in the water transmits through his movements sound frequencies or vibrations that can call in or attract sharks. In turbid, murky, or discolored water, the dangers of attack would be greatly increased for anyone in the water behaving in this manner because the shark would be responding to attractive sound stimulus and might attack without making visual contact with its prey. The safest way to move through the water in the vicinity of a shark or sharks is to employ a relaxed, slow form of breast stroke devoid of splashing.

What to Do When You Meet a Shark: Leave the water slowly, purposefully, never thrashing. Always face a shark rather than turn away from it; look alive, even scornful and threatening. It may be as afraid of you as you are of it.

It may be necessary to push a shark with a shark billy, camera, or other handy object. Do not wound the shark or you may infuriate him, but if necessary, hit him on the snout, eyes, or gills. This may drive him off.

Type of Wound: Severe bites, massive bleeding, usually curved, clean cuts. Fatalities are estimated at higher than 80 percent.

Treatment: Administer standard first aid. Get medical attention at once.

SHARK DEFENSE SYSTEMS

In areas where sharks are frequently encountered, many divers elect to carry some form of shark defense, a variety of which are available and have been proven effective. These devices are designed only as defense mechanisms.

Probably the oldest anti-shark device is a 3- to 4-foot-long wooden club with a short nail in one end, commonly called a "shark billy." It is used to fend off or strike the shark, preferably on the nose. Years of experience have proven the usefulness of this device in discouraging annoying sharks.

A power head can be used if the diver desires not only to discourage a shark, but to eliminate him altogether as a threat. This device, commonly called a "bang stick," consists of a specially constructed chamber designed to accommodate a powerful pistol cartridge or a shotgun shell. It is attached to the end of a pole and shot or pushed against the shark, the shell firing upon impact. This device is effective against marine life other than sharks. Although it has a built-in positive safety, it should be handled with extreme caution.

A device known as a "shark dart" is commercially available and is designed to disable or kill a shark instantly by the injection of a burst of compressed gas. This device consists of a hollow stainless steel needle approximately 5 inches long, which is connected to a small carbon dioxide cylinder or extra scuba tank, and is available in dagger or spear form. The dart is thrust against the shark's abdominal cavity, penetrating into the body cavity and discharging the contents of the CO_2 cartridge. The gas expanding into the shark creates a nearly instantaneous embolism and forces the shark toward the surface.

Hitting the shark in a vulnerable area and killing it quickly is of great importance. Different-model shark darts accept different-sized CO_2 cartridges, and the larger the cartridge, the greater the effective depth. Like the power head, a positive safety is provided, but the shark dart can still be dangerous and must be handled with care.

KILLER WHALES (ORCA)

Danger: Depends on how you act, whether you appear to be palatable prey, how hungry the whale is. Its size and power alone make it inherently dangerous. Hardly a record exists of man-killing.

Appearance: Jet-black head and back, white underparts, lengths up to 30 feet in males, 15 feet in females.

Behavior: Killer whales usually travel in herds. Carnivorous mammals, they feed on warm-blooded animals. They could attack man, not out of the lust or killer instinct attributed to them; but when hungry they may take man for their natural prey.

Where Found: All oceans and seas, tropical to polar.

How to Avoid Attack: Leave the water at once. Cruise home. A small vessel may look like prey and be attacked.

KILLER WHALE

Type of Wound: Massive bites, generally fatal; intense hemorrhaging, shock.

Treatment: Standard first aid and anti-shock therapy. Medical help.

SEA SNAKE

Danger: Not very aggressive, but its venom is possibly lethal.

Appearance: Resembles snakes, has venomous fangs. Up to 9 feet in length.

Behavior: Boldness varies. Generally passive.

Where Found: Tropical Pacific and Indian oceans, from river mouths to far at sea.

How to Avoid Attack: Unprovoked attacks are rare, but since its venom is extremely potent, keep your distance.

Type of Wound: Generally there may be little or no pain at bite. Symptoms, therefore, could be overlooked for at least twenty minutes to about an hour. Reaction then sets in: general malaise and anxiety in some cases; or a mild, false sense of well-being in others. There is a sensation of thickening of the tongue, and a generalized feeling of muscular stiffness, aches, sense of shock, and type of paralysis. Later symptoms include: drooping eyelids, tightening of jaw

SEA SNAKE

muscles, difficulty in speaking and swallowing, thirst, burning or dryness of throat, unconsciousness. Mortality rate, 25 percent. There are no later effects if recovery occurs.

Treatment: Leave water immediately. Place a restricting band up the blood stream of the bite to slow the course of the venom to the heart. The band—*it is not a tourniquet*—should be loosened every 30 minutes. Keep the victim rested. Get medical attention at once.

GROUPER (SEA BASS)

Danger: Generally playful although according to some reports, a menace to humans. U.S. Navy lists them as dangerous—a case of guilty until proven innocent.

Appearance: Bulky body, up to 12 feet in length, 700 pounds.

Behavior: Curious, bold, voracious feeders.

Where Found: Around rocks, caverns, old wrecks.

How to Avoid Attack: Face him, make threatening advances, fend him off with a stick.

Type of Wound: No information available. It is probable that his bite can cut or lacerate but not as seriously as that of a shark, barracuda, or moray.

Treatment: If wounded, use appropriate first aid.

SEA LION

Danger: Not ferocious except during breeding season, when bulls may become irritable.

Appearance: Resembles a seal but larger.

Behavior: Curious, fast swimmers.

Where Found: Northern waters.

How to Avoid Attack: Keep away especially during breeding and feeding times.

Type of Wound: Nips if in an irritated state.

Treatment: The nip of a sea lion is not expected to be terribly serious. Treat with appropriate first aid for bruises or flesh wounds.

STINGRAY

Danger: Few of its fellow sea creatures can equal the number of injuries inflicted annually on man by the stingray—several hundred annually—although it is not vicious and does not attack. Victims in almost every case tread on the ray or mishandle it unintentionally or unavoidably.

Appearance: Hard poisonous barb located almost a quarter of the way from the end of its tail, flat body, many kinds. Averaging less than 2 feet wide.

Behavior: Drives barb (or spine) upward into leg or foot when stepped on. It is also quite possible to receive a body wound if you swim too close to a stingray.

Where Found: Tropical to temperate waters, shallow waters.

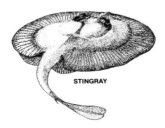

STINGRAY

How to Avoid Attack: Avoid contact, especially with the tail. Step carefully when walking or swimming in shallow waters. Wear protective foot gear; shuffle, don't walk. Use a stick to probe sand where stingrays conceal themselves. Do not belly flop into tropical surf: A chest or abdominal wound inflicted by a ray can be fatal.

Type of Wound: Deep, penetrating stab, producing ragged, dirty wound. Barb often remains in wound; venom produces severe pain.

Treatment: Since fainting is common, get victim out of the water promptly. Commence treatment at once. Wash wound with salt solution, if available; otherwise, cold, clean water. Remove any remaining parts of barb. Next soak the wound in plain water as hot as can be tolerated for about 30 minutes. Use hot compresses on areas that cannot be immersed. (Heat is believed to destroy venom.)

When the pain has subsided, cover the wound and elevate the limb. Obtain medical assistance and further treatment. Be sure to get tetanus toxoid injection.

Special Treatments: If victim is wounded in the chest or abdomen, get him to a hospital at once. If signs of shock (fainting, weak pulse) appear, keep the victim lying down, elevate his feet, cover him, and seek a physician's help immediately (see First Aid for Shock, pages 231–32).

MORAY EEL

Danger: Not aggressive but defensive if molested, cornered, frightened. Capable of inflicting a bad bite.

Appearance: Long, narrow, snake-like; some reach lengths of 10 feet. Jaws bear rows of sharp, vicious-looking teeth.

Behavior: Attacks defensively when provoked or frightened. Does not hunt its prey but lies in wait hidden and unmoving until a

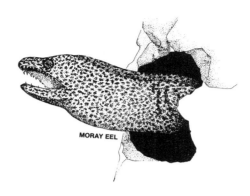

MORAY EEL

likely fish swims within range. Then it lunges out lightning-like to finish the helpless victim in a gulp.

Where Found: Tropical and subtropical; bottom dwellers, lurking in crevices, coral caves, wrecks, seaweed, rubble.

How to Avoid Injury: Don't reach into dark holes or crevices except with caution. Morays are waiting there for prey to eat and in self-defense instinctively strike out at any threat or commotion.

Type of wound: Maintains grip tenaciously, crushingly. If eel won't let go, use your knife to kill it, then get home.

Treatment: Administer appropriate first aid. Call a physician immediately.

GREAT BARRACUDA

Danger: No verifiable cases of attacks on divers.

Appearance: Long slender, up to 8 feet in length; large mouth filled with sharp teeth.

Behavior: Swift, fierce, attracted easily, curious, unpredictable, the barracuda is a sight feeder attracted mainly by what it sees. A lone barracuda is more apt to attack than those in schools.

BARRACUDA

Where Found: Tropical and subtropical waters, West Indies, Brazil, northern Florida, in the Indo-Pacific from the Red Sea to Hawaiian Islands.

How to Avoid Attack: Do not corner or goad, avoid wearing bright colors, shiny objects. Avoid murky waters. Do not tow speared game. Don't molest or spear barracuda unless you are prepared for a real run for your money.

Type of Wound: Jagged cuts, followed by shock and severe hemorrhaging.

Treatment: Appropriate first aid. Get physician immediately.

OCTOPUS

Danger: The octopus is not aggressive, will not attack. Some divers make sport of grappling with them.

Appearance: Round head with tentacles radiating from it. Up to 25 feet in size.

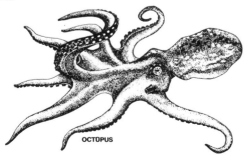

OCTOPUS

Behavior: Holds on with tentacles, will use beak to bite if molested.

Where Found: Generally, undersea caves, wrecks, crevices.

How to Avoid Injury: Avoid caves, crevices, and wrecks when possibly. Avoid mouth at root of tentacles.

Type of wound: Bites that produce stinging, swelling, redness, and heat around wound. Much bleeding possible.

Treatment: Lie down, elevate feet, apply cold compresses to wound, control bleeding if any. Get medical attention.

GIANT CLAM

Danger: Evidence of trapping men is but hearsay. No verifications reported.

Appearance: Large shell, several hundred pounds.

Behavior: You have only to look at the clam's great size to acknowledge its capability of trapping a man's limb, but no records are verifiable that it ever happened. Shells do not snap shut bear-trap fashion. However, a diver trapped between shells can drown. If caught, a victim can be released by inserting a knife between shells and severing the clam's adductor muscle. The closing of a shell is so ponderously slow it isn't likely a sane man would stay around long enough to become trapped.

Where Found: Abound on tropical sea floors.

How to Avoid: Should be easy to avoid. They are brightly colored and conspicuous.

SEA URCHIN

Danger: A common danger to the unsuspecting wader or bare-footed swimmer.

Appearance: Small, spiny animals, generally black; spines are needle sharp; small venomous pincers.

Behavior: Usually remain passive and stationary but do move around the sea bottom.

Where Found: Tropical and temperate zones, ocean floor on rocks and coral reefs scattered about in large numbers.

How to Avoid Injury: Don't handle, avoid when sighted.

Type of Wound: Penetration of skin with spines, intense burning, swelling, redness, aching. Severe cases may produce intense radiating pain, fainting, numbness, generalized paralysis, loss of voice, respiratory distress, and even death.

Treatment: Remove spines and cleanse wound area. Hot candle-wax applied on wounds kills the pain. Apply a large, loose dressing. If infection or other complications set in, seek medical attention promptly.

CONE SHELLS

Danger: Six of the species are dangerous if picked up by hand and mishandled. See Behavior below.

Appearance: An inverted, porcelainous cone with a long, narrow aperture, a sharp-edged outer lip, a cone shell is solid and rather heavy for its size (about 6 inches). Its spire takes the form of a flattened disc. All are generally attractive with flecks of brown white, or yellow, even pink. Cone shells are highly prized by collectors.

CONE SHELL

Behavior: Although there are hundreds of species, only the following six are known to inflict toxic stings: the court cone, the textile cone, the marbled cone, the geographic cone, the tulip cone, and the striated cone.

The cone is armed with a long, fleshy, barbed proboscis, which can extend beyond its shell if disturbed and be used as a hypodermic needle to paralyze prey with venom. The wound in a man can result in paralysis and death.

Where Found: Southern and tropical seas, deep waters, coral reefs, crawling in or on bottom sands, and under rocks.

How to Avoid Injury: Avoid contact with the soft parts and handle the shell gently. Don't carry except in a container. Wear gloves.

Type of Wound: Sharp, needle-like puncture. Sharp sting followed by numbness and local cutting-off of blood supply evidenced by a blueness. Numbness and abnormal sensitivity might spread through the body, especially to the lips and mouth. In severe cases, paralysis, coma, and death by cardiac failure can result.

Treatment: Local analgesics, rest, and medical attention at once.

BARNACLES

Danger: Not necessarily great, but contact is probable around debris, wrecks, and pilings.

Appearance: Clustered masses of sharp gray-white cone-like shells with holes on top out of which feather-like antennae project.

Behavior: Passive, stationary.

Where Found: Worldwide, particularly on rocks, pilings, ship bottoms, and almost anything solid they can cling to.

How to Avoid Injury: Be watchful in areas where found.

Type of Wound: Cuts, lacerations.

Treatment: Administer first aid appropriate for lacerations and cuts. Same treatment as for coral wounds.

ABALONE

Danger: Shells can close over a diver's fingers or hand.

Appearance: Shells are irridescent and resemble that of a large clam except for spiral whorl. Has large, flat muscular foot by which it holds fast to rocks. Water passes through a row of holes visible on the outer rim of the shell.

Where Found: California Pacific waters.

Behavior: Clings to rocks especially when disturbed but is generally passive.

How to Avoid Injury: Avoid use of bare hands when prying abalone off rocks; use an abalone knife or iron.

Type of Wound: Can pinch or cut flesh.

Treatment: Apply appropriate first aid for pinch or cut.

PORTUGUESE MAN-OF-WAR

SEA WASP

JELLYFISHES (COELENTERATES), SEA NETTLE, PORTUGUESE MAN-OF-WAR, SEA WASP

Danger: Stings with extremely painful results are, in some instances, inevitable if contact is made.

Appearance: Tentacles of varying lengths (often several feet long) streaming out of a transparent mushroom-shaped jelly-like head which propels the creature in rhythmic motions. The Portuguese man-of-war floats and is propelled along by the wind blowing a puffed-up bladder which acts as a sail. Its tentacles trail behind in the water.

211

Behavior: Stings with cells on its tentacles, injecting venom. The sea wasp and Portuguese man-of-war produce stings of more serious nature than do the others. All jellyfishes are passive and can be avoided in good visibility by a diver wearing a mask.

Where Found: All jellyfishes are found in large numbers in tropical waters, warm brackish waters, bays, rivers. The sea wasp appears in Indo-Pacific oceans only.

How to Avoid Injury: Difficult to avoid when any of these are numerous and visibility is poor. Wear protective clothing—a rubber exposure suit, long johns, or a flight suit. Be watchful and keep out of their way; they haven't the brains to keep out of yours.

Type of Wound: Puncture-like, with a venomous sting, from a prickling sensation to intense burning, throbbing, or shooting pain; the wound results in redness of area stung, welts, blisters, and small skin hemorrhages. In severe cases muscular cramps, abdominal rigidity, nausea, shock, paralysis, delirium, convulsions, and, on rare occasions, death.

Treatment: If severely stung, signal for help at once, leave the water, and protect hands by using seaweed or sand to avoid spreading the sting material. Get to or send for a physician. Apply weak ammonia or a sodium bicarbonate (baking soda) solution if available; otherwise, rub the area gently with wet sand, then wash with fresh water. Use cortisone ointment, antihistamine cream, or local anesthetic ointment if available. Otherwise try olive oil, sugar, soothing lotions, or ethyl alcohol. Apply cold compresses. Check for shock. Keep victim lying down, feet elevated.

CORAL

Danger: Because coral is widespread, accidents are plentiful.

Appearance: Coral throughout the world is a conglomeration of built-up living organisms. In the tropics these organisms are the builders of reefs. Coral consists of various multicolored and mul-tiformed plants and animal life found taking the form of isolated clusters, scattered masses, and most often widespread jungle-like seascapes stretching for miles. Some varieties of the conglomeration of the life forms are spongy and soft resembling plants with branches swinging with the current. Some resemble tiny human hands, mas-sive human brains, columns, tubes, spires, and fantastic architec-tures of all descriptions. Some growths such as antler coral, elkhorn, and staghorn corals are hard, jagged, and brittle to the touch. They can easily cut an unprotected diver or rip his exposure suit. Fire coral is a form to avoid touching. It appears in various smooth shapes but is always mustard yellow in color. With contact you will experience a burning sensation and see a redness where touched. However, in an hour you will feel better again.

How to Avoid Injury: Swim cautiously when near coral. Wear shoes and gloves and protective clothing if contact is to be prolonged and inevitable. Beware of current and swells, which can drive you into coral heads.

Type of Wound: Cuts, scratches, lacerations, generally superfi-cial. Pain and itching, reddening skin, welts.

Treatment: Rinse the affected area with baking soda solution and weak ammonia, if available; otherwise, with clean water. Use cor-tisone ointment or antihistamine cream on the wound, or give anti-histamine by mouth to reduce initial pain and reaction. As soon as pain eases, cleanse the wound thoroughly with soap and water to remove foreign matter. Apply an antiseptic and cover the wound with sterile dressing. In severe cases, get medical help.

MARINE PLANTS

Appearance: Seaweed, vegetation, green, from leafy to huge fronds.

Where Found: Widespread. Kelp, one of the more dangerous forms, thrives off the coast of California.

How to Avoid: Do not make fast, entangling moves. Carry a knife in case you or your propeller become entangled.

FISH THAT INFLICT VENOMOUS STINGS

Types: Horned sharks, catfish, weeverfish, scorpionfish, ratfish, toadfish, surgeonfish, rabbitfish, triggerfish, zebrafish, stonefish.

Danger: Injury is produced by contact with poison-bearing spines.

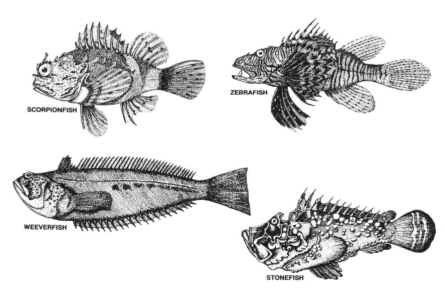

Appearance: The triggerfish has a retractable hidden barb near its tail which springs out when the fish is excited by contact. Common to almost all types of venomous fish is the fact that they are spiny, elaborate, and vicious-looking, with large, protruding eyes near the tip of large bony or spiny heads, and large mouths. Various moderate sizes. They are usually so well camouflaged you may brush their toxic spines unaware.

Behavior: Behavior varies. They spend much time on the sea bottom, swimming a few feet, then resting. They inflict a venomous sting when contacted. They are by nature relatively passive and do not attack.

Where Found: Generally tropical and temperate zones, along reefs and rocks and bottoms.

How to Avoid Injury: Absolute avoidance of contact. Beware when reaching for any object; it may be well-camouflaged fish.

Type of Wound: Symptoms vary. Though smaller, the wound resembles that inflicted by a stingray, or it is similar to a snake bite. Pain results from actual injury produced locally by the spine, from the effects of the venom, and from the irritation of slime and other foreign substances in the wound. Some wounds appear like punctures, others like lacerations. Venom injected by the spines causes redness, pain, swelling, muscle spasms, general malaise, difficulty in breathing, and, in severe cases, convulsions and death.

Treatment: Treat for shock and get medical assistance. Irrigate wound with clean, cold water. If injury is of the puncture type, make a small incision to bleed out the poison. Flush with sterile saline or clean, cold water. Remove the foreign matter, apply suction. Soak the wound for at least 30 minutes in water as hot as can be tolerated. Epsom salts may be added to the water. After soaking, continue cleansing.

SPECIAL PRECAUTIONS IN TROPICAL WATERS

Since attack by fish is more likely to occur in tropical waters than elsewhere, the following guide for safe diving is suggested:

Carry a good knife.

Always wear cotton gloves in tropical waters.

Don't stay down if you are bleeding. *Remember it is almost impossible to see bleeding while submerged.*

Don't carry any speared fish with you in the water. Warn other divers to keep their game out of the water, too.

Be especially watchful when visibility is reduced by murky water; chances of attack by a barracuda or shark are then greater. Best advice: Don't dive in "dark" water.

Don't poke around dark holes or crevices. Moray eels generally lurk in such places and may strike with painful results.

Don't wear brightly colored, flashy clothing or shiny objects such as jewelry; they attract predatory fish.

Don't drag your legs behind a moving boat.

HAZARDS OF DESCENT

Under Boyle's Law, when a diver descends, the external pressure literally squeezes the outer walls of the air spaces, causing pain and injury. Relief is possible by equalizing pressure or ascending. Pressure is equalized by introducing into the air spaces a volume of air equal to the outside pressure around the air space affected. As long as you equalize you can make descents unharmed. The solids of your body will not suffer squeeze since over 90 percent of your body is liquid.

DRY-SUIT SQUEEZE

Causes: With a poorly fitting loose dry suit the external pressure causes the suit to pinch the skin because of lack of equalizing.

Symptoms: Welts and skin hemorrhages develop, and discomfort is felt.

Prevention: Use a wet instead of a dry suit, or admit a little air into the suit before diving.

FACE SQUEEZE

Cause: On descent, the increased ambient pressure crushes mask against face if you have failed to breathe enough air into your mask to equalize.

Symptoms: You will feel a tightness of your mask pressing into your face.

Prevention: Wear only a recommended equalizing face mask. *Never wear goggles.* Exhale through the nose to maintain a cushion of air to offset the pressure of the surrounding water causing the squeeze.

INTESTINAL SQUEEZE

Cause: Excessive air in stomach caused by swallowing of air.

Symptoms: Bloating and discomfort on ascent.

Prevention: Prior to diving, eat a light meal with no spicy foods or soda drinks.

EXTERNAL-EAR SQUEEZE

Causes: On descending while wearing a dry-suit hood, air pressure outside of the ear is less than the pressure exerted against it from the middle ear. The hood seals over the external ear. The use of ear plugs also causes this squeeze. Never use them.

Symptoms: Pain on descent even though able to "pop" ears. Pain stops if eardrum ruptures. Don't be fooled by sudden relief, as this is an almost sure sign of rupture.

Depending on the extent of damage, redness and swelling of the eardrum. Often a diminution of hearing. Spitting up of blood. Bleeding into eardrum or middle-ear space; bleeding to outside of ear if eardrum is ruptured.

Possible Damage: The internal-ear pressure, if sufficient, may cause bursting of the ear outwardly, or inwardly when using a wet-suit hood.

Treatment: See a physician. Avoid pressures until damage heals and ears can be cleared readily. If the eardrum has been ruptured, do not dive until it has healed, but this must be checked by a doctor. Keep water, all objects and materials (including patent "medications") out of the ear. *Hands off!* Return to your physician without delay if pain increases or drainage appears, as these signs may indicate infection requiring antibiotic treatment.

Prevention: Admit air into the dry-suit hood during descent.

MIDDLE-EAR SQUEEZE

Causes: Diving with blocked eustachian tube. Failure to "pop" ears (equalize) on descent.

Symptoms: Same as for external-ear squeeze.

Possible Damage: Rupture of eardrum. Bleeding in middle ear.

Treatment: Same as for external-ear squeeze.

Prevention: "Pop" ears on descent by swallowing, yawning, moving jaw, blowing gently against closed nostrils. Don't dive with a cold.

SINUS SQUEEZE

Cause: As with ears, failure to equalize.

Symptoms: Pain and nosebleed.

Treatment: In serious cases, see a physician.

Prevention: Divers with nasal congestion due to colds should not dive. If pain persists, since sinuses cannot be equalized voluntarily, discontinue dive.

THORACIC SQUEEZE

Causes: Too-deep (about 132 feet) descent during snorkel dive, or holding breath during descent with self-contained air-breathing equipment. Failure of air supply during descent.

Symptoms: Sensation of chest compression during descent; pain in the chest (sometimes); difficulty in breathing on return to surface; bloody, frothy sputum.

Possible Damage: Bleeding of sensitive membranes of lungs.

Treatment: Bring diver to the surface. Place in face-down position in order to clear blood from the mouth. Give artificial respiration if not breathing. Treat for shock. Get help of physician promptly. (Most cases should be hospitalized at least for observation.) Give antibiotics under physician's directions to prevent infection.

Prevention: Avoid snorkel dives in excess of 100 feet, where symptoms will occur. Never hold your breath while diving with an air rig.

TOOTHACHE (AERODONTALGIA)

Cause: Air pocket under a cavity.

Symptoms: Pain in the affected tooth.

Treatment: See dentist for corrective filling of tooth.

Prevention: If pain is severe enough, do not dive.

SHALLOW WATER BLACKOUT

Shallow water blackout often occurs when a snorkel diver tries to increase his breathholding or underwater endurance by overbreathing on the surface before diving in. This is called hyperventilation. Divers who hyperventilate and then dive cause a carbon dioxide lack in the body and since respiration is actuated far more by a buildup of carbon dioxide than a lack of oxygen, hyperventilating on the surface extensively eliminates carbon dioxide from the blood. With heavy exertion under water the oxygen content of the body will be so rapidly consumed that the diver will become unconscious from oxygen lack before the carbon dioxide has reached a sufficiently high level to actuate a strong desire to breathe. The danger in hyperventilating lies in the fact that the oxygen starvation may go unnoticed by the diver. Hyperventilating is therefore strongly ill-advised unless closely monitored by one stand-by diver topside and one in the water. In cases of anoxia, immediate rescue is sufficient to restore normal breathing, and consciousness will return in about a half minute. If an unconscious diver who has suffered anoxia is left under water too long, artificial respiration must be applied and medical advice sought. See page 74 on breath-holding and hyperventilation.

HAZARDS AT DEPTH

ANOXIA

Cause: Anoxia can occur in snorkel diving when the breath is held too long. It cannot occur with an open-circuit air rig as long as you use certified pure compressed air in your tanks.

Symptoms: Little forewarning. Diver loses his sense of judgment and may not realize he is suffering from anoxia, and is therefore rendered helpless.

Treatment: Simply get the diver to fresh air if he is still breathing; if he is not, apply artificial respiration. Get a doctor.

Prevention: In snorkel dives, avoid excessively long and deep dives. In air diving, use carefully maintained, tested equipment and pure air.

ASPHYXIA

Causes: Loss or inadequacy of air supply, often involving anoxia and carbon dioxide excess. Obstructed breathing—strangulation—may result.

Symptoms: Usually labored breathing, headache, weakness, dizziness; mental changes as in anoxia and carbon dioxide excess (see below); cyanosis (blueness of skin); unconsciousness if the case is severe; may have violent increase in breathing followed by cessation of breathing.

Treatment: Loosen clothing; apply artificial respiration if breathing has stopped. Expose victim to fresh air or, if available, to pure oxygen, under a physician's supervision. If asphyxia is caused by carbon monoxide, oxygen will clear it considerably.

Prevention: Follow the rules of safe cylinder care, handling, and refilling; never use a tank known to be contaminated until it is "bled" and refilled with certified pure air for breathing.

CARBON-DIOXIDE POISONING

Causes: Loss or inadequacy of air supply; too much carbon dioxide in body; overexertion. Excessive "controlled breathing." Ordinarily this is no hazard to open-circuit air-equipment users except when a full face mask is used, then carbon dioxide may build up excessively for lack of ventilation of the mask. It can occur if the cylinder is charged with air containing carbon dioxide, or because of insufficient breathing resulting in inadequate elimination of carbon dioxide. The greater the depth, the greater the toxicity.

Symptoms: Sometimes occurs without warning as in anoxia. Usually there is labored breathing, air hunger, possibly headache, dizziness, weakness, excessive sweating, nausea. Other effects include an inability to think clearly and confusion, slowing up of responses, clumsiness, foolish actions, unconsciousness, possible muscular twitching in extreme cases, even death.

Treatment: Diver should stop, rest, ventilate, surface if possible. Provide fresh air and rapid recovery will follow—except in severe cases. If the victim is unconscious, treat accordingly. If he is not breathing, apply artificial respiration. Get a physician.

Prevention: Sport divers should avoid use of the full face mask or closed-circuit air rigs. Use open-circuit equipment only. Breathe normally. Do not skip-breathe.

CARBON-MONOXIDE POISONING

Cause: Contamination of all supply in tank by exhaust fumes from gasoline-driven compressors at the time of filling. With increased depth the partial pressure of carbon monoxide becomes deadlier.

Symptoms: Unconsciousness occurs with little or no warning. Detection of the danger for oneself is difficult except that there may be a strange taste to your air supply. If your air is not odorless and tasteless, it may be contaminated. Detection of carbon-monoxide poisoning in another diver is easier, for the victim's lips, face, and mucous membranes take on a bright red color.

Treatment: Apply artificial respiration if breathing has stopped. Expose victim to fresh air or to pure oxygen if available. Oxygen considerably accelerates the cleaning out of carbon monoxide.

Prevention: Follow the rules for safe cylinder care, handling, and refilling; never use a tank known to be contaminated until it is "bled" and refilled with certified air.

NITROGEN NARCOSIS (RAPTURE OF THE DEEP)

"What makes this disease so odd," said the doctor, "is that the man who has it shows no outward sign of illness, in fact he has no sensation of sickness at all—he looks and feels as if he were in perfect, robust health."

"My god," shrieked the hypochondriac, clutching at his chest, "those are my symptoms exactly!"

Cause: The nitrogen in the air supplied by your tank can have an intoxicating effect on you from about 100 feet on down.

Symptoms: The sensations of nitrogen narcosis are very much like those of alcoholic intoxication, but the effects vary with each individual. They are mainly loss of judgment and skill. This lack of judgment is of greatest importance because the victim is unable to tell that he has become a victim of nitrogen narcosis. He has a false feeling of well-being; he is giddy and silly, he lacks concern for his own safety; he experiences difficulty accomplishing even simple jobs, his behavior is foolish and inappropriate, and near-unconsciousness can result for a highly susceptible person.

Treatment: No special treatment is required. The effects disappear rapidly with ascent. There are no aftereffects.

Prevention: Nitrogen narcosis can be prevented only by avoiding exceptionally deep dives with breathing apparatus. If you must make very deep dives, be sure to understand the effects just described and be prepared to act accordingly in conjunction with your buddy.

OIL-VAPOR POISONING

Cause: The presence of oil in the air tank which accumulates in your lungs under pressure.

Symptoms: Choking, shortness of breath, inability to relieve irritation by coughing.

Possible Damage: Permanent shortness of breath, suffocation, possible drowning owing to asphyxiation.

Prevention: Follow strictly the rules of safe cylinder handling, and, in refilling, never use a tank known to be contaminated until it is "bled" and refilled with certified air at a reliable and reputable air station. Extra care must be used during the filling process to prevent lubricants from entering the tank. Be suspicious of air with any hint of taste or odor.

OXYGEN POISONING

Cause: No danger to users of pure compressed air except at depths of 250 feet or more. On the surface in our normal environment, oxygen is a life-giving component of the air we breathe. However, at 250 feet or more, as a result of increased volume (Dalton's Law of partial pressures), oxygen can become deadly even when using pure air.

Symptoms: Muscle twitching, nausea, dizziness, eye or ear disturbances, mental confusion, severe convulsions. Convulsions may occur without other warnings and can cause immediate unconsciousness and drowning.

Prevention: Use *only* open-circuit compressed-air scuba. Closed or semiclosed circuit gear are emphatically *not recommended* for amateurs. They require special training skills and facilities restricted to professional dive operations. Do not dive below 300 feet: Rapture of the depths (nitrogen narcosis) will get you long before you reach oxygen-poisoning depths.

HAZARDS OF ASCENT

AIR EMBOLISM

Cause: Air embolisms are caused by the forcing of air through the lung walls into the bloodstream when holding one's breath while ascending with a breathing apparatus. They can occur when one ascends from a depth as shallow as 7 feet. Boyle's Law applies as in squeeze, only this time in reverse, to wit: As the outside pressure decreases, the inside pressure of your lungs simultaneously increases, and when you reach the surface of the water, such overexpansion (like that of a toy balloon) reaches the breaking point with a possible rupture of the lung and subsequent leakage of air bubbles from the lungs into the bloodstream. Air bubbles are apt to lodge in the brain and cause permanent damage or death.

Symptoms: A small amount of blood coming from the mouth at surfacing may be caused merely by the rupture of a small vessel in the mucous membrane muscle wall of your throat, eustachian tubes, or nasal cavity. However, if bleeding from the mouth is accompanied by a sharp pain in the chest, then a rupture in the lung wall has taken place, indicating air embolism. Air embolism occurring under the surface is accompanied by a bulletlike pain in the chest and at surfacing a pink foam bubbling from the mouth.

Treatment: Rush the diver immediately to the nearest recompression chamber where he can be recompressed and air bubbles can be reduced in size. Waste no time. To treat the victim in the water offers little hope of success. Call the Coast Guard and a physician for aid. If only a slight air embolism has occurred and the victim is in control, he should still be treated as above. By recompressing, the bubbles of air causing these symptoms will be recompressed to a point where they can be exhaled normally. There are usually two causes for breath-holding underwater: panic or exertion.

Prevention: Avoid panic, panic-creating situations, and overexertion. When ascending, rise a little slower than your smallest bubbles (no more than 60 feet per minute). Don't hold your breath. You can't anyway: you have to breathe in order to see those bubbles.

DECOMPRESSION SICKNESS

(Known also as the Bends, Caisson's Disease, Compressed-Air Illness, and Diver's Disease)

Cause: The bends occur when a diver ascends too rapidly from depth. As a result the pressure on the body is reduced too rapidly and nitrogen in the bloodstream turns from solution into gas bubbles in the bloodstream.

Symptoms: Appearance of symptoms depends on the depth and duration of submersion and the rate of ascent. Symptoms generally appear shortly after surfacing or within 24 hours after exposure to pressure. Itching skin, rash, pain in the limbs (most frequent), muscle spasms, and/or convulsions. Paralysis means that a bubble or bubbles have lodged in the spinal cord or brain; disturbances of sight or hearing mean that bubbles have lodged in the brain. Until otherwise proved, any such sign or symptom or peculiar behavior should be treated as decompression sickness, especially when you know the diver has been deep diving.

Possible Damage: Local blocking of circulation. A bubble can lodge in fatty tissues (worse in overweight divers). Bubbles can lodge in heart or brain, causing permanent or fatal injury.

Treatment: Place the victim under pressure either in a recompression chamber or back in the water (only if in complete control) so that nitrogen bubbles go back into solution in the bloodstream—then return him gradually to atmospheric pressure. Observe the victim carefully throughout the treatment. Call for medical help, an ambulance, or the U.S. Coast Guard search and rescue team.

Prevention: Avoid deep dives. Avoid repetitive dives within a 12-hour period. Under certain circumstances, if you must exceed the No-Decompression limits, be sure you know, consult, and follow the U.S. Navy Air Decompression Tables.

SPONTANEOUS PNEUMOTHORAX

Cause: Air getting into the space between the lungs and the lining of the chest wall causing the lung to collapse, particularly at least as pressure increases. Enough such pressure will impair breathing and heart action seriously.

Symptoms: Shortness of breath, chest pain, and turning blue (cyanosis).

Treatment: Recompression will give temporary relief. A physician must be in attendance as he will have to remove trapped air by means of a needle and syringe; therefore, recompression itself is only one part of the treatment.

Prevention: Follow safe procedure in your ascent to the surface. Ascend at 60 feet per minute. Don't hold your breath; breathe normally.

SUBCUTANEOUS AND MEDIASTINAL EMPHYSEMA

Cause: The expansion of air upon ascent in the tissue spaces of the mediastinum (air space in the middle of the chest).

Symptoms: Pain under the sternum within chest, difficulty in breathing and swallowing or speaking, possible shock. In less severe cases, there may be no symptoms at all. There may be fullness or great swelling in the victim's neck and a change in the sound of his voice, crepitation of the skin and difficulty in breathing or swallowing.

Treatment: Whatever the degree of emphysema, air embolism may be present. Recompression is probably the best treatment.

Prevention: Follow safe diving procedure in your ascent to the surface. Ascend at 60 feet per minute (don't pass your smallest bubbles), and don't hold your breath. Breathe normally.

GENERAL FIRST AID

Your First Duty Is To Do No Harm: Size up the situation rapidly and correctly—this will tell you what to do first. Ask yourself these questions:

Is He Breathing? If not, artificial respiration takes precedence over everything except the need to control massive bleeding.

Is He Bleeding? Rapid loss of blood must be controlled at once or death can follow in minutes. Stop bleeding instantly.

Is He in Shock? Shock follows almost any type of injury and can cause death.

In the absence of problems demanding immediate attention, examine the victim thoroughly to find all injuries he may have sustained. Be gentle and do not move him any more than absolutely necessary. Especially avoid unnecessary moving of the head and neck in case of fracture, or you may cause permanent paralysis or death.

If a broken bone is found or suspected, immobilize that part without moving the victim. Keep the victim lying flat, preferably on a deck or floor, head level with body, until you are sure of the full extent of injury. Do not move the victim until you are sure it is safe to do so, and then not without a stretcher or reasonable substitute. Send for medical help immediately if you can.

BLEEDING

Methods of Stoppage: When bleeding is massive, the important thing is to stop the flow of blood. Apply pressure on the wound either by hand or with a pressure dressing (sterilized or clean cloth in several folds) taped or tied in place. Apply the dressing firmly but not tight enough to hamper circulation. Hand or finger pressure on the artery supplying blood to the area near the wound will stop or sufficiently slow most bleeding from extremities until a dressing and bandage can be applied. In an arm injury, the most widely used pressure point is located on the interior side of the arm where the brachial artery can be compressed against the arm bone. In leg injuries the pressure point most widely used is located on either side of the groin where the femoral artery can be compressed against the thigh joint below the pelvis. Also, elevation of the wounded area will reduce the flow of serious bleeding.

Use a Tourniquet Only as a Last Resort: If the tourniquet is incorrectly placed, venous bleeding is increased and arterial bleeding is unaffected. When a tourniquet is placed incorrectly, the blood supply to the area below the tourniquet is completely shut off and the tissues will die from loss of oxygen and food unless surgical attention is obtained forthwith.

Tourniquets are applied only to arms and legs and cannot be used for bleeding of the face, head, neck, or trunk of the body. If a tourniquet is essential, use a triangular bandage in a necktie shape. The band should be about 2 inches wide. A necktie, belt, or stocking can be used for lack of something better. Ropes, strings, wires, and narrow strings of cloth make less ideal tourniquets because they cut into the flesh, but as a last resort these too may be used.

Place the tourniquet close to the wound, not at the wound's edge, and always between the heart and the wound, never below the wound. Apply it only as tightly as is necessary to stop bleeding. Do not release it once it is applied no matter how long it has been in place except when a physician is present.

To apply an emergency tourniquet made from something like a handkerchief, towel, or belt, wrap the material once around the limb and tie an overhand knot. Place a short stick on the overhand knot and tie a square knot over it. Then twist the stick rapidly to tighten the tourniquet. The stick may be tied in place with another strip of material.

If the patient is covered so that the tourniquet is concealed, be sure the doctor is informed that a tourniquet is being used.

WOUNDS

A few simple rules, when followed, will greatly reduce the chance of infection or other complications and add to the comfort of a wounded victim.

When applying first-aid care to any opening in the skin, the first-aider should have clean, washed hands.

Soap and clean water (preferably boiled) may be used to cleanse the wound area. Care must be exercised to prevent dirt or foreign material from entering the wound.

If the wound is to receive further care by a physician, it is best that no antiseptic be applied. Cover the wound with a sterile dressing and bandage it in place snugly without impairing circulation.

Even with minor wounds, if signs of infection appear (redness, warmth, swelling, pain, and pus) consult a physician. Remember to have a tetanus shot.

LOSS OF CONSCIOUSNESS

Loss of consciousness during or after a dive is an acute emergency. It may result from many different factors: a serious form of decompression sickness, simple fainting, or any mishap such as air embolism or a head injury which stops breathing or any part of the respiratory process.

The supposed nature of the accident will seldom change the steps you should take in treatment. Therefore, it is far more important to start treating the victim at once than to try to figure out the cause.

Treatment of an Unconscious Diver: If the victim is not breathing, start artificial respiration at once.

Get to a recompression chamber at once if the victim was engaged in dives beyond No-Decompression limits.

Examine him for injuries and other abnormalities. Apply first aid as required. If possible, send for a physician without delay. But keep up artificial respiration.

SHOCK

Shock is a depressed condition of the body functions when a sufficient amount of blood fails to circulate through the body following serious injury to body tissue from a burn, wound, or fracture, and it is particularly the result of loss of a large amount of blood. In general the greater the damage to the body, the greater the danger that shock will occur. Death can result from shock even though the injury causing it would not otherwise be fatal. Therefore, proper first aid to prevent or deal with shock is essential in the care of the injured.

Symptoms of Shock: Weakness of victim, pale, moist, unusually cool skin, lackluster eyes, dilated pupils, shallow and irregular breathing, weak or absent pulse, sometimes nausea, sometimes beads of perspiration on the face, palms, and in armpits. Thirst is common.

Caution: Do not confuse shock with simple fainting. Fainting often results from minor injuries or the sight of blood or other reasons not related to serious injury. (See Fainting, page 237.)

First Aid for Shock: Give first aid for shock to all seriously injured victims. First aid applies to both prevention and care of shock. Keep the victim lying down unless he shows difficulty in breathing. Then—and only then—elevate his head and chest.

In case of extreme loss of blood or severe injury elevate the lower part of the body unless there is a head injury—to do so would make breathing difficult—or if the victim complains of pain due to a leg or abdominal injury.

Keep the victim warm but not sweating.

Rule of Thumb: Do not add heat; simply prevent loss of heat.

Do not give fluids if the patient is nauseated, unconscious, or half-conscious, or has suffered a penetrating abdominal wound. Otherwise, water is best for quenching a victim's thirst. Sips will do until medical help arrives. If medical help is not available or is considerably delayed, give half-glass doses of water along with one-half level tablespoon of salt and one-half level teaspoon of baking soda per quart at about 15 minute intervals. While treating for shock, give attention to hemorrhaging and other injuries.

Keep the victim quiet; soothe him with encouraging words.

FRACTURES

First aid for fractured bones consists mainly in careful handling (or no handling, unless necessary) in order not to aggravate the injury. If the victim must be moved or transported other than in an ambulance, the fracture should be immobilized. Use whatever suitable materials are at hand (appropriate length, weight, and strength) for splints, and at the same time prevent movement of the adjacent joints. Careful transportation and shock care are a must.

Splint for the Forearm: Use two splints. One should extend from the elbow to the fingers on the palm side; the other, of the same length, should be placed on the opposite side. Bind the splints snugly in place with several triangular bandages folded in cravat shape.

Upper Arm (Humerus): Use two well-padded splints. Place pad in the armpit to protect blood vessels and nerves from undue pressure. Place one padded splint between arm and chest wall, the other on the lateral surface of arm. Secure splints in position with triangular bandages folded as cravats. Place forearm in sling.

Splint for the Palm or Wrist: One splint extending from below the elbow to the fingertips on the palm side and securely bandaged in place is sufficient. Then place the arm in an armsling.

Splint for an Ankle Fracture: See that the victim lies down. If he is to be transported, carry him or use a stretcher. Pad the ankle before placing a splint on each side extending from the heel to a point an inch or 2 below the knee.

Splint for a Leg Fracture at a Point Between Ankle and Knee: If medical help appears readily available, wait for it. Meanwhile, immobilize the injured part by placing a blanket, pillow, or folded coat or sweater against it. Be alert for shock symptoms and treat accordingly. Splints should be on both sides of the leg from the ankle to the upper end of the thigh.

Fracture of Thighbone (Femur): Splint both sides of leg almost from the groin and hips to below the heel with padding at the ankle and the knee. Foot must be immobilized and at right angles to the long axis of the leg as viewed from the side.

BURNS

First aid for burns depends on the degree and the amount of area involved. Burns are classified as:

First degree—reddening of the skin
Second degree—blisters
Third degree—charring or deep destruction of tissues

Pain can be relieved by exclusion of air through the application of many-layered sterile dressings (dry). Small first- or second-degree burns may be treated by the careful application of medically approved preparations and sterile dressings.

Shock care is imperative when large areas of any degree are involved. Shock, even when psychically induced, is generally a threat even where relatively small areas have suffered third-degree burns. Since infection and other complications might follow even simple burns, get medical help.

Sunburn: The commonest type of burn suffered by divers is sunburn. Long exposure, both in and out of water, has taken all the pleasure out of many an otherwise well-planned diving trip. To prevent painful, or even serious, burns, use tanning lotions or light clothing and curtail exposure until a tan is gradually built up.

SEASICKNESS

Causes: Wave motion, prolonged exposure to the motion of the sea, whether at surface or when diving at depth.

Symptoms: Nausea and dizziness.

Possible Damage: Loss of efficiency, and vomiting resulting in choking and possible drowning if in the water.

Prevention: Those susceptible to seasickness should avoid dives in waters having any wave motion or turbulence. Divers should control their diet rigidly, chew their food thoroughly, and wait at least three hours after eating before diving. Meals should be high in protein with no gas-forming or heavy foods. Anti-seasickness medicine may be used but only under a doctor's supervision because of the possible side effects of such drugs.

PANIC

Causes: Variable, but generally triggered by the diver's encounter with what he believes to be a dangerous situation. Panic is characterized by unreasoned fear. The victim is obsessed with an instinct to save himself, abandoning all logical and intelligent thought.

Prevention: Do not exceed your abilities, stay within your limitations, avoid situations you cannot cope with. Always dive with a buddy. Be thoroughly familiar with your equipment and its limitations. Master emergency procedures so well that you can react immediately and automatically and with enough presence of mind to overcome panic.

LEG CRAMPS

Causes: Excessive fatigue, cold, or overexertion, causing a knotting up or tightening up of various muscles of the leg causing sharp pain.

Treatment: Stop all activity. Knead affected muscles with hands. Stretch out the ailing leg. Leave water unless you have an ample air supply and control enough to cure cramp.

STOMACH CRAMPS

Causes: Entering the water too soon after eating, overexertion, or radical temperature changes in the water.

Symptoms: Severe pain, involuntary drawing up of knees to the chest, doubling up.

Treatment: Go to the rescue of the victim, and tow him to the surface. If he is still conscious and breathing through his regulator mouthpiece, tow him on his back, leaving his mouthpiece in place. Tell him to breathe through it except when out of air. Once ashore, place him in a position so that his knees are flexed to relieve tension.

EXHAUSTION

Causes: Exhaustion or fatigue is a major cause of drowning, not necessarily while submerged but often as a result of an exhausting swim after surfacing. Exhaustion follows an excess of physical exertion, which, in turn, causes a buildup of carbon dioxide in the body.

Problems of exhaustion are failure of muscles to function, panic, emotional stress or excitement, which may induce rapid movements and excess physical work coupled with faulty breathing, which curtails the supply of oxygen to the lungs. Excess submersion in cold water contributes to the slowing down of all mental and physical bodily functions.

Symptoms: Difficulty in breathing, tired-out feeling, possible dizziness, possible nausea, unconsciousness.

Treatment: Stay calm. Stop activity and rest to regain composure and normal breathing rate. Concentrate on exhalation. A fatigued diver should get out or be taken out of the water to rest and be kept warm. Be alert for shock symptoms.

Prevention: Maintain a discipline of regular off-season physical exercises and moderation of exertion. Keep fit year round with physical exercise. Do not overexert while diving. For propulsion use a slow easy scissor kick, trail your arms loosely at your sides, and take deep slow breaths to conserve air and strength.

DROWNING

Causes: Any number of causative factors precede the final paroxysm known as drowning: failure of air supply, flooding of mouthpiece or mask, severe exposure, exhaustion, panic, unconsciousness, etc. Drowning is the greatest cause of death in self-contained diving. The most common cause of drowning is physical exhaustion resulting from swimming *after* surfacing. Drowning is, in effect, the blockage of air passages, causing strangulation, unconsciousness, and death.

Symptoms: Choking, coughing, gagging, wild, uncontrollable gestures, a desperate attempt to surface—all signs of panic.

Prevention: Adequate training and drill in emergency procedures, proper equipment in good condition, physical and emotional fitness.

FAINTING

Causes: Unusual stress. Fall of blood pressure to the point where insufficient oxygen reaches the brain.

Symptoms: Nausea, "turning green," eventual loss of consciousness. If these signs are visible, sit down and lean over with head between knees. If in water get to shore as fast as possible.

Treatment: If a person has fainted, stretch him out and watch him carefully until he regains consciousness, elevate his feet and legs slightly. If breathing stops commence artificial respiration at once. Call a doctor if recovery is not evident. Take into account the possibility that the victim, if diving, might be suffering from air embolism or decompression sickness and act accordingly.

STRANGULATION

Causes: Strangulation refers to obstruction of breathing. If severe, it will produce asphyxia. The accidental inhalation of foreign material is the most likely cause of strangulation in diving. The diver may have spasm of the larynx owing to inhalation of water. Strangulation may require artificial respiration.

Symptoms: Very difficult breathing, noisy breathing, choking, gasping.

Treatment: Seek obstruction and remove it if possible. Get the victim to cough. Call for medical help. In an extreme case, as a desperate solution, perform a tracheotomy: Open the windpipe below the larynx by making an incision in the midline of the neck (not across) two fingers' breadth below the point of the Adam's apple. Use ice pick or knife and hold the incision open. Victim can then breathe through it without obstruction.

INJURY FROM LIGHTNING

Treatment: If the victim is struck unconscious, give cardiopulmonary respiration as diaphragm or lung muscles are often paralyzed by the bolt. Treat burns later. Get a doctor; there may be internal injuries.

Prevention: If a thunderstorm is imminent, leave the water, head for port. Don't go near the water as the flow of current carried by water from a bolt striking at some distance can cause electrocution.

FISH POISONING—GENERAL (see pages 173–74)

Cause: The meat of porcupine fish, boxfish, puffer fish, triggerfish, and filefish are poisonous. Also poisonous are some barracuda, the yellow fin grouper, some jacks, weeverfish, horned sharks, some catfish, scorpion fish, ratfish, toadfish, surgeonfish, rabbitfish, stonefish, zebrafish, and any unfresh or spoiled fish. Poisoning can result from eating the meat of poisonous fish (ichthyosarcotoxism) or eating fish that is not in itself poisonous but is spoiled (ichthyotoxism).

Symptoms: Stomach cramps, nausea, malaise, upset stomach, diarrhea, dizziness, shortness of breath.

Treatment: Induce vomiting (tickle the back of the throat or drink warm soapy or salty water) and see a doctor.

Prevention: Eat the freshest fish of known edible varieties. Avoid poisonous fish and beware of other fish during certain seasons when even a normally edible fish can become poisonous, such as the grouper or snapper.

FISH POISONING, MOST USUAL SPECIFIC VARIETIES

Ingestion Poisoning

Internal: Internal poisoning results from the consumption of contaminated marine life. It can be broken down into two general categories, that contracted from eating contaminated fish and that contracted from eating shellfish during certain months of the year.

Ciguatera: This poisoning results from eating certain unrelated fish which contain a poison (ciguatoxin). The reason for this poison being present is unknown, although it is thought that it comes from certain species of algae eaten by fish. There is no way to distinguish fish with ciguatera from harmless fish except by laboratory analysis or by feeding the suspected fish to animals and watching for a reaction. Ciguatera can occur in a species of fish that was harmless the day before. Fish known to carry ciguatera include barracuda, grouper, snappers, and jacks. About 800 species have been known to produce ciguatera. Diseased fish seem more prevalent in tropical areas and because the concentration builds up over time, large fish of a given species are more likely to be toxic. The internal organs of diseased fish are particularly toxic.

Symptoms: Reversal of thermal touch sensation (hot feels cold and cold feels hot); abdominal pains; nausea, vomiting; diarrhea; numbness of lips, tongue, throat; fever.

Treatment: A doctor should be consulted as soon as possible, and informed that fish has been consumed within the last 30 hours. In some cases, death may result in only 10 minutes, but a period of days is more common. If untreated, death may follow as a result of paralysis of the respiratory system. Assisted ventilation may be effective in those patients with respiratory paralysis. Once contracted, the symptoms may persist for months, particularly the reversal-of-temperature sensation. It is recommended that fish not be eaten while any symptoms remain, as this may cause a serious recurrence.

Scromboid Poisoning

Some fish which have been left exposed to sunlight or left standing at room temperature may develop a toxin. Within a few minutes of consumption, symptoms will develop.

Symptoms: Nausea, vomiting; severe headache; massive red welts; severe itching.

Treatment: Seek medical aid as soon as possible.

Shellfish Poisoning

During the summer months, many shellfish which inhabit the Pacific Coast and Gulf of Mexico become poisonous. This poison results from the ingestion of poisonous plankton and algae, which does not affect the shellfish, but can be poisonous if the shellfish is consumed by humans. Mussels and clams carry this poison. Abalone and crabs do not feed on plankton and are therefore not affected. In most cases, cooking will not neutralize the toxin. The poison works directly on the nervous system and the usual signs, such as nausea and vomiting, are not generally present. The poison impairs respiration and affects the circulation of the blood. Death, which results in severe cases, is normally the result of respiratory paralysis.

Signs and Symptoms: Onset is variable but may occur within 20 minutes of ingestion; difficulty breathing, getting progressively worse; cessation of breathing; infrequently, nausea, vomiting, and other gastrointestinal ailments.

Treatment: If shellfish poisoning is suspected, seek immediate medical attention.

CHILLS

To stay alive the human body needs to maintain a body temperature close to the normal of 98.6° F. Waters in which you will be diving are always colder than this, and generally water grows colder with depth. You will, therefore, always be losing body heat in the water. The body compensates for the loss temporarily by increased chemical activity within the body. Don't be fooled: After a prolonged stay in the water you may suffer chills as well as cramps and exhaustion. Even if chills are not severe enough to threaten life or cause permanent harm, they can cause loss of sense of touch, clumsiness, shivering, loss of coordination, and difficulty in hanging onto your mouthpiece. They even may affect your ability to think clearly. Whenever diving in water temperatures of less than 75° F wear long johns; otherwise, after an hour or so, you will be chilled. In water of 70° F or colder, rubber suit protection is necessary.

Treatment: Get out of the water, dry yourself, put on warm, dry clothes, exercise for a few minutes to stop the shivers, drink a hot beverage.

SUGGESTED FIRST AID KIT

A simple, well-constructed metal or plastic moistureproof box to contain first aid materials should be standard equipment on every dive. There must be no lock; the box should be sealed with tape but only when its contents are complete: The tape should be a sign that they are. The following items are suggested:

Tube for mouth-to-mouth resuscitation
2 one-in. adhesive compresses
1 two-in. adhesive compress
1 three-in. adhesive compress
1 four-in. adhesive compress
1 package (2 doz.) 3 × 3 in. plain gauze pads (sterile)
1 two-in. gauze roller bandage
1 tube burn ointment

2 plain absorbent gauze, ½ sq. yd
2 plain absorbent gauze, 24 × 72 in.
3 triangular bandages
1 pair of scissors, a pair of tweezers, and a 6-in. piece of ½-in. dowel to be used as the windlass when applying a tourniquet (optional) Emergency tracheotomy kit

Supplementary items desirable in the first aid care of marine life injuries would include:

Baking soda
Nonprescription ointment for relief of pain (applied locally)

Antihistamine tablets
Antihistamine ointment

Read and follow directions for the dosage or application of any drugs included in the kit. Examine and renew the contents of your kit regularly. Have *The First Aid Textbook of the American Red Cross* in your possession and keep it in a convenient spot so that it is easily found when needed.

FLYING AFTER DIVING

Should a diver fly after diving or should he allow a certain amount of time to elapse before taking to the air? The answer is that there should be no danger of bends provided the diver has made dives within the depth-time ratios not requiring decompression. There should be no danger even if he has made a dive requiring decompression provided he has made adequate decompression stops. If proper and adequate decompression has not been taken the diver is likely to get the bends whether or not he flies. Under normal diving conditions and following the normal decompression procedure there is no risk of decompression sickness occurring in a subsequent flight.

To a diver whose blood and tissues are partially saturated with nitrogen, flying in a pressurized plane can cause serious decompression problems. To prevent bends, wait at least 12 hours after diving before flying. If you are planning to fly after diving, make short, deeper dives. Reason: The tissues of the body affected in shorter, deeper dives will lose nitrogen more rapidly than those on long shallow dives. Dive only within the No-Decompression limits. After a single No-Decompression dive at sea level, you may fly commercially within 4 hours. If, for reasons of a serious injury, you have to fly for treatment immediately after a decompression dive or dives, the altitude of the aircraft should not exceed 800 feet.

Care of Your Equipment in Flight or at High Elevations: Unless it is a capillary type, your depth gauge can be damaged by lower pressures. Keep it in a sealed container in flight or when at mountain elevations. The law requires that your tanks be empty in flight.

Caution: If a diver suffering symptoms of the bends must be flown to a decompression chamber, warn the flight crew to fly as low as is permissible—unless the plane is pressurized. Of course, pilots who engage in sport diving should be especially certain to have cleared themselves of any decompression problems.

LOSS OF CONSCIOUSNESS DURING
OR AFTER DIVE

1. If the victim is not breathing, start artificial respiration at once.
2. Get the victim to the nearest recompression chamber if the need is suspected.
3. Get a physician. Apply first aid if necessary.
4. Continue artificial respiration on the way to the chamber and during recompression.
5. Recompress unless:
    a. The victim regains consciousness and is free of symptoms before recompression can be started.
    b. The possibility of air embolism or decompression sickness can be ruled out without question.
    c. Another life-saving measure is absolutely required and makes recompression impossible.
6. Try to reach a recompression chamber no matter how far it is.

For the most up-to-date location of the nearest chamber and medical advice, call the following telephone numbers. A helpful physician is on duty 24 hours a day, seven days a week. He will offer first aid suggestions and help you get transportation to a decompression facility near you.

Brooks Air Force Base*
(512) 536-3278 or (512) 536-3281

U.S. Navy Experimental Diving Unit
EDU Duty Phone
AC904-234-4353

Naval Medical Officer
(202) OX 3-2790 (5 days per week)

* The decision to go and how to get there is your responsibility.

RESCUE OPERATIONS

EMERGENCY ASSISTANCE PLAN (EAP)

For the well-trained, well-equipped skin diver, serious emergencies are rare, as he knows how to avoid situations that create them. With a good training program behind him, he will have been drilled to cope with almost any problem that might confront him. All divers should formulate an emergency assistance plan. The chances are that you will never need your plan, but be prepared anyway. Learn the dive signals (see pages 64–69), and be sure that each diving companion is thoroughly familiar with them.

Your dive plan should be concise and clear to everyone throughout a normal diving sequence. Emergency procedures should be memorized.

Know the location of all hazards in the vicinity of the dive and warn all divers accordingly.

Know the name, location, and telephone number of organizations that can render emergency assistance, such as:

Police Department
Fire Department
First aid stations
Physicians
Hospitals
The nearest recompression chamber
Coast Guard

Write this information on the back pages of this manual.

All the divers in your party should be familiar and proficient in the techniques of artificial respiration and first aid. Equipment essential to lifesaving must be handy.

Buddy Breathing (Assisted Ascent): Any diver who runs out of air at moderate depths (say under 100 feet) will surface instinctively and safely without assistance. He may be helped, however, by sharing the air supply of a buddy. This is known as buddy breathing. If the depth and duration of the dive calls for stage decompression stops, buddy breathing may be the safest step until a spare air rig can be strapped onto the airless man.

If your buddy loses his breathing apparatus or has run out of air, he gives the "give me air" signal unless he surfaces without incident, then proceed as follows:

When ready to pass your mouthpiece to him, tap him so that he will be ready to receive it.

Lose no time after this signal. Start the *4-cycle* breathing technique with an easy rhythm as follows:

Exhale—inhale—exhale—inhale; then, holding last breath, pass mouthpiece to buddy.

With the air he still has in his lungs, your buddy uses the 4-cycle breathing technique, then returns the mouthpiece to you. The 4-cycle technique calls for 2 breaths at a time by each buddy. Buddy breathing can be done while in motion as well as at a standstill. Keep the space between you and your buddy at a minimum while breathing, approximately half an arm's length away. Hold each other's tank harness to avoid drifting apart.

If you are the air supplier using a two-hose regulator and your buddy is out of air, swim with your left (exhaust hose) side down. Your buddy swims right-side down, holding your harness with his left hand. This procedure is not applicable if you are using a single-hose regulator, with which no special positioning is required.

Whenever anyone in a diving party is equipped with an octopus rig, all fellow divers should be briefed on its use.

Final Word: The great danger of buddy breathing is that on the occasion when it is most needed a diver may panic and make successful buddy breathing impossible. Practice buddy breathing until you are familiar enough with it to feel confident that you will not panic when it is required.

FOULING AND ENTANGLEMENT

When a diver becomes trapped, entangled, or fouled, he must remain calm. Struggling to free himself immediately will probably result in even worse entanglement and loss of equipment. His best assets are calm, a knife, and the aid of a buddy. Emergency ascent should be used only as a last resort.

SELF-RESCUE

Ditching Equipment: In most emergency ascents you should not ditch your breathing apparatus. If you must ascend without it because it has become fouled, use the following procedure.

Signal your buddy.

Unfasten the quick-release tank harness or back pack. If you are wearing a wet or dry suit, don't ditch your weight belt except as a last resort.

After you pull the quick-release harness, the tank will swing slowly upward behind you. Reach back with both hands to grab the body of the tank. Pull the tank up and over your head and horizontally down in front of you. Take a full breath.

Pull the mouthpiece out of your mouth and leave the tank on the bottom. Weight it if time allows so that you can retrieve it later.

Exhale as hard as you can: blow and go.

Begin to ascend to the surface, blowing the compressed air out of your lungs. Tilt your head back to avoid any blockage of air passages. Maintain an ascent at 60 feet per second.

Never hold your breath when making an ascent. Continue exhaling.

Note: when you sense a greater need to exhale as you rise, don't panic: The residual air in your lungs is merely expanding. No matter how forcefully you exhale, there is always some residual air remaining in the lungs. To elaborate, a normal human lung when full of air contains about 8 pints of air. A forceful exhalation will expel about 6 pints, leaving 2 pints of residual air remaining in the lungs.

How to Make a Free Ascent:
Jettison your weight belt if you are not wearing a wet suit.
Do *not* remove your breathing apparatus. Keep it on.
Take a breath and float upward.
Maintain a rate of ascent of 60 feet per minute—no faster.

As you ascend, the air volume in your lungs will increase with the lessening of water pressure. If your air rig failed you before you had a chance to inhale a breath, you may not have enough buoyancy to rise without kicking your way up. As the water pressure lessens (again remember Boyle's Law), the volume of remaining air in your lungs will increase and come to your aid in your ascent.

Exhale continually as you go. If you sense a slight pressure or pain in your chest, you are beginning to feel the effects of overexpansion, meaning that you are either rising too fast or not exhaling adequately. *Caution:* An air embolism can occur without warning of pain. Because of the reduction of pressure and the increase of air and oxygen volume in your lungs, you will not feel as powerful a need to breathe as you might expect after a long, steady exhalation. The crucial point of ascent occurs in the last 10 feet, where pressure change is the greatest. From this depth upward, exhale as vigorously as possible.

Free ascents are of utmost importance in emergencies. Practice often under supervision. Use only as a last resort.

Inflating Your Flotation Device (BC vest) in Emergencies: Be careful if you inflate your vest while you are making free ascents. An air embolism may result from an uncontrollably rapid rate of ascent. If use of your vest is imperative, first exhale the air out of your lungs to the greatest extent tolerable, then inflate your vest. Do not fail to exhale from your lungs the residual air, which will expand as you go up.

Running Out of Air: Every tank has its limits. When your air is low, notify your buddy. Then if you are equipped (as you should be) with a manual reserve air valve feature, the J-valve, pull the pressure lever as breathing becomes difficult. This will release a remaining 300 pounds per square inch of air in reserve, giving you ample time to reach the surface. Once you go on reserve, do not descend. With increasing depth, your reserve air will be cut off and stay off until you ascend. Reserve air is sufficient to provide only enough breathing time to get to the surface. When on reserve—go up. If you do not have a J-valve reserve feature, read below.

Running Out of Air When You Don't Have a Reserve Mechanism: Remember, the exhaustion of your air supply is always something to be expected in self-contained diving. By keeping time, you should know just about when your supply will run out. Even with an empty tank, you may have 3 to 4 breaths remaining in ascent. Use them, for as you ascend, the reduced ambient pressure will make available a little more air in the tank, just enough to get you to the surface. Stay calm: There's no great danger. Rise slowly and exhale continually after each breath. If you feel pain or discomfort because of lung expansion, increase your exhalation. While you are under, remember that according to Boyle's Law your air expands as you rise. You will have enough to get to the surface safely, but always remember to exhale. Though it is a rule more easily prescribed than observed, don't panic or worry. Think of the submarine crews who in free-ascent trials come up from 300 feet with no air supply other than the lungful they started with at the bottom. It has been proved that they are able to exhale all the way to the surface.

Final word: If you are out of air, get to the surface.

Why You Should Not Throw Away Breathing Equipment in Emergencies: Even if your air supply is exhausted, don't throw away your rig at depth. As you rise, even in an emergency, you will lose valuable seconds taking off the gear. Swim with it to the surface. Get rid of it only if it is somehow hopelessly entangled and in your way. Remember, owing to reduced pressure in the surrounding water, even an empty cylinder will give you a few breaths of air as you rise. The cylinder will also give you a buoyancy that you may be thankful for. In an emergency, drop off your weight belt, unless you can manage to ascend with the added weight. Once at the surface, remove the tank and use it as a flotation buoy, especially if you don't have your snorkel or flotation device with you.

Emergency Ascent Procedure If Your Buddy Is Not Nearby: An emergency ascent requires returning to the surface in the shortest possible time when you can't resort to buddy breathing (assisted ascent). Your buddy should be there with you, but if he is not, and presupposing a combination of mishaps including a total failure of your air supply, here's how to ascend alone.

Release and leave your weight belt if it impairs ascent. With a wet suit you may flip up too fast for safety, and it may be wiser to keep your belt on. When wearing a wet suit you'll have difficulty controlling the speed of your ascent if you jettison your weight belt, because the nitrogen gas bubbles manufactured into the suit will expand as you rise. Leave the belt on and inflate your BC vest. By this procedure your emergency ascent then becomes a buoyant ascent. Keep on exhaling. In an emergency without air, you have little choice but to get up fast.

Exhale forcefully and continually as you ascend because remaining air will expand from where you are then, particularly from 33 feet (1 atm) to the surface.

Ascend as quickly as possible.

Keep your mouthpiece in place to reduce your activity and use of time. The mouthpiece also helps keep water out of your mouth.

Keep one hand above your head to ward off any obstruction. Look up and around for obstructions. Note: In a free ascent, the diver exhales gradually on the way up. In an emergency ascent the diver must exhale all the air he can before commencing the ascent. The popular nomenclature for the latter is "blow and go." You blow out all the air you can; then go up as fast as you can.

Lost, Exhausted, or Far from Base: Use your BC vest for flotation, conserve energy. Try to establish your position. Signal for help if necessary. When rested, resume your swim homeward.

RESCUE OF ANOTHER

Rescuing a Diver Who Has a Cramped Leg and Is Calm: Tell the victim to lie on his back and float. The rescuer faces and grabs the victim's arms at the elbows so that his arms are extended in front of his chest and the rescuer's arms are extended forward. Use a normal kick and push the victim backward to shore.

Rescuing a Victim Who Has a Stomach Cramp: In a severe case the sufferer usually has no control over his movements and he can do little to help himself without someone else to bring him to safety. Often his breathing is inhibited. The rescuer should act accordingly and proceed with the applicable rescue method. Get the victim to the surface. Keep his head above water. Tow him on his back, keeping his mouthpiece in place. Tell him to breathe through it. If the victim is so doubled up that he cannot easily be floated or towed on his back, and he has lost his mouthpiece, let him float face down and try floating by bobbing. If he can't bob try to get his head out of the water by tugging his hair, persuading him to act on his own while you stand by. Use whatever flotation is available including the victim's BC vest.

Two Rescuers Surfacing and Towing an Unconscious Diver to Shore: Always inflate the victim's BC vest if he is wearing one. Both rescuers swim on their backs behind the victim while holding him on his back and finning backward. The rescuer at the right holds the right arm of the victim above the elbow with the right hand. The same rescuer's left hand supports the back of the victim's head to keep it out of the water. The rescuer on the left holds the victim's left arm with both hands. Be close to the victim. Fin to the surface and homeward in this position. Rescuers need not use snorkel but their masks may be kept on if circumstances dictate. (Breathing may be easier without masks for both rescuer and victim.) If a tank is worn, jettison only if the circumstances so dictate, remembering that an empty tank is buoyant and can be a useful float. Weight belts probably should be dumped if no BC vest is worn, as the extra

weight impedes rescue. Remember, under no circumstances should
the saving of equipment impede the saving of a life.

One Rescuer Surfacing with an Unconscious Diver: Jettison the
weight belts at once. If victim is wearing a BC vest, inflate it—
unless he is wearing a wet suit. If the victim is wearing a wet suit, it
will keep him afloat. Get a grip on the victim by the hair or the harnesses and slowly and cautiously swim to the surface. Beware of the
possibility of air embolism. Remember that the victim may have a
lungful of compressed air and it should be bubbling from his mouth.
As you ascend, press the victim's chest to get the air out of his
lungs. Keep his head tilted well back to prevent blockage of air passages.

If the weight of the victim is too heavy to tow and you have a
short length of line handy, attach it to the victim's harness and
secure the other around your waist in a slip knot. You will then have
an extra swim arm with which to propel yourself to the surface.

TIPS ON RESCUE

The sight of a diver in trouble is not what you might expect.
Chances are he is not hailing you with a proper distress hand signal
or blowing a whistle. He usually surfaces in an upright position high
in the water, looking as if he were trying to climb out of the water.
His mask is probably off and he is fighting for breath around his
snorkel. He may be in the grip of panic.

At the first sign of distress, a rescuer must respond quickly. Don
fins, mask, and weight belt (if you already have donned a wet suit).
The time it takes to get equipped will be repaid in reaching the victim faster and with greater control. If possible take or toss a float to
victim. Hurry, but conserve your strength; you will need it not only
to reach him but to tow and probably rescuscitate him. An effective
rescue is phyically demanding.

If victim insists on clinging to some piece of equipment, as is
often the case, persuade him to discard and he probably will surren-
der it at your reassuring appeal.

Dump victim's weight belt and see that it falls clear.

When victim is unconscious and not breathing, the most important concern is to reach the surface as quickly as possible.

When towing victim keep his face above the water so that you can monitor his face for signs and symptoms and in a manner enabling you to swim freely. The next concern is to get air into the diver.

If a surface float is available, it should be used under the rescuer if he is going to administer in-water resuscitation. The rescuer needs to be above the victim in order to resuscitate effectively. Without a float, the rescuer must kick to gain enough height to resuscitate. This tires the rescuer quickly. With a float placed beneath the rescuer, no energy is needed to gain height and the rescuer can resuscitate for an indefinite period of time. Inflate neither yours nor victim's vest. At the surface, the wet suit will support the victim with the weight belt removed. In fact, the inflatable vest is nearly all out of the water with the victim lying face up. If both vests are inflated, they usually interfere with resuscitation. Inflating the rescuer's vest may also interfere with resuscitation. The rescuer could let his own weight belt drop to gain more buoyancy in order to be higher than the victim the better to administer resuscitation.

In order to administer cardiopulmonary resuscitation, remove the diver from the water and place on a firm surface. Cardiopulmonary resuscitation cannot be effectively administered in the water. The sternum must be depressed 1½ to 2 inches every second. This requires a direct force of approximately 120 pounds. The victim's lungs must also be ventilated. There is no known method to accomplish these requirements in the water. If heart stoppage is suspected, ventilate the victim while moving quickly to get the person out of the water and to a firm surface where compression can be effective.

If resuscitation must be interrupted for any reason while making an in-water rescue, give several quick inflations. No interruptions should exceed 15 seconds.

Rescuing a Victim Who Has Not Panicked: Remain behind him, holding him to the surface with a firm grip under his arm or by his tank valve.

See that he jettisons his weight belt or do it for him, but only if necessary.

Chat with him calmly to give him reassurance.

Be watchful for signs of panic. Particularly avoid his getting a chance to grip you. Stay behind him until he is towable.

When he is ready to be towed, hand him a stick, snorkel, or towel and tow him along, benefiting from his own active assistance and reducing the hazard of being grabbed.

Rescuing a Panicked Victim: The risks in saving a panicked victim are very great for both victim and rescuer. Stay behind the victim, out of his reach. If he grabs you, his instinct will be to climb on you to raise his head above water. In this instance you should submerge, since he does not wish to go down again and will automatically attempt to stay above water and will disengage himself from you.

When you are again free of him, grasp him by the legs, turn him so that when you surface he is in front of you, facing away from you.

Jettison his belt. Now you can take further rescue measures.

Breaking a Front Headlock: If the victim has a front headlock on you, first submerge. If he still holds on, grab his lower arm by the wrist and elbow. Turn your head to the side and push upward. The result will be that you will descend and free yourself.

Another method of getting free of a headlock is to grab the victim at the hip, pushing outward and upward, turning your head to the side. This should free you. An excellent rule to follow in freeing yourself is *sink—think—act.* Sinking is the very thing the victim does not wish to do.

Breaking a Hold from the Rear: If the victim has a grip on you from behind, sink. Grab the victim's lower arm at the wrist and elbow, push his elbow up and wrist down. This will free you but allow you to maintain contact with the victim.

Turn him away from you.

Jettison his weight belt as you ascend.

Rescuing a Victim Wearing a Tank: Approach the victim from the rear and grasp his arms. Submerge and inflate his vest or safety float. Dump his weight belt by pulling the quick-release strap. When you surface him, remove his mask and mouthpiece. Keep his head out of the water. If circumstances permit, retain his breathing apparatus for buoyancy (though his inflated vest, or even wet suit, should suffice). *Act fast!* Retain your mouthpiece and continue breathing with your air rig, as you will be submerged part of the time. Don't inflate your own inflatable safety float unless you are exhausted.

Get the victim on his back to keep his head above the water. To do this, grasp the tank by the valve with one hand and the bottom of the tank with the other, pushing up the bottom until the wearer is horizontal. The rescuer is now on his back, with his legs grasping the victim's tank, keeping a good grip on the tank valve to prevent the victim from breaking away, panicking, and grabbing the rescuer. In this manner, if the victim does turn, the rescuer can roll with him. The victim is then face down in the water with the rescuer on top. If the victim is thrashing uncontrollably with his head under, he will soon become unconscious and easier to handle. Do all you can to calm the victim with words of reassurance. Talk about any subject but the situation at hand to distract him from his enormous sense of peril.

Persuade him to help by using his fins and keeping himself horizontal. With one hand keep the victim's chin out of the water. Once the victim recognizes that he is in good hands and the rescuer has won his confidence, his panic should disappear and he will cooperate.

Another method of propelling a victim wearing a tank is to grasp the tank valve in one hand, swim on your side, using a scissor kick or trudgen kick, supporting the victim's tank on your hip.

Should You Ditch Victim's Breathing Apparatus? Whether or not you should depends on the circumstances. Although the victim has ceased to use his air supply the tank is a convenient handhold for the rescuer. It also provides some buoyancy when empty (see previous section).

Should Rescuer Continue Using His Own Tank? Retention of his own tank by the rescuer depends on the circumstances. In case of a foreseeable long tow home and/or the rescuer's air supply is low, it may be wise to jettison all breathing gear to minimize encumbrances in the performance of rescue.

Rescue by a Snorkeler of a Snorkeler: Make your rescue without the encumbrance of mask and snorkel. During the rescue, the victim's snorkel should be removed because the victim will be floating on his back. His mask should be removed to free his nose for breathing.

Using a Float for Towing the Victim: During all dive excursions include as part of your equipment a flotation device such as a good inner tube anchored near the dive site. It will serve as a resting station and valuable rescue device. If the float is available for rescue, tow the stricken diver to it—after having inflated his safety device and jettisoned his weight belt. Move him onto the float so that his arms hang loosely over the side and his nose and mouth are out of the water. Then grasp the victim by the arm and tow. Keep your mask on and continue using your breathing apparatus or snorkel as circumstances dictate.

ARTIFICIAL RESPIRATION

Tube Method of Artificial Respiration While Towing Victim to Safety: If breathing has stopped you can start artificial respiration at once with the tube method if feasible while towing him. The procedure may seem almost impossible in mid-towage but it's worth a try if you can save a life.

Make certain that the victim is well supported on the rescue float and that his nose and mouth are out of the water.

Cut or break off your snorkel just below the mouthpiece so that you have a straight tube left.

Put your finger in the victim's mouth and slide the tube past his tongue and down his throat to the trachea. You can then remove any foreign matter from his mouth.

Keep his chin up and forward to prevent obstruction of the airway.

Seal off the victim's nose and mouth with your hands.

Take a deep breath, then exhale into the tube to blow up his lungs. Allow him to exhale automatically. Blow again, filling his lungs with your breath each time. Repeat rapidly the first minute, then follow the procedure at a rhythmic normal breathing rate for the next 30 minutes or so.

Waste no time at all getting started. Don't bother with pulse or heartbeat check—get right to the artificial respiration.

Notes on Artificial Respiration: If the victim has stopped breathing, start artificial respiration at once. Seconds count. Make certain his air passage is clear, then start artificial respiration and don't stop. Send someone for a doctor but continue artificial respiration without interruption. Watch to see that the victim does not choke on regurgitated material.

In the absence of equipment or of help from a second person, regardless of the cause of cessation of breathing, the mouth-to-mouth (or mouth-to-nose) technique of artificial respiration is the most practical method for emergency ventilation of an individual of any age who has stopped breathing.

Where there is evidence that breathing has stopped for any reason, *start artificial respiration at the earliest possible moment.*

The mouth-to-mouth (or mouth-to-nose) technique has the advantage of providing pressure to inflate the victim's lungs immediately. It also enables the rescuer to obtain more accurate information on the volume, pressure, and timing of efforts needed to inflate the victim's lungs than is afforded by other methods.

When a person is unconscious and not breathing, the base of the tongue tends to press against and block the upper air passageway. The procedures described below should provide for an open air passageway when a lone rescuer must perform artificial respiration.

Mouth-to-Mouth (Mouth-to-Nose) Method of Artificial Respiration: If there is foreign matter visible in the mouth, wipe it out quickly with your fingers or a cloth wrapped around your fingers.

The most important factors in keeping the airway passage open are to tilt the head back so that the chin is pointing upward and to pull or push the jaw into a jutting-out position.

Remember that if the airway is not open between the mouth and lungs, efforts at mouth-to-mouth resuscitation will be useless. Tilt that head back firmly!

These maneuvers should relieve obstruction of the airway by moving the base of the tongue away from the back of the throat.

Open your mouth wide and place it tightly over the victim's mouth. At the same time pinch the victim's nostrils shut or close the nostrils with your cheek or fingers. Or close the victim's mouth and place your mouth over the nose. Blow into the victim's mouth or nose. (Air may be blown through the victim's teeth, even though they may be clenched.)

The first blowing efforts should determine whether or not obstruction exists.

Remove your mouth, turn your head to the side, and listen for the return rush of air that indicates air exchange and be sure the victim's chest, not stomach, is moving with each breath. Repeat the blowing effort. For an adult, blow vigorously at the rate of about 12 breaths per minute. For a child, take relatively shallow breaths, appropriate for the child's size, at the rate of about 20 per minute.

If you are not getting air exchange, recheck the head and jaw position. If you still do not get air exchange, quickly turn the victim on his side and administer several sharp blows between the shoulder blades in the hope of dislodging any obstruction. Again sweep your fingers through the victim's mouth to remove foreign matter.

Those who do not wish to come in contact with the person may hold a lightweight cloth over the victim's mouth or nose and breathe through it. The cloth does not greatly affect the exchange of air.

Evaporation of water from the victim's skin will result in lowering still further a body temperature that may already be dangerously low. It is imperative, therefore, to keep the victim from becoming chilled. See that this is done without interrupting artificial respiration.

Related Information: Time your efforts to coincide with the first attempt of the victim to breathe for himself. If vomiting occurs, quickly turn the victim on his side, wipe out the mouth, and then reposition him.

Normally, recovery should be rapid, except when the victim has suffered electric shock, drug poisoning, or carbon monoxide poisoning. In these instances, nerves and muscles controlling the breathing system are paralyzed or deeply depressed, or the carbon monoxide has displaced oxygen in the bloodstream over a period of time. When these cases are encountered, artificial respiration must often be carried on for long periods.

When a victim is revived, he should be kept as quiet as possible until he is breathing regularly. He should be kept covered and otherwise treated for shock until suitable transportation is available—if he must be moved.

Artificial respiration should be continued until the victim begins to breathe for himself, or until a physician pronounces the victim dead, or until the person appears to be dead beyond any reasonable doubt.

A doctor's care is necessary during the recovery period, as respiratory and other disturbances may develop as an aftermath.

12

YACHTING, SEAMANSHIP, AND DIVING

Not all diving is near shore and beach. Some of the best exploration is found from one hour to a day's journey offshore. Trips to far-out reefs and wrecks require convenient surface transportation. Whatever else you call a diver, he is, to some degree, also a sailor. At least he should be. And it should be the other way around. Boatowners and skippers should seriously consider learning to dive for work and pleasure.* Think of the money one can save on boat haulouts. The material in this chapter is for those who own or plan to own a boat or who plan to charter a bare boat.

SOUND SEAMANSHIP

We humans are land creatures and we know that inevitably we face risks when venturing into one of the other elements, so we need hardly belabor the point of "safety first." All experienced seafarers accord a high place to sound seamanship, and this includes

---

*"A sailor who never dives is like the driver of a Paris autobus who passes the Louvre every day but has never been inside."—Jacques Yves Cousteau

proper care to safeguard the craft and those aboard her. Sound yachting is as much to your benefit as sound diving.

Training in Seamanship: If you or your dive companions lack experience in seamanship, I'd advise you, particularly on long runs, to hire a boat manned by a professional, or otherwise experienced, skipper. The first step to being a good skipper of your own boat is to enroll in the course given by either the United States Power Squadron or the Coast Guard Auxiliary. With successful completion of either of these excellent training programs you should be ready to handle your boat skillfully.

CHARTERING A BOAT

Go to a reputable charter agent or broker. He has an obligation to help you and the owner. The terms of chartering are clearly spelled out in the Yacht Party Charter Agreement. These terms cover delivery and redelivery of the boat, crew, insurance, accidents, running expenses, navigation limits, parts replacements, restricted use, nonassignment of the charter agreement, charter authority over crew, defaults, brokerage fees, disputes, and others. Know what gear you will need, and consider whatever else the broker suggests. Know the limitations of your crew, but be sure each of its members is reliable. You can charter a boat for periods of various lengths. With a long period you may get an option to buy. Charter-before-buying is a sensible way to find out how suitable your boat is for your purposes, especially if diving will occupy most of your time afloat.

BUYING YOUR OWN BOAT FOR DIVING

Shopping: Whether buying a new or used boat, plan to have someone along who knows boats.

Insurance: Always obtain insurance coverage for your boat. Call a good marine insurance broker.

Financing Your Boat: Bank financing of boats is common today. Banks usually require a down payment of one-third the cost with the balance due over a 3-year-period, with no penalty for paying the note ahead of schedule. By financing directly through a dealer, payments can be stretched to 5 years with the same down payment. Insurance costs can be included in the purchase price. Financing can also be obtained for motors, trailers, and maintenance. Bear in mind that as long as you possess a boat there will be operating upkeep, maintenance, storage, dockage, and equipment costs. Before buying be sure your budget can sustain these anticipated obligations.

Length: A boat 16 to 18 feet in length from stem to stern with a wide beam should be large enough to carry four fully geared passengers for air diving, or a total weight of 1600 pounds.

Beam: Wide enough to be steered in choppy water or heavy seas. Look for good, sturdy construction.

Transom: About 18 inches out of the water.

Speed and Power: Up to 20 miles per hour. Select a motor, recommended by a boat manufacturer, with enough horsepower for a planing speed, say 45 horsepower.

Motor: For diving purposes an outboard motor, or better still, an outboard-inboard, rather than an inboard, is recommended. Following are some of the advantages of an outboard over an inboard:
An outboard weighs at least 50 percent less than its inboard counterpart.
Its design is simpler.
It is less expensive.
It is more easily removed for minor repairs, overhaul, and storage.
It presents no fire hazard.
It is smaller per equal horsepower rating than the inboard.
Most outboard boats are trailable.

Being of 2-cycle design, the outboard can take larger periods of rpm operation without being easily damaged.

Although it uses more fuel per hour because of its 2-cycle design, it gets more mileage per gallon because of its lighter weight.

Outboard hulls have no underwater hull obstructions such as the strut, propeller shaft, and rudder of an inboard.

With its tilt adjustment feature the outboard can cruise in shallow waters, close to reefs without hitting bottom or other obstructions, making possible the discovery of many good dive locations.

An outboard can be tilted out of the water and your boat can easily be beached.

The steering mechanism of an outboard is simpler and more responsive to controls owing to the thrust of the propeller, which aids in the steering function.

The outboard-inboard has all the advantages of outboard flexibility combined with inboard efficiency. A particularly attractive feature is that the drive unit will automatically swing up if it strikes an underwater obstruction.

Range: At least 100 miles without refueling, allowing trips up to 25 to 30 miles offshore with enough gas left to compensate for rough water or errors in navigation. Be sure to ask whoever sells you a boat about gas consumption, capacity of fuel supply, and the weight of extra gas. Make a practice of logging known distances in nautical miles; divide the distance by the number of gallons of fuel used, and keep records of actual miles per gallon.

Storage: There should be enough room under the seats and behind the bulkhead to store gear without clutter. Reserve a watertight storage cabinet for dry gear. For example, if a seat has tubular legs remove them and use the space under the seat for plywood cabinets.

Floors and Cockpit: Nonskid, flat floors with an area of 6 feet by 10 feet. A cockpit cover (canvas or hardtop) is essential for protecting personnel and equipment.

Galley: The kind of galley equipment you install on a dive cruise boat depends on space, safety, and finally your personal preferences. Alcohol stoves have been favored for years because of the safety factor. If alcohol spills and catches fire, the flames can be extinguished with water, which is not so with gasoline or kerosene. Select a stove with a sea rail or other pot-holding device to keep cooking containers in place when the boat rolls or pitches.

Bottom: A double bottom can ensure a boat's chances of staying afloat should it suffer damage from ramming jagged rock or coral.

Hull Surfaces: A boat should have a smooth surface with no protruding hardware, which might snag exposure suits and other diving equipment.

Pumps: Have a bilge pump aboard.

Freeboard: A boat should be low to the water to facilitate climbing in and out with diving gear as well as the hauling of equipment over the side.

Entry and Exit: A platform built onto the stern of a boat a few inches below the surface of the water is superior to a boarding ladder. When reentering the boat you can place your rig on the platform, which also makes a good climbing platform. A disadvantage of most manufactured boarding ladders is that they are not designed for swim fins, so the lower rungs should be angled away from the hull to permit some room for fins. The bottom rung should be at least 20 inches below the surface of the water. The best tactic when about to board by ladder is to doff your fins and hand them to your topside tender or toss them on board. The ladder top should have hand holds high enough above the rail so that a diver climbing aboard wearing a tank can pull himself up.

Navigation Equipment: A pair of good binoculars, a time-speed distance calculator, a course protractor or parallel ruler, a sharp pencil, an eraser, a compass, and area charts are the basic navigating tools.

Radio Communication: Keep a 2-way radio on board for expeditions in excess of 20 miles. A marine radio telephone is your hot line for information and assistance. One recent model is a small boatman's dream. It is factory pretuned and can be installed in minutes. With it you can send and receive messages on 3 channels within a 30-mile range.

Depth Finder: This accessory bounces high-frequency waves off the bottom and measures the time it takes for the echo to return. This is a handy aid to locating schools of fish, wrecks, and shallow bottoms in time to prevent running aground. Be sure you have at least 20, even 40, amps of available generator power for operating the depth finder and other gear.

Tachometer: A tachometer measures the number of revolutions per minute (rpm) of the outboard motor. As such, it acts as a counting check on performance. Its usefulness for all types of outboard owners is obvious. You can spot trouble months before it develops into something serious and, in the process, avoid a major repair bill.

Construction Material of Boats: Whether the boat you buy or charter is of aluminum, Fiberglas, or wood depends on your personal taste. An inflatable rubber boat is suitable for short-range, close-in work for a couple of divers.

Trailability: For the mobility that divers want for fullest enjoyment, your boat should be conveniently trailable to jumping-off points for dive expeditions. Good trailability is another advantage of the outboard over the inboard.

Type and Size of Anchor: The kind and size of the anchor you carry, as well as how much line, will depend on a number of factors:

1. The weight and length of your boat.
2. Her windage, or resistance to the wind caused by freeboard, cabin house, and rigging.
3. The amount of tide and current in your area.

4. The number of protective harbors or landfalls your area affords.
5. The average depth of water of the area.
6. The kind of bottom.

For small craft, any type of anchor patented since World War II is appropriate. Keep two anchors on board. A 24-35 pound Northill for rocky areas and a Danforth for sandy bottoms. Do not use the kedge type. In nautical lingo, anchors and related anchor lines are referred to as "ground tackle."

ANCHORING TECHNIQUES

Except for your float and BC vest, your boat is probably your only refuge when diving far from shore. In emergencies you will need it for rescue, rest, medical attention, and transportation homeward. Moor your craft close to the planned dive site. Assurance of your boat's whereabouts may depend on your skill in the execution of anchoring techniques. Master them.

Navigational charts covering the area of your anchorage will identify bottom conditions—type of bottom and how well your anchor will hold. Here are the types of bottom you will encounter and their characteristics.

Type	Characteristics
Firm sand	Excellent and consistent
Clay	Excellent if very dense; if plastic enough use good anchor engagement
Sticky	Good
Loose sand	Fair, if anchor engages deeply
Soft mud or silt	Questionable
Rock	No good unless anchor hooks under or in a crevice
Grass	Questionable; usually prevents engagement

Try to pick an anchorage without excessive current. If the wind and currents are from opposite directions, there is a good chance that the anchor line is highly susceptible to fouling.

When near other boats it is always best to keep ample distance in case of a swing of your boat or someone else's. One technique often used by diving teams is to drop one anchor forward and one aft, especially when leaving a boat totally unmanned. This technique supposedly has an added advantage of giving the diver a constant directional reference if the compass direction of the anchor lines is known in advance. *Caution:* Use the double-anchor technique only in predictably calm, flat water, unchanging wind and current directions, and only when you are reasonably sure that other anchored boats will not collide with you because of their swing. When one vessel is double-anchored in the vicinity of another that isn't, chances of collision are good. Also, with anchors fore and aft, a stiff breeze or current from abeam striking broadside can create havoc with the vessel and its passengers. With dislodgment of anchors the boat can run aground, ram a reef, float away, or collide with another vessel.

When selecting a spot to anchor, keep well out of channels and sea lanes, and be sure you have plenty of room to swing in all directions without hitting other boats or obstructions. Study the effects of wind and currents on your boat or others in the vicinity to determine the eventual lie of your boat after the drop.

Make sure the anchor line is properly fastened to a suitable fitting on your boat. Avoid entangling yourself in the anchor line.

Drop the anchor (never throw it) as your boat reaches a standstill just before it gathers sternway. Be sure the anchor line is untangled so as to drop the anchor crown first. Then as the boat backs slowly, pay out the line, hand over hand. When the line is payed out, snub it (yank it) to allow the anchor to get a good hold on the bottom.

Another technique for setting the anchor after the line is down and payed out is to put a couple of turns around a Samson post or a forward cleat and put the engine in reverse. Make sure the line is securely fastened and stop the engine. To find out if the anchor is holding, pull on the line. If the line comes to you, the anchor has not set; if the line is taut and pulls you, the anchor is set. Since you are on a diving trip, if you have trouble anchoring, one diver should submerge to the anchor to set it properly.

For boats with an over-all length of less thn 20 feet, an anchor line of 100 feet is recomended for a light anchor or 150 feet for a heavy anchor, with a diameter of ⅜ inch if nylon and ½ inch if of first-class manila.

RECOMMENDED ANCHOR LINES FOR OTHER POWER CRAFT

Dimensions	Anchor	20'–25'	25'–30'	30'–40'	40'–50'	50'–65'
Length of	Light	100'	100'	125'	150'	180'
Anchor Lines	Heavy	150'	180'	200'	250'	300'
Diameter	Light	⅜"	½"	9/16"	¾"	⅞"
if Nylon	Heavy	½"	9/16"	¾"	1"	1⅛"
Diameter if	Light	½"	⅝"	¾"	1"	1¼"
1st-Class	Heavy	⅝"	¾"	1"	1⅜"	1½"
Manila						

How to Fasten Anchor Line: The anchor line may be made fast to the anchor ring by a fisherman's bend, but it is better to use an eye splice with a metal thimble and a shackle, which will reduce chafe. The pin in the shackle should be tied with a heavy string so that it will not back out or unscrew itself.

Anchor Cable Length: A length of 7 to 8 times the depth gives good holding power. In nautical terminology you would then say the anchor has a scope of 7 or 8, meaning 7 or 8 times the depth. For example, with a depth of 10 feet a scope of 8 calls for 80 feet of anchor line. With a scope of 8, if the anchor still drags, you have no business being out, as you are probably up against severe weather conditions. For small craft under 20 feet use ⅜-inch nylon or ½-inch manila line. Incidentally, have enough line available to increase your scope for possible heavy seas. Light ⅜-inch nylon is the best kind of rope if you're planning to use an anchor in extremely deep water and you need a lot of scope, because the ⅜-inch nylon apparently has the strength equal to 4000 pounds. The first 20 feet of anchor line should be of $^3/_{16}$-inch anchor chain attached to the anchor. Rope can chafe on jagged coral reefs, but chain will not. The weight of the chain also helps set the anchor, for the chain will sink despite current action and hold the shank parallel to the bottom. Chain also diminishes the tugging effect of heavy swells. In any event, examine your anchor line frequently against wear and tear.

Weighing Anchor: Make sure the water is clear of personnel, start the engine, and under power run the boat up to the anchor, taking line as you approach. Break out the anchor by whipping the line up and down, and move slowly to prevent the anchor flukes from banging the hull. Wash off the anchor to avoid bringing mud on board. Secure the anchor on the deck; never leave an anchor loose on deck.

A first check against the drifting of an anchored boat is to take a bearing on two identifiable objects on shore (like church steeples) by sighting them in range over another object in front of them. Recheck bearings later. If the ranges change, the boat is dragging anchor. The local object picked should be 90 degrees away from you.

Make sure you recheck your position about fifteen minutes after setting the anchor and periodically thereafter. If you are drifting, your anchor is probably badly engaged, which sometimes happens when a turn of the line or chain catches one of the anchor's flukes and pulls it out of the bottom.

Trip Line: When anchored on a rocky or coral bottom, have a trip line on the anchor attached to the anchor crown. The trip line should be a little longer than the depth of the water and tied to a float. When ready to lower the anchor, pay out this line with the anchor rode (line) and secure it on the deck after the anchor is set. If when you weigh anchor it refuses to budge, a good tug on the trip line is usually all that is necessary to lift it out. If it still won't budge, send a diver down to dislodge it.

Remember to keep your craft free to cast off immediately should there be an occasion to recover a diver in difficulty. Try to warn all persons in the water to stay clear of engine and boat.

Boat Maintenance: Keep your boat clean. Hose off salt water. Wax and polish hull and hardware surfaces. Keep all moving parts lubricated. Keep the boat dry in port.

If your boat is small enough, haul it out to drydock once a month and clean the bottom. Do this job while the boat is still wet. Once dried, a fouled bottom is harder to clean.

For engine care, always follow the manufacturer's recommendations.

Pre-cruise Safety Checklist:

1. Do you have on board and in working order lights, bells, whistles, fire extinguishers, and lifesaving devices required by the Coast Guard? Have you checked to see if your equipment meets current Coast Guard requirements for a boat of your class?
2. Is an anchor on board, attached to a line, the line attached to boat? Extra line? Mooring lines? Extra anchor?
3. Is a corrected compass properly installed?
4. Are all necessary Government Navigational Charts on board?
5. Are such items as a flashlight, tool kit, bilge pump, bailer, and paddle on board?
6. Have expected weather conditions been checked?
7. Has someone on shore been told your destination and arrival time?
8. Has the compass been checked and a course laid out?
9. Have the lights and motor been tested?
10. Have all life preservers been checked? Are there enough of them?
11. Is there a first-aid kit at hand? Stocked?
12. Do you have sufficient fuel and oil supplies?
13. Is dive gear aboard and secured?
14. Is there a diver's flag aboard?
15. Are all lines neatly coiled?

Suggested List of Spare Parts to Take on Boat: Disregard those items in the following list not applicable to your type of boat.

Set of plugs
Fuel filter gasket
Pump and generator belt
Ignition coil
Condenser
Distributor cap
Rust solvent
Extra light bulbs

Electric wire tape
Fuel pump gasket
Carburetor flange gasket
Water pump repair kit
Breaker point set
Rotor
Tube of Permatex Form-a-Gasket
Spool of insulated wire

Suggested Tools to Take on Board:

Set of screw drivers
Wrenches 7/16 in. to 1 in.
    in size
Crescent wrenches
Pliers
Hammers
Knife

Cutting pliers
Spark-plug wrench
Breaker point file
Hack saw
Can of oil
Empty oil can

Note: Protect all tools against exposure by coating them with oil and wrapping them in oil cloth.

NAVIGATION

Where Am I? How to Fix a Position: Tools of navigation include a magnetic compass and nautical charts. Used with a compass, charts will pinpoint a location by means of *bearings,* the straight-line direction of distant objects. Compass and chart are interrelated by means of the *compass rose* found on every official nautical chart.

Compass readings are to be taken on every official nautical chart.

Compass readings are to be taken after a factor called *deviation* is compensated for and correction is made from a factor known as *variation.* Although I discussed earlier the fundamentals of compasses and how they are used any discussion of so vital a science as navigation calls for a review and further elaboration. The text here is not meant to be a course of instruction in navigating. Any diver who takes on the responsibility of operating a boat with some degree of frequency is duty bound to seek thorough instruction in either the Power Squadron or the Coast Guard Auxiliary schools, or by his own readings on the subject bolstered by practical experience. All I can offer here are some handy essentials should you need to refer to them from time to time.

The Magnetic Compass: The safety of a yacht and her party is the sole and inescapable responsibility of the owner or appointed skipper. Always carry a compass (not to be confused with a diver's underwater compass, discussed in Chapter 4). Keep it secured against rolling away and breaking. Trust it. All types of magnetic compasses have the following general characteristics:

The magnetized compass needles align themselves with the earth's magnetic field.

The needles are fastened to a card that is in the form either of a disc or a cylinder and is marked with the cardinal points (that is, the main directions) of the compass: north, east, south, and west.

The card and needles are supported on a pivot. No matter how the ship or boat swings, the card is free to rotate until it has re-aligned itself with the magnetic north pole.

The moving parts of the compass are contained in a liquid which buoys them up and takes some of the load off the pivot, thus reducing the friction and letting the card turn more easily toward the north. At the same time, the liquid slows the swing of the card and brings it to rest more quickly. A special oil called Varsol is in common use as a damping fluid.

The moving parts are contained in a bowl or similar housing provided with a window through which the compass card may be seen. Ships' compasses usually have a flat glass top for all-around visibility and for taking bearings. Smallboat compasses often have spherical tops, so that courses can be read more easily from the smaller compass cards.

In the window of the compass, or marked on the compass bowl, is a line called the lubber's line, which agrees with the fore-and-aft line of the ship or boat. Thus, by noting the compass card direction lined up with the lubber's line, one can tell in what direction the ship is headed.

What You need to Know Before Using a Compass: Compass error: The magnetic compass does not point directly north most of the time. Usually there is a difference of several degrees. This difference is known as the compass error and is made up of *variation* and *deviation.* The variation of a compass arises from the fact that the magnetic north pole and the true, or geographic, north pole are not the same. The magnetic field of the earth also varies from place to place and from year to year; hence the needle follows the magnetic field and "varies" from the real north. Variation is marked on charts; hence a chart of the locality must always be used when computing the compass course or the true course.

The *deviation* of a compass is due to the presence of metal objects around the compass, such as the iron and steel of the ship, equipment, and so forth. A knife in the pocket of the helmsman can cause the compass to deviate. (Never bring a metal object near a compass. And always be sure a boat is 100 yards or more from a ship before setting a magnetic boat-compass course.) It is different for different headings of the ship since the metal is distributed in different amounts over the length and breadth of the ship or boat. Before she puts to sea she is swung through the complete circle from 0 to 360, and the amount of her compass deviation is noted at every 15° or 30°. Put your boat through a number of courses the direction of which can be determined by your chart. Steer the boat over these courses and note the direction shown by the compass. For example, choose two points on the chart which are directly North and South of each other. The points could be lighthouses or buoys, anything that is readily distinguishable. Steer this course. Suppose the compass shows North by East. Note the direction shown. Repeat this every 15° or 30°, noting down what the compass shows. By comparing the compass headings with the actual magnetic courses shown by the chart, you can readily determine your compass deviation on various headings. Compile your notes on a table such as the one below and mount it near the compass.

SAMPLE DEVIATION TABLE*

Ship's Heading psc †	DEV	Ship's Heading psc †	DEV	Ship's Heading psc †	DEV
000	14 W	120	15 E	240	4 E
015	10 W	135	16 E	255	1 W
030	5 W	150	12 E	270	7 W
045	1 W	165	12 E	285	12 W
060	2 E	180	13 E	300	15 W
075	5 E	195	14 E	315	19 W
090	7 E	210	12 E	330	19 W
105	9 E	225	9 E	345	17 W
				360 (000)	14 W

*Values are excessive for a properly compensated compass should not have deviation greater than 6.
† Per standard compass.

True Course True course is the track of the ship or boat in degrees measured from true north in a clockwise direction.

Magnetic Course: Magnetic course is the track of the ship in relation to the directions of the magnetic lines of force around the earth. Correcting the magnetic course for variation gives the true course. Applying the variation to the true course gives the magnetic course.

Compass Course: Compass course is the reading of a particular ship or boat compass, that is, the course the compass actually shows. Correcting the compass course for deviation gives the magnetic course; correcting the magnetic course for variation gives the true course. The process of adjusting for both deviation and variation is called correcting.

Correcting for deviation and variation: Deviation and variation cause the compass to turn somewhat to the east or west of true north. The problem is to find out how much, and whether both pull the compass in the same direction, in which case their effect is a combination of the two forces: If they pull in opposite directions, the effect of one cancels the other to some extent.

The following example shows how to correct a compass course.

A ship or boat is following a compass course of 270°. What is the true course? First we must correct for deviation, then for variation.

1. The deviation card shows that the deviation for the ship's heading psc (per standard compass) 270° is 7° west.

2. From a chart of the vicinity (or from one's own knowledge or memory) we find the variation. Assume it is 12° east.

3. The information so obtained is written down in a table as follows:

Compass Course	Deviation	Magnetic Course	Variation	True Course	Total Error
270°	7°W		12°E		

4. To find the true course the 7°W deviation is subtracted from the compass course (270°) which gives a magnetic course of 263°. The variation of 12°E is then added to the magnetic course, giving the true course of 275°. The total compass error is 5°E, which is the difference between the 7°W and the 12°E. But how to decide whether to add or subtract the deviation or variation?

The rule to follow when correcting, that is, going from compass course to true course, is: When correcting, *add* easterly errors and *subtract* westerly errors. For more on this re-read What Is the Variation?, page 58.

Compass Course	Deviation	Magnetic Course	Variation	True Course	Total Error
270°	7°W	263°	12°E	275°	5°

Note that true differs from magnetic by the amount of variation, and that magnetic differs from compass by the amount of deviation.

An easy way to remember the setup of the table given here is to use the phrase: "Can Dead Men Vote Twice?" The first letter in each word corresponds to the first letter in the headings of the table: Compass, Deviation, Magnetic, Variation, and True, respectively.

How to Determine a Course: To go from, say, Point A to Point B draw a straight line on your chart between the two. Using parallel rules this line is "walked over" to the compass rose and drawn through its center to the inner circle where magnetic degrees are shown. To the degree figure your rule touches add or subtract the deviation and variation corrections. The result is the true course you will steer by compass to reach Point B.

Bearings: A bearing is an imaginary line drawn, pointed, or taken from one object to another. For accurate navigation it is too vague to say that an object, ship, or lighthouse is "off there," or "over to the right," or "almost due west." Accordingly, a system of *true* and *relative* bearings has been worked out to reduce directions to bearings which are measured in degrees.

True bearings are those based, like the compass, on a circle of degrees with north as 000° (or 360°), east as 090°, south as 180°, and west as 270°. Remember that in navigation all circles are customarily divided for measurement purposes into 360°.

Relative bearings are those based on a circle drawn around the ship itself, with the bow taken as 000°, the starboard beam as 090°, the stern as 180°, and the port beam as 270°. Thus, if a ship is on a course due north (000°), another ship sighted dead ahead would bear 000° *true* and 000° *relative*. But if the ship were on a course due east, the object would bear 090° *true* but would still be dead ahead or 000° *relative*.

True bearings are based on the geography of the earth; *relative* bearings are relative to the ship itself.

More About Relative Bearings: Relative bearings are those based on a vessel at the point of reference. The bow of the vessel is taken as 000° regardless of what its course or geographic direction may be. Relative bearings are for use wherever there is no compass so there must be some way for them to point out where objects lie, and this method must be fast, accurate, and unmistakable. Irretrievable time could be lost if a man reported a distressed diver "off to the right." "Off to the right" could leave his companions wondering if the man meant his right, or the ship's starboard, or off to the right of the bow, the beam, or the stern.

On Coast Guard ships the standard method of reporting the location of objects around a ship is to use relative bearings in degrees from the bow of the ship. It is also the standard method used by most well-trained boatmen. The ship or boat is assumed to be in the center of a 360° circle. Hence an object dead ahead would be "Object zero-zero-zero" (which is the same as 000°). To avoid misunderstandings always use three digits. Say, "Ship zero-four-five." Never say, "Ship bearing forty-five degrees." With practice a man quickly learns to estimate the relative bearings closely and can report objects in such a way that others can locate them immediately.

Taking True Bearings: True bearings can be obtained directly from a magnetic compass so situated as to make bearings on outside objects possible.

Taking a Cross-Bearing: Sight over your compass at a distant object, say a water tower on the shore. Note down the degrees on the sight line, and using the deviation card plus the compass rose on your chart, convert to a true bearing, 085°. With the parallel rules draw a line on the chart through the tower at an angle of 080° true. This is a *line of position,* and your boat is located somewhere along the line. But where? To find out select another object on the horizon, say a church steeple to the north. Take another reading over the compass, convert again, and draw the line on the chart 015° true. Your boat is located where the two lines cross. You can be even more thorough by selecting a third object.

How to Determine a Line of Position by the "Range": When two objects, say a buoy and a water tower, line up one behind the other in the eye of a distant observer, they are described as "in range." On a chart, extend a line through the two; the observer's position is at some point along the line. Find a second range, say at 90° from the first range, and cross the lines to determine position.

General Yachting Practice: Use up-to-date charts. Keep a log of your trip. Learn and log your boat's performance, speeds, range, and gas consumption. Protect charts and navigational data against soakage, preferably by covering them in plastic bags. Keep at least 50 percent fuel reserve over and above the need of every day. Don't relax your lookout while at the helm. If caught in a fog and in doubt of your position, anchor. Turn off the engine and give sound signals, such as the rapid ringing of a bell once every minute. If you are still underway in fog, sound your horn. If your boat is under 26 feet, you are not required to carry a bell, but you can improvise a sound. Familiarize all your passengers with the boat and boat terminology. Demonstrate the use of the life preservers and fire extinguishers to all. Diving, no less than cruising, should not be carried on so long that the crew is overly exhausted for the voyage home. Surfacing from a dive does not constitute a safe homecoming until the boat is navigated safely back to its home port. Get in before dark.

Teach at least one guest how to manage should you, the skipper, become incapacitated.

Drill all youngsters in their duties and responsibilities.

When wearing dive gear, stay put. Don't move around. Put your fins on last.

Brief everyone on accident, fire, and survival procedures.

Permit no dives except when your boat is at anchor with the motor off—and the key out of the ignition, if you please. Have a spare key on board.

On larger vessels on long-range trips, keep foul-weather gear and warm, dry clothing aboard for all guests.

Instruct guests not to throw objects of any size overboard. Tell them which is the windward and which is the leeward side of the boat. Windward is the side from which the wind is blowing; leeward is the downwind side.

Falls are one of the greatest causes of injury on board a boat, especially with diving gear on board. Eliminate tripping hazards. Have adequate grab rails and use appropriate footwear, skid-proof, slip-proof.

Remove varnishes and oily rags to reduce fire hazards. For cooking on board, use kerosene or alcohol in a pressure stove, never gasoline.

Remember that the skipper is responsible for the safety of the boat and all aboard her. Allow nothing to distract you at any time. Be watchful of everything affecting the security of the boat and crew: weather, position, seas, movements of guests, functioning of the vessel.

If a man goes overboard, the skipper should not be the one to jump in after him except when he is the only person available.

Don't speed in congested areas like harbors or recreation sites.

Keep down your wake when passing other boats.

Keep your boat shipshape and tidy.

Distribute weight evenly to keep your boat in balance.

Carry extra gasoline only in an approved container and stowed in a safe place.

Turn off the motor when adding fuel.

Fuel tanks should be removed from the boat for refueling. No smoking during refueling.

Don't jump into the boat; step gently into the center.

Check minimum government requirements for boats and outfit yours accordingly. The Coast Guard and the state will enforce the law.

See to it that your equipment (life preservers, ring buoys, buoyant vests, fire extinguishers, etc.) meets Coast Guard specifications and clearly bears the inspector's stamp. Show passengers where they are stowed.

Be thoroughly familiar with your engine mechanism and its maintenance.

Report to the state or the Coast Guard authorities any accidents resulting in death or injury. It is mandatory to report within 5 days to the state authorities any accident resulting in property damage of $100 or more and/or in injuries incapacitating the victim 72 hours or more. Death or disappearance must be reported to authorities as soon as possible. Check your state law.

Have a good textbook or two on seamanship.

Keep a first-aid kit on board.

Never overload with passengers or excessive gear.

Lash down equipment, especially compressed air cylinders.

Stow your full cylinders apart from empties.

Avoid horseplay and excessive moving around.

Do not start your engine with divers in the water except in an emergency, but warn persons in the water to swim clear of the boat.

Have a safety man topside geared for diving in case of emergency while others are diving. Don't dive from a moving boat whether under power or with the engine stopped.

On rowboats, carry at least three oars in case one gets lost.

Separate dry gear from wet gear.

Carry plenty of spare rope coiled up neatly in readiness for quick use.

Carry a boarding ladder. The ladder should be designed to project or angle outward, away from the side of the boat by means of frames or angles. The bottom rung should be well under water.

Carry warm, dry clothing and some beach towels.

Keep your equipment dry.

Bring plenty of tools and spare parts for trouble shooting.

Boat Handling in Stormy Seas:

Secure all loose equipment.

Keep the bow or stern directly to the wind or waves.

In outboards, ride bow on.

Don't get into the trough of waves so that they pound your beam and roll you.

If taking water, bail or pump out excess to maintain stability.

Don't speed in rough water except as needed for maneuvering.

When landing, mooring, anchoring, or approaching other boats, head into the wind or current, whichever has more effect at the time.

Heading an Outboard into the Waves:

Head into the waves at a slight angle to avoid pounding.

Maintain enough power to maintain this heading because the action of waves tends to swing the boat broadside to them.

In a strong blow do not try to maintain planing speed against heavy pounding.

Entering an Inlet When a Heavy Following Sea Is Running: The action of waves may turn a boat broadside to them, which could lead to broaching (rolling over in a wave trough).

Maintain enough speed to steer under control, but don't go so fast that the boat runs down one wave and digs into the wave ahead. This could cause a boat to be "pitchpoled" and overturn.

PLANNING MEALS FOR A CRUISE

If a cruise is for several days or more, plan to take only enough perishables to last from one stop for ice to the next. Precook as much food as possible at home, and remember that your appetite will increase surprisingly on the water (see Chapter 10 for suggested foods).

BEACHING A BOAT

Study charts or use a face mask to see what kind of bottom exists at the beach. Avoid beaches with a heavy surf. As you approach the landing, drop an anchor over the stern while about 75 feet away from the shore. As the boat drifts shoreward set the anchor by placing tension on it until it holds. The stern anchor has two functions: It keeps the stern of the boat away from the beach and acts as a hauling anchor against which to pull away from the beach when getting under way.

When the boat reaches the beach, set a bow anchor ashore or tie a bowline to a sturdy log or tree on shore. Try to keep the boat off the beach as much as possible. Keep tab on the tides so that you won't be left high and dry. Move the boat out as the tide recedes.

Leaving a beach anchorage is easy. Simply haul in the bow anchor or cast off the shore mooring line, pull on the stern anchor, and when in deep enough water, start the engines. Get under way slowly, picking up your stern anchor as you go.

GETTING OUT OF TROUBLE

Out of Gas: Anchor. Borrow gas from a passing boat or get a tow. Row ashore in a dinghy or get a lift in a passing boat. If your craft is small, paddle.

Running Aground: Check the tide. If it's rising, wait for the tide to lift you off. Shift passengers and weight to heel the vessel and try reversing your motor. Get overboard and push. Use an oar or boat hook to pole off. Carry an anchor out to deep water and kedge off by pulling the anchor. Get help or a tow from a passing boat or call the Coast Guard. Often the wake created by a passing boat can lift you off.

Engine Failure: Check your fuel system for clogged air vents, fuel line, or filter, a stuck needle valve or choke. Or maybe you are just out of gas. Check ignition for fouled or cracked plugs, loose plug wires, shorting ignition wires, cracked distributor cap, bad points, bad rotor, loose plug, worn coil. It's a good idea to keep spare plugs, points, coil, and distributor cap on board.

Man Overboard: Heave a life buoy (ring buoy or floating seat-cushion type) near the victim, not at him. Keep a steady eye on him. Turn the boat in a circle, approaching the leeward side of victim. If anyone dives into the water for rescue, see to it that he is wearing a life vest and is attached to a line from the boat. Use a dinghy or boarding ladder if time permits.

Taking Water: Bail or pump at once. Look for the source of the leak. Plug as best you can.

Lost in a Fog: It will be almost impossible to take bearings once you are engulfed in a fog. Therefore, if fog is anticipated take bearings, marking your position on your chart and continue logging courses and speeds. Blow fog signals. Slow down. Keep a crew on sharp lookout as far forward as possible. Stop engines from time to time to listen for lighthouse fog signals. Take bearings on them if at all possible. Beware, however: Fog distorts sound. When heading into a harbor, head upwind of the harbor and run down to it along the shoreline. If in doubt, anchor and keep sounding fog signals.

Storm: Watch the horizon. Listen to radio reports on AM radio. When you hear static, the storm is in your area. Get home. Slow down and lash gear securely as the seas build. Wear life jackets. In larger boats, run out a drogue (a sea anchor, usually a conically shaped canvas bag) to keep the stern or bow into the seas. Attach an oil bag to the drogue or, if lacking a drogue, run out a canvas bag, even a cabin table or locker door, to the weather side of the boat. Stay off the lee shore in case of engine failure, using only enough power to maintain steerage. Use the heading that gives the easiest riding, even if you have to head into the seas.

Seasickness: Avoid alcohol, fatty foods, sweets, carbonated drinks, and orange juice. Eat solid foods, especially salty ones. Wear sunglasses. Don't read. Avoid fumes. Take antimotion pills, and don't dive for at least 3 hours after. If sick, don't go diving. Wait until you are well.

Freeing Propeller: If you heave to in shallow water your prop may become tangled or fouled in kelp or other seaweed. If so, do as follows:
Power forward, then throttle back and go into neutral. Tilt the engine out of the water and coast until stopped. Tilt the prop back into the water and throttle forward again.
If you are not then freed, repeat this process several times until you are. If this procedure fails after repeated attempts, sever entangling plants with a knife. Be sure ignition is off and stays off during this operation. For added safety to the diver below, take the key out of the ignition so that no one can inadvertently start the engine.
Should you be operating an inboard-equipped boat and become seriously entangled, stop the engines, turn off the ignition, remove the key, and send a diver down with a knife to cut away the entangling material.

Rudder Failure: Check the rudder cables, etc. If the rudder is broken, use a paddle or bucket overside toward the direction of desired turns while in motion.

Fire: Use your fire extinguisher at the base of the flame. Use water on wood or cloth fires. If the fire is in machinery, cut the fuel supply. Stop the boat to reduce the wind effect. Order all hands into life jackets. If the fire is serious, call for help. Work fast.

Distress signals: If giving distress signals by marine radio-telephone, use the "Mayday, Mayday" call followed by your emergency message. The frequency is 2182 KHC but use it only in an emergency. The VHF calling and distress frequency is 156.8 MHz. Wave the new rectangular international orange flag, the international code flags NC, or a square flag with a ball above or below it. Fire a gun. Yell, wave. Bang a pan. Light a flare. Shoot rockets. One of the best signals is an orange smoke bomb. Continue sounding distress signals or produce noise to attract attention. By day, show smoke by burning oil rags in a fireproof container. At night, if in need of rescue on a distressed vessel use flares, rescue light, or flashlights.

Towing: Use a fresh line. Toss it over to the boat to be towed. Make fast the towline to the forward cleat or bitts of the towed boat and the after cleat of the towing boat, keeping all gear out of the path of the towline. Be ready to cast off the line in an emergency. Watch that the crew avoids injury from a sudden snap of the line. Take up the line slowly and evenly when moving off. The towed boat should keep its weight aft. Minimize the steering on the towed boat. On craft larger than runabout size, keep an ax handy to cut the line quickly if anything goes wrong.

Swamping and Capsizing: If your boat starts taking on water, swamping can result. Bail fast, plug leaks, repair damage. Retrim the weight of the boat and adjust your course to minimize the effect of seas. Wear life jackets. If capsized, get your crew to pull on the gunwales in order to right the vessel. Keep gear from floating away. Stick with the vessel as long as it stays afloat; rescue is more probable. Should sinking occur, use the floating techniques unless you are (as you should be) wearing a life preserver.

Collision: In the event of collision, check damage before separating the boats involved. Both vessels should stand by to be of mutual help. If your boat has been punctured by the bow of another boat, separate the boats and nail a canvas patch over the hole, using wood strips to clamp it down. Retrim the weight of the boat to keep the worst damage above the water line, reducing seepage and facilitating your efforts to repair. Get into life jackets. If the other boat is sinking, give aid.

Lost: Attempt to reconstruct your position on the chart, recalling speeds, courses, and times. Head shoreward and when in sight of land follow the shoreland, taking soundings until a landmark is sighted. You might watch for steamers and estimate your distance from the steamer lanes. Use a transistor radio to locate a major city by rotating to the loudest signal, usually at right angles to the face of the set. Maintain a direct course toward a probable landmark. Keep a log of your course, speed, and time. Be patient. Don't panic.

A PERSONAL OBSERVATION

What to Look for When Hiring a Diving Guide: Be sure your guide knows diving, that he is an expert familiar with the local area. Check that his equipment is the best. Tell him you insist that there be good boat discipline, that equipment is safely stowed out of the way. What gearing up on board see that each of your party has a steady hold and a buddy assigned to help him. Insist on flotation devices or bring your own. The use of the latter should be the rule. Always direct your dives upcurrent and upwind of your boat. All the surfaced diver need do is drift effortlessly to the boat without overexerting, working with the elements. When going out as well as returning make it a rule of thumb to rendezvous at the anchor. For divers who overshoot the boat see that a flotation device or two have been lashed to the stern with a line of at least 50–75 feet. Such a device could prevent the loss of an exhausted diver. Exhaustion is more likely to overcome a diver when he is surfaced and struggling through heavy swells to stay afloat and get back to his boat than when at depth.

ROPE

Rope will be used for lifelines, lines linking buddies, signaling, hauling gear, directional guidance, anchoring, mooring, temporary rope ladders, towage, marking, hitching, and tying. Keep plenty of it for these many purposes.

Rope, as used on or around water, boats, and diving, is called *line*.

Shot Lines: It is a comfort to have a shot line to give you directional guidance, a point of departure, and a kind of umbilical cord of security. Shot lines should be used from a boat when diving in bad visibility, around wrecks, or to hazardous seabeds. It should be heavily weighted so that it hangs vertically in the water, resisting strong current. It should hang free, not rest on the bottom, so that it will always be taut. To set it, let it touch bottom and then lift it a few inches off the bottom. If decompression stops in deep dives are anticipated, the stop stations should be clearly marked by knots or ribbon along the line.

Buddy Line: Connect a rope to a diver by fastening it to his harness or backpack beneath the demand valve, against his back. The balance of the tether should be taken under the diver's left or right armpit, down his forearm, and wound twice around his open hand. *Not* around his wrist or forearm. Never secure it.

Type of Rope: Nylon stretches well under load and is exceptionally capable of absorbing shock. It is preferred for anchor line (also known as rode) and mooring or dock lines. If stretching is undesirable, use manila or Dacron rather than nylon. In general, nylon has greater elasticity and durability for all-purpose use.

Polypropyline is an excellent synthetic rope that floats. It is therefore ideal for towing in men overboard.

Manila is good all-around rope. If stored wet it will mildew and rot in time. Synthetic rope like nylon, Dacron, polypropyline, and polyethylene won't rot even if stored wet.

Care and Maintenance of Rope: When storing line, loop it neatly and hold it with a hitch. Rope of natural fibers should never be stored wet, as dry rot will weaken it. Inspect all lines against chafes and frays. Spread the fibers of manila rope to inspect the core. If the core is soft and black throw the rope away and get a new one. To prevent chafing and prolong the life of rope, wrap it in rags or tape where friction is likely to recur. Every "well found" (nautical term meaning well-equipped) boat should carry the following lines:

2 anchor lines
A line for towing
A line for heaving to a distressed diver or man overboard

In addition to these basic needs, plenty of line for diving purposes such as a buddy line, line for hauling gear or treasure, shot lines for decompression, lines for marker buoys should be on hand.

KNOTS

Square or Reef Knots: Probably the most useful of all knots, easily tied but tends to jam. Reliable also for packages and bundles. Don't use this knot for linking two hawsers together since it unties too easily when yanked.

Two Half Hitches: Very secure and useful for moorings and making fast to piles, spars, or stanchions. Quickly tied and reliable.

Clove Hitch: This is one of the most common hitches for making fast temporarily to spars and pilings.

Bowline, the Running Bowline, and the Bowline on a Bight:
Used for lowering a man over the side and for rescue work or tying
two lines together. The running bowline is often used for making a
good knot or for tying a package.

Sheepshank: Used to shorten a rope. This knot will hold under
tension.

Sheet or Becket Bend, Single and Double: The best knot for join-
ing two lines together. It will not slip even if there is a great difference in the sizes of the line.

Fisherman's Bend (Also Called the Anchor Bend): For securing
rope to a buoy or a hawser, also good for securing anchor lines to
anchor ring.

Figure Eight Knot: This is a stopper knot to keep rope ends from
slipping through an opening or running through a block. Does not
jam.

Rolling Hitch: Used to bend (nautical term meaning to secure or
fasten) a line to a spar or rope. Close turns up tight and take the
strain on the arrow-tipped end.

NAUTICAL CHARTS

A chart is similar to a map except that a chart is concerned with
the water and its dangers and only those landmarks that can be used
by the mariner. Most charts that concern us are small sections of the
globe flattened out by way of the method called a Mercator Projec-
tion. They are published by the National Ocean Survey (NOS) of the
United States federal government and can be obtained from it or
from marine supply stores.

Available, too, at most east-coast suppliers is the excellent nautical chart book series called the Marine Atlas Series, prepared by
William B. Matthews, Jr., and published by National Book Corpora-
tion, P. O. Box 81, Andover, Massachusetts 01810. The three cur-

rent atlases include the New England Edition, the Long Island Sound and South Shore Edition, and the New Jersey Edition. All are continually updated by professional cartographers. Considering the wealth of information they give and also the fact that each edition reproduces the equivalent of $150 worth of NOS charts, the price of $12.95 per copy is a bargain these days.

Charts furnish information necessary for safe navigation. They show bottom depths and characteristics, dangers, channels, landmarks, aids to navigation, fish-trap limits, anchorages, restricted or prohibited cable and pipeline areas, wharves, cities, etc. Nautical chart scales vary. Use the largest scale chart available in the area to be navigated. Your charts are of utmost importance as a reference (this applies to divers almost as much as to mariners). However, look to local divers or boatmen to provide you with a wealth of information about their native waters. Note down facts of particular interest on your chart.

13

WEATHER AND DIVING

Weather will often determine if, when, and possibly where you dive and what equipment you will need. Accurate weather forecasting is, therefore, vital before and during diving operations. Analyze published reports, weather maps, signals, and atmospheric conditions, then let prudence guide your actions.

The Dangers of Unfavorable Weather: The dangers of unfavorable weather lie in poor subsurface visibility, loss of contact with your buddies, turbulent waters, seasickness, possible loss of boat, gear or personnel, collisions, and injury to others.

Where to Find Weather Information: Call the nearest U.S. Weather Bureau, U.S. Coast Guard station or base, or possibly a local airport.

Consult local daily newspaper reports. Most papers publish a good general picture including wind, temperature, and atmospheric pressure data.

Listen to AM radio weather broadcasts at announced intervals. Usually static on an AM radio on board indicates a storm nearby.

Sources of Storm Warning Signals: Weather Bureau of maritime boats. Some vessels, shore, or surface stations of the U.S. Coast Guard. Yacht clubs, marinas, and other waterfront establishments.

A black pennant shown with the weather flag indicates temperature. If the black pennant is above the weather flag, temperature will rise; if below, temperature will fall.

USEFUL GUIDES FOR JUDGING STATE OF SEA AND WEATHER

SEA AND SWELL

Sea is defined as the waves caused by wind at a given place.

Swell is caused by waves formed by past wind, or wind at a distance.

Short swell: where the length or distance between each successive top of the swell is small.

Long swell: where the length or distance as above is large.

Low swell: where the height between the lowest and highest part of the swell is small.

Heavy swell: where the height as above is great.

INTERNATIONAL SEA SCALE

Scale No.	Description	Height of waves— crest to trough (in feet)
0	Calm	0
1	Smooth	0–½
2	Light	½–2
3	Moderate	2–5
4	Rough	5–9
5	Very Rough	9–15
6	High	15–24
7	Very High	24–36
8	Precipitous	over 36

Note: Numbers 4 and over—diving and use of small craft dangerous.

INTERNATIONAL SWELL SCALE

Code figure	State of the swell in the open sea	
0	None	
1	Short or average length	Low
2	Long	
3	Short	
4	Average length	Moderate height
5	Long	
6	Short	
7	Average length	Heavy
8	Long	
9	Confused	

FOG AND VISIBILITY SCALE FOR SHIPS AT SEA

Code No.	Description	Definition	
0	Dense fog	Objects not visible at	50 yards
1	Thick fog	" " " "	1 cable
2	Fog	" " " "	2 cables
3	Moderate fog	" " " "	½ mile
4	Mist or haze or very poor visibility	" " " "	1 mile
5	Poor visibility	" " " "	2 miles
6	Moderate visibility . . .	" " " "	5 miles
7	Good visibility	" " " "	10 miles
8	Very good visibility . .	" " " "	30 miles
9	Excellent visibility . . .	Objects visible more than	30 miles

WEATHER FORECASTING EQUIPMENT

A truly well-equipped diver, no less than a yachtsman, should fortify his weather prediction with the following aids, all of which can be purchased at any marine supply house.

The Barometer: The barometer is an instrument that records the rise and fall of atmospheric pressure, which indicate changes of weather as air masses approach. A rapid fall indicates a storm coming. Changes in barometric pressure are caused by factors such as air temperature, the amount of vapor in the atmosphere, and the movement of masses of air. Changes in the glass are usually so slight they may not be noticeable to the inexperienced user; therefore, tap the glass to show the trend. The tap will usually show the barometric reading rising or falling.

Portable AM Radio: For periodic reports.

Thermometer: Thermometer registers temperature readings. A drop in temperature generally means bad weather approaching.

Guest or Kenyon Weathercasters: Either of these (available at marine suppliers) are books with rotatable dials set for sky conditions, barometric changes, barometric readings, and wind direction. By combining these elements with the table in the book, you can come up with an accurate forecast.

Cloud Chart: Weather maps in newspapers usually include a cloud chart. Reference to printed reports for several days prior to setting out on a dive trip can tell you what weather is building up.

Sling Psychrometer: A pocket-size sling psychrometer is handy, although not especially required, when cruising in areas where fog is probable. It consists of two thermometers mounted so that they can be whirled about. One thermometer is wrapped in a wet cloth. When whirled, the drier the air, the faster will be the evaporation and the lower will be the temperature reading on a wet-bulb thermometer. The greater the difference in the wet- and dry-bulb temperatures, the lower the humidity and dew point. The dew point is the temperature at which moisture in the atmosphere will begin to form dew. The dew-point spread is the number of degrees between the actual temperature and the dew point. When the spread is 3 degrees or less, fog is likely.

Keeping a Weather Eye While Afloat: Keep a weather eye peeled for any of the following:

The approach of dark, threatening clouds. They may foretell the approach of a squall or a thunderstorm.

A distant but approaching thunderstorm. Lightning may be seen but no thunder heard.

Any steady increase in wind force or the height of waves or both.

Any increase in wind velocity opposite in direction to a strong tidal current. A dangerous rip current condition may form with steep waves capable of broaching a boat.

Keep checking radio weather broadcasts for any warnings that may be issued.

General Characteristics of Weather Across the Continental United States: The entire weather pattern in our latitudes tends to move roughly from west to east, covering as much as 600 miles per day but often less, particularly in the summer. Therefore, study the weather especially to the west of you because it is very likely that this will be the weather you will be getting in the next day or so.

Fair weather is usually associated with high atmospheric pressures shown on the weather map as winds blowing in a clockwise direction away from the center of a high.

Wind-Barometer Indications (United States): A high barometer reading means good weather, while a low means bad weather, but this should not be oversimplified. One must look for a trend of a barometer, whether it is rising or falling. This can be determined by noting the present reading (usually noted by manually setting the brass hand that lies over the top of the black pressure-indicating needle), then making a later reading to determine the amount of rise or fall.

Some general rules regarding barometers:

1. Barometers following winds from easterly quadrants—good chance of foul and rainy weather.

2. High barometer: wind veering clockwise to westerly quadrants.

3. Slow-rising barometer: weather should be fair. For south winds, the barometer usually falls. For north winds the barometer usually rises. A rising glass with a veering wind indicates fair weather. Falling glass with a backing (changing counterclockwise) wind usually means bad weather. Sudden rise indicates unsettled weather and often strong winds ("quick rise after low, portends a stronger blow"). A gradual, steady fall indicates rainy and unsettled weather. A rapidly falling and extremely low glass indicates foul weather and perhaps severe storms.

Two of the best guides we have for determining future weather conditions are the indications afforded by the wind and the barometer.

Winds from the east quadrants of the compass and a falling barometer indicate foul weather.

Winds shifting to the west quadrants indicate clear and fair weather.

The rapidity of a storm approaching and its intensity are indicated by the rate and the amount in the fall of the barometer.

If low barometer readings usually attend stormy weather and high barometer readings are generally associated with clear or fair weather, it follows that a falling barometer indicates precipitation and wind and a rising barometer fair weather, or the approach of fair weather.

South winds bring warmth; north winds bring cold.

East winds in the middle latitudes indicate the approach from the west of an area of low precipitation or storm area, and the west winds show that the storm area has passed to the east. The indications of the barometer generally precede the shifts of the wind.

During the cold months, when the land temperatures are below the water temperatures of the ocean, precipitation will begin along the seaboards when the wind shifts and blows steadily from the water over the land, without regard to the height of the barometer. In such cases the moisture of the warm ocean winds is condensed by the cold of the continental area. During the summer months, on the contrary, the onshore winds are not necessarily rain winds, for the reason that they are cooler than the land surface and their capture of moisture is increased by the warmth that is communicated to them by the land surface. In such cases thunderstorms commonly occur when the ocean winds are intercepted by mountain ranges or peaks. If, however, the easterly winds increase in force with a falling barometer, the approach of an area of low barometer precipitation from the west is indicated and rain will follow within a day or two.

From the Mississippi and Missouri valleys to the Atlantic coast and on the Pacific coast, rain generally begins on a falling barometer. In the Rocky Mountain and plateau districts and on the Rocky Mountain slope, precipitation seldom begins until the barometer begins to rise after a fall. This holds true in the eastern United States, however, only during the colder months and in the presence of general storms that may occur at other seasons.

In the warmer months summer showers and thunderstorms usually come about the time the barometer turns from falling to rising. Note: Precipitation on the Great Plains and mountainous regions between the plains and the Pacific Ocean does not usually begin until the center of the low barometer area has passed to the eastward or southward and the wind has shifted to the north quadrants with a rising barometer.

The wind and barometer indications for the United States are generally summarized in the following table:

WIND BAROMETER TABLE

Wind Direction	Barometer Reduced to Sea Level	Character of Weather
SW to NW	30.10 to 30.20 and steady	Fair, with slight temperature changes for 1 or 2 days
SW to NW	30.10 to 30.20 and rising rapidly	Fair followed within 2 days by rain
SW to NW	30.20 and above and stationary	Continued fair with no decided temperature change
SW to NW	30.20 and above and falling slowly	Slowly rising temperature and fair for 2 days
S to SE	30.10 to 30.20 and falling slowly	Rain within 24 hours

Wind Direction	Barometer Reduced to Sea Level	Character of Weather
S to SE	30.10 to 30.20 and falling rapidly	Wind increasing in force, with rain within 12 to 24 hours
SE to NE	30.10 to 30.20 and falling slowly	Rain in 12 to 18 hours
SE to NE	30.10 to 30.20 and falling rapidly	Increasing wind and rain within 12 hours
E to NE	30.10 and above and falling slowly	In summer, with light winds, rain may not fall for several days. In winter, rain in 24 hours
E to NE	30.10 and above and falling fast	In summer, rain probably in 12 hours. In winter, rain or snow will often set in when the barometer begins to fall and the wind set in NE
SE to NE	30.00 or below and falling slowly	Rain will continue 1 or 2 days
SE to NE	30.00 or below and falling rapidly	Rain with high wind, followed within 36 hours by clearing and, in winter, colder
S to SW	30.00 or below and rising rapidly	Clearing in a few hours and fair for several days
S to E	29.80 or below and falling rapidly	Severe storm imminent, followed in 24 hours by clearing and, in winter, colder.
E to N	29.80 or below and falling rapidly	Severe NE gale and heavy rain; winter, heavy snow and cold wave
Going to W	29.80 or below and rising rapidly	Clearing and colder

Note: The table includes general statements about the weather and can be very useful. However, the latest Weather Bureau forecast should be used whenever available. These forecasts are given on scheduled marine radiophone broadcasts, commercial radio stations, and from Weather Bureau offices.

FRONTS

There are four kinds of fronts mariners and divers ought to know about—cold fronts, warm fronts, occluded fronts, and stationary fronts. The atmosphere is made up of vast moving air masses. Fronts occur where two air masses of different atmospheres collide. When cool air is met and overrun by a warm air mass, a warm front is produced. The leading edge of the warm air mass which is the front slides up over the cool air and produces rain. The warm front is characterized by great sheets of low clouds, fog, poor visibility, and a steady rain. The winds are generally not violent, but foul weather is likely to continue for some time. On the other hand, when a cold air mass collides with and plows under warm, a cold front is produced. The cold air flows low under the warm air because warm air rises and cold air sinks. With a cold front, the warm air is pushed rapidly to high altitudes and thunderstorms are built up. A cold front is usually accompanied by strong, shifty surface winds, squalls, and thunderstorms. The predominant cloud formations will be cumulus. Cold-front weather is severe but quickly passes.

When a cold and a warm front meet, stop, interlock, and remain stationary, a stationary front results. When a fast-moving cold front overtakes a warm front that is moving in the same direction, the cool air in front of and the cool air behind the warm front meet to force the warm air upward. Such is a closed or occluded front, and it can have the characteristics of either a warm front or a cold front or both.

Include in your weather check an estimate of the possibility of cold fronts, where they are, where they are coming from, and if they are likely to affect your plans for the day. Once under way, keep a sharp lookout and listen to your radio. While under way, make the following check for cold fronts:

1. The direction in which clouds first appear, probably W or NW.

2. Look for the first cloud formation appearing, probably alto-stratus. Its distance should be about 300 miles in front of the cold formation.

3. Following alto-stratus clouds generally alto-cumulus, nimbo-stratus, or cumulus-nimbus.

4. With cold-front activity the barometer should be checked. It will be erratic at first, falling and rising several times. Finally it will fall as the front gets nearer, and rise sharply after the front passes.

5. Wind will first appear from the south increasing in velocity, then shifting to north as the cold front passes.

6. Temperature will go down after the front approaches and passes by.

To check warm-front activity, evaluate your weather map and all weather predictions, listening attentively to radio reports. Your check-list of warm-front warning signs is the following:

1. Clouds will probably first appear to SW.

2. First clouds cirrus about 600 miles ahead of the front.

3. Sequence of clouds following cirrus will be cirro-stratus to alto-stratus to nimbo-stratus. If the air is stable this means the air will be relatively mild, but fog and rain will prevail for some time. If the sequence is cirrus to cirro-cumulus to alto-cumulus to cumulo-nimbus, as it is when the air is not stable, anticipate strong winds, heavy rain, and thunderstorms.

4. The barometer will fall at a rapid rate.

5. Wind from SE to SSE and increasing; it will shift to SSW or SW as the front passes.

The temperature will rise gradually. Also look out for extra tropical cyclones, which are a combination of a warm front, a cold front, a low-pressure area, and a wind system.

Review the latest weather information available. Try to time the approach of bad weather and govern yourself accordingly.

CLOUDS

Clouds are indicators of weather to come. Recognize their message, then use good judgment in planning your day of diving.

Cloud Formations Under 6500 Feet:
Cumulo-nimbus or thunderheads—extremely tall, vertical-shaped, very dark gray, dangerous, sometimes covering a 200-mile area. They indicate thunderstorms, high winds, and very turbulent sea.
Nimbo-stratus—flat, uniformly gray, indicating rain over a large area.
Strato-cumulus—sometimes precede or follow storms. Puffy looking, with a possibility of developing into nimbo-stratus shape. Generally fair weather can precede as well as follow a storm.
Stratus—low, with indefinite shapes, creating hazy atmosphere. They can be classified as fog.
Cumulus—series of calm, puffy clouds. Sometimes resembling a flock of sheep. Fair weather.

Cloud Formations Between 6500 and 20,000 Feet:
Alto-cumulus—flat bottoms with intermittently massive, puffy tops. Fair weather.
Alto-stratus—high sheets of clouds, which can develop into nimbo-stratus. Storm possible in 12 hours.

Clouds Generally Appearing Over 20,000 Feet:
Cirro-cumulus—resembling fish scales, sometimes called mackerel sky, creating no shadow and indicating changeable weather.
Cirro-stratus—high and cobwebby-looking like white, frosty fingers. Indicate possible rain in 24 hours or so.
Cirrus—sometimes called mare's tail. Stringy, resembling ice crystals, which refract beautiful light. Cirrus and cirro-stratus forms make a halo around the sun and moon and foretell weather to come in at least 24 hours.
Cumulo-nimbus, thunderheads, thunderstorms, or squalls—DANGER!—If a thunderhead appears in the southwest or northwest

horizon, with dirty gray bottom and anvil-like top, beware of an impending storm in the area within a half hour. *Head Home.* A line squall or squall line is a series of thunderstorms.

FOLKLORIC WEATHER WISDOM, PROVERBS, AND SAYINGS

A diver has to be engaged in a working partnership with nature as a matter of pure necessity. This handful of rich sayings reflect the cumulative weather wisdom of many centuries.

> Sailors who these jingles doubt
> Should say a prayer before going out
> —A. P. Balder

The Barometer
"When the glass falls low, prepare for a blow;
When it rises high, let all your kites fly.
When the wind backs and the weather glass falls
Be on your guard against gales and squalls."

Cirrus Clouds
"Mackerel scales and mares' tails
Make tall ships carry short sails."
                    and
"Trace in the sky the painter's brush,
The winds around you soon will rush."
"Whene'er the clouds a cloth shall weave,
Look for storms before they leave."

Cumulus Clouds
"Morning towers bring evening showers."

Cumulo-Nimbus Clouds
"When the clouds appear like rocks and towers,
The earth's refreshed by frequent showers."

The Sun
"Above the rest, the Sun who never lies
Foretells the change of weather in the skies."

"The sun sets weeping in the lowly west,
Witnessing storms to come, woe and unrest."
                                                    —*Virgil*

Color of the Sky
"A red morn: that ever yet betokened
Wreck to the seaman, tempest to the field,
Sorrow to the shepherds, woe unto the birds,
Gusts and foul flaws to herdsmen and to herds."

"Red in the morning, sailors take warning,
But red at night is the sailor's delight."

Wind
"When the wind is in the north
Sailors seldom venture forth;
When the wind is in the east
Sailors venture forth the least.
When the wind is in the west
Then the weather's at its best;
But when the wind is from the south
It blows the rain from the storm king's mouth."

"A veering wind means weather fair.
A backing wind, foul weather's near."

Fog
An early morning fog generally indicates a clear day.

"Mists dispersing on the plain
Scatter away the clouds and rain;
But when they rise to the mountain tops
They'll soon return in copious drops."

Rain
"Long threaten, long last;
Short notice, soon past."

"Rain before seven, clear before eleven."

The Rainbow
"Rainbow to windward, foul fall the day;
Rainbow to leeward, damp runs away."

Dew
"When the dew is on the grass,
Rain will never come to pass."

"When the grass is wet at night,
Look for rain before the light.
When the grass is dry at morning light
Look for rain before the night."

FISH AND MARINE LIFE AND WHAT SOME CAN TELL US ABOUT WEATHER

Cuttlefish swimming on the surface presage a storm.

When the codfish's eyes are bloated, wind is coming. The cod is said to take in ballast before a storm.

When trout refuse bait or fly
There ever is a storm a-nigh.

Sea urchins trying to dig in the mud or to cover their bodies with sand foreshadow a storm.

Sharks swim out to sea when a wave of cold weather approaches.

Before the storm the crab his briny home
Sidelong forsakes, and strives on land to roam.

If eels are very lively, it is a sign of rain,
They are nought but eels, that never will appear
Till that tempestuous winds or thunder tear
Their slimy beds.

When porpoises and whales spout about ships at sea, storms are coming.

Whales sounding foretell a storm.

Like dolphins when a signal they transmit
To mariners by arching of the back,
That they save their ships take counsel fit.

Cockles and most shellfish have gravel sticking to their shells during a storm, which is nature's way to help weigh them down and protect them from being tossed around in surging water.

14

EPILOGUE

OCEANOGRAPHY—A SHORT COURSE

Oceanography is not a science separate in itself. It is an ocean-oriented area of physics, chemistry, biology, and geology. The basic sciences are the foundation of oceanography. Its pursuit starts, not from the seabed, but in classrooms and laboratories.

APPLIED OCEANOGRAPHY

Applied oceanography uses descriptive and theoretical knowledge for technological developments of benefit to mankind. Here are some of the new fields to conquer.

Oceanic Engineering: This is the application of standard engineering disciplines to the ocean environment. Oceanic engineers are designing structures, vehicles, components, or processes that can be used in the sea. They create pressure-resistant devices capable of surviving currents, corrosion, and the onslaught of marine organisms.

Marine Geology: Marine geology or geological oceanography is the study of the ocean floor, the oceanic crust, and the processes acting on them.

Marine Biology: Some of the most exciting problems in oceanography are biological—mainly how to understand, predict, control, and manage the populations of the oceans, including the development of global fish production, to meet the world's nutritional demands.

As we breed and farm fish there will be a need for fish veterinarians, pathologists, and experts on the diseases and parasites that may plague our flocks in the sea or our plants.

Water Pollution Control: Current water pollution control needs are still formidable.

Telemetry: Telemetry involves sensing, transmitting, and displaying oceanographic data.

Plant Harvesting: The oceans are a source of a vast amount of vegetation, but so far only a limited number of plants are considered valuable enough to harvest. Seaweed, for example, is harvested in a number of countries and converted into animal feed in France and human food in Japan.

Ocean Behavior Studies (Descriptive Oceanography): Man- and brain-power will be needed for studies of tides, waves, turbulence, water types, currents, distribution of marine organisms, and topography.

Acoustics: The behavior of sound transmitted through the sea water is of vital importance in undersea warfare.

Electric Power: It is expected that in the future we will obtain electric power from the sea.

Recreation Activities: Water recreation includes activities as diverse as surfing, skin diving, fishing, sunbathing, water skiing, and yachting. Activities such as weather forecasting, shark control, and pollution abatement directly influence the decision of thousands of people to take that Sunday ride down to the beach.

Long-Term Weather Forecasting and Weather Control: Another field will be that of the study of air-sea interaction processes for a better understanding of weather processes.

Marine Radioactivity and Fallout: The disposal of radioactive wastes is a problem that must be met with increasingly effective methods.

Fleets and Crews for Oceanographic Field Work: Oceanographic fleets must be manned and vessels must be constantly modified to meet new demands. Civilian as well as naval crews will be needed.

New Sources of Fresh Water (Desalinization of Sea Water): Science must provide the technology needed to produce greater amounts of fresh water converted from the salt seas, especially when and if water shortages threaten to become critical.

Search and Salvage: Considerable technical advances must be achieved in order to meet the growing demands of government and commerce in search and salvage. Search and salvage operations will require better tools for identification, equipment and divers for recovery, highly maneuverable and controllable vehicles operated by nuclear and non-nuclear power for extended search, and improved bathymetric charting to define the contours of the sea floor with exactness. In the search phase of salvage, industry is developing scanning sonar, high-resolution sonar, bottom-penetration sonar, and other sophisticated detection devices such as magnatometers and gravimeters.

Photography: There will be a demand for photographic and television techniques and equipment capable of operating at the remotest depths.

Marine Chemistry: New gases and mixtures will be needed so that men can breathe under water for prolonged periods without ill effects. The primary concern of the marine chemist is with the chemical composition of ocean waters. Research projects include dissolved salts, temperature, gases, minerals, and radioactivity.

Underwater Archaeology: Because the sea has preserved ancient works of art that were carried by ships in antiquity, underwater archaeology should bring to light many important finds, precious sources of evidence in historical research. Scientific excavation calls first for exact and detailed plans of each phase of the work. Better wreck-finding techniques equal to the normal archaeologist's budget must be devised. In many instances actual excavation of a wreck will probably call for saturation diving either from an underwater house or from a submersible decompression chamber. Until now marine archaeology has been sorely underfinanced, and the few significant discoveries on record have been made accidentally by amateurs or fishermen.

CONCLUSION

For me, to have glimpsed even a small part of the sorcery and poetry of the universe beneath the foam is all that I ask of diving. To escape the land mass and the shore, to slip the bonds of gravity, merge and mingle with our eons-old ancestors—this and no more.

There in the upper, safer reaches of this now strange, now familiar element, vaster in all its dimensions than the land masses above, one can sport, frolic, soar, climb, nosedive, and hover weightlessly, effortlessly. There, amid a grandeur as awesome as Everest and as rich in color, hue, and form as anything under the sun, one can marvel, ponder being, and come to terms with that world above that is often too much with us.

Loren Eiseley wrote of that strange door to the past: It swings open and things pass through it, but they pass in one direction only. No man, he wrote, can return across its threshold, though he can look down "and see the green light waver in the water weeds." No man can return across the evolutionary threshold; but is there a child among us who has never held a seashell to his ear and listened, all mystified and in happy confusion, to the roar of a distant sea? We who have learned to swim and dive belong to an elect group. We *can* cross that threshold again and again and again. And each time we return we are never quite the same.

APPENDIX

SUGGESTED FIELD MAINTENANCE AND REPAIR KIT FOR EXTENSIVE DIVE ACTIVITIES

Tools:

Crescent wrenches
    1 size 16″
    1 size 8″
    1 size 4″

Screwdrivers
    Flat ⁵/₁₆″ with 6″ shaft
    Flat ¼″ with 6″ shaft
    Phillips No. 2 with 6″ shaft

Files
    1 rat-tail, medium coarseness
    1 flat, medium coarseness

awl or icepick—for removing O-rings or punching holes in belts or straps

single-edge razor blades pack—for trimming wet-suit material

pliers—assorted

sail needles—small, both straight and curved

sailor's palm

nylon strapping crimping tool

penknife

claw hammer—medium weight
wire brush—long handle
vice-grip pliers
sharpening stone
wire-cutters—medium size
hacksaw and blades
tool container—either plastic box or canvas bag

Spares:
O-rings—necessary sizes
mask straps
buckles
purge valves and components
quick-release "D" rings
scuba mouthpieces
scuba hoses—for double-hose rigs
snorkle mouthpieces
exhaust vents—single-hose rigs
weights
spare masks
spare swim fins
spare weight belts

Supplies:
spare wet-suit material (1 yd.)
nylon or brass wet-suit zippers
⅛" nylon strapping and nylon clips
waxed linen, nylon, or Dacron thread (dental floss is also used)
adhesive plastic tape (¾")
spray can of silicone (not for O_2 service)
spray can of silicone-based grease (not for O_2 service)
spray can of light oil
miscellaneous nuts, bolts, washers, etc.
paraffin candles—for burning nylon ends, heating tip of awl to
    penetrate heavy rubber materials such as swim fins
masking tape (½")
matches
neoprene cement for wet suits
wire—bailing or leader type

waterproof felt pens
contact cement
epoxy glue
manila line—(¼ ")
talcum powder—or cornstarch
liquid detergent
towel—(paper towels)

DIVER'S EQUIPMENT CHECKLIST

[ ] diving gear bag
[ ] mask
[ ] snorkel with snorkelkeeper
[ ] fins
[ ] swimsuit
[ ] towel
[ ] wet-suit jacket
[ ] wet-suit pants
[ ] wet-suit hood
[ ] wet-suit boots
[ ] weight belt
[ ] Buoyancy-Compensator vest
[ ] gloves
[ ] diver's knife
[ ] tube-float with line
     and diver's flag
[ ] scuba tank with back pack
[ ] regulator
[ ] depth gauge
[ ] diver's watch with bezel
[ ] diver's compass
[ ] diver's thermometer
[ ] decompression meter
[ ] game bag
[ ] game-measuring device
[ ] underwater flashlight
[ ] first-aid kit with supplies
[ ] underwater slate and pen

[ ] lift bag
[ ] safe-line reel and buddy line
[ ] marker floats and line
[ ] rescue-flare and dye-marker
[ ] lung bag and thermos
[ ] current fishing license
[ ] diving log book
[ ] scuba certification card
[ ] tickets and money
[ ] warm clothing
[ ] extra tank
[ ] spare CO_2 cartridge
[ ] extra weights
[ ] spare O-rings
[ ] spare mask and fin straps
[ ] pliers, wrench, screwdriver, etc.
[ ] wet-suit powder
[ ] tank pressure gauge
[ ] spearfishing equipment
[ ] photogaphy equipment
[ ] metal-detecting equipment
[ ] plastic bags and containers
[ ] area charts and notepaper
[ ] _____
[ ] _____
[ ] _____
[ ] _____
[ ] _____

311

SAMPLE DIVING LOG

PERSONAL INFORMATION

This is the Diving Log of:

NAME _____

AGE_____ BLOOD TYPE_____

Address_____

City_____ State/Prov. _____ Country_____

Zip_____ Phone: Res. ( )_____

Bus. ( )_____

PERSONS TO CONTACT IN CASE OF EMERGENCY

Name	*Address*	*Phone*
Name	*Address*	*Phone*
Name	*Address*	*Phone*

Drug sensitivities_____

RECORD OF PERSONAL EQUIPMENT

REGULATOR _____

Brand　　　*Model*　　　*Type*　　　*Serial No.*

TANK _____

Brand　　　*Size*　　　*Serial No.*　　　*Test Date*

OTHER SERIAL NUMBERED ITEMS

_____ NO. _____
_____ NO. _____
_____ NO. _____
_____ NO. _____
_____ NO. _____
_____ NO. _____

ACCESSORY EQUIPMENT

_____
_____
_____
_____
_____

DATE _____ Dive No. _____

Location _____

OBJECTIVE _____ Equip. Used _____
Weather _____ Water Visibility _____
    In _____ Air _____
Dive Time: Out _____ Temp. Surface _____
    Bottom _____ Bottom _____
Depth: Average _____ Air Pressure Start _____
    Maximum _____ Finish _____
REMARKS/OBSERVATIONS: _____

_____
_____
_____

Dive Buddy Verification _____ Accum. Dive Hours _____

DIVING LOCATIONS

LOCATION _____
Directions/Map:

U.S. NAVY STANDARD AIR DECOMPRESSION TABLE

Depth (feet)	Bottom time (min)	Time first stop (min:sec)	Decompression stops (feet)							Total ascent (min:sec)	Repetitive group
			70	60	50	40	30	20	10		
40	200								0	0:40	*
	210	0:30							2	2:40	N
	230	0:30							7	7:40	N
	250	0:30							11	11:40	O
	270	0:30							15	15:40	O
	300	0:30							19	19:40	Z
50	100								0	0:50	*
	110	0:40							3	3:50	L
	120	0:40							5	5:50	M
	140	0:40							10	10:50	M
	160	0:40							21	21:50	N
	180	0:40							29	29:50	O
	200	0:40							35	35:50	O
	220	0:40							40	40:50	Z
	240	0:40							47	47:50	Z

*See No Decompression Table for repetitive groups

Depth (feet)	Bottom time (min)	Time first stop (min:sec)	Decompression stops (feet) 70	60	50	40	30	20	10	Total ascent (min:sec)	Repetitive group
60	60								0	1:00	*
	70	0:50							2	3:00	K
	80	0:50							7	8:00	L
	100	0:50							14	15:00	M
	120	0:50							26	27:00	N
	140	0:50							39	40:00	O
	160	0:50							48	49:00	Z
	180	0:50							56	57:00	Z
	200	0:40						1	69	71:00	Z
70	50								0	1:10	*
	60	1:00							8	9:10	K
	70	1:00							14	15:10	L
	80	1:00							18	19:10	M
	90	1:00							23	24:10	N
	100	1:00							33	34:10	N
	110	0:50						2	41	44:10	O
	120	0:50						4	47	52:10	O
	130	0:50						6	52	59:10	O
	140	0:50						8	56	65:10	Z
	150	0:50						9	61	71:10	Z
	160	0:50						13	72	86:10	Z
	170	0:50						19	79	99:10	Z
80	40								0	1:20	*
	50	1:10							10	11:20	K
	60	1:10							17	18:20	L
	70	1:10							23	24:20	M
	80	1:00						2	31	34:20	N
	90	1:00						7	39	47:20	N
	100	1:00						11	46	58:20	O
	110	1:00						13	53	67:20	O
	120	1:00						17	56	74:20	Z

* See No Decompression Table for repetitive groups

Depth (feet)	Bottom time (min)	Time first stop (min:sec)	Decompression stops (feet)							Total ascent (min:sec)	Repetitive group
			70	60	50	40	30	20	10		
	130	1:00						19	63	83:20	Z
	140	1:00						26	69	96:20	Z
	150	1:00						32	77	110:20	Z
90	30								0	1:30	*
	40	1:20							7	8:30	J
	50	1:20							18	19:30	L
	60	1:20							25	26:30	M
	70	1:10						7	30	38:30	N
	80	1:10						13	40	54:30	N
	90	1:10						18	48	67:30	O
	100	1:10						21	54	76:30	Z
	110	1:10						24	61	86:30	Z
	120	1:10						32	68	101:30	Z
	130	1:00					5	36	74	116:30	Z
100	25								0	1:40	*
	30	1:30							3	4:40	I
	40	1:30							15	16:40	K
	50	1:20						2	24	27:40	L
	60	1:20						9	28	38:40	N
	70	1:20						17	39	57:40	O
	80	1:20						23	48	72:40	O
	90	1:10					3	23	57	84:40	Z
	100	1:10					7	23	66	97:40	Z
	110	1:10					10	34	72	117:40	Z
	120	1:10					12	41	78	132:40	Z
110	20								0	1:50	*
	25	1:40							3	4:50	H
	30	1:40							7	8:50	J
	40	1:30						2	21	24:50	L
	50	1:30						8	26	35:50	M

Depth (feet)	Bottom time (min)	Time first stop (min:sec)	70	60	50	40	30	20	10	Total ascent (min:sec)	Repetitive group
	60	1:30						18	36	55:50	N
	70	1:20					1	23	48	73:50	O
	80	1:20					7	23	57	88:50	Z
	90	1:20					12	30	64	107:50	Z
	100	1:20					15	37	72	125:50	Z
120	15								0	2:00	*
	20	1:50							2	4:00	H
	25	1:50							6	8:00	I
	30	1:50							14	16:00	J
	40	1:40						5	25	32:00	L
	50	1:40						15	31	48:00	N
	60	1:30					2	22	45	71:00	O
	70	1:30					9	23	55	89:00	O
	80	1:30					15	27	63	107:00	Z
	90	1:30					19	37	74	132:00	Z
	100	1:30					23	45	80	150:00	Z
130	10								0	2:10	*
	15	2:00							1	3:10	F
	20	2:00							4	6:10	H
	25	2:00							10	12:10	J
	30	1:50						3	18	23:10	M
	40	1:50						10	25	37:10	N
	50	1:40					3	21	37	63:10	O
	60	1:40					9	23	52	86:10	Z
	70	1:40					16	24	61	103:10	Z
	80	1:30				3	19	35	72	131:10	Z
	90	1:30				8	19	45	80	154:10	Z
140	10								0	2:20	*
	15	2:10							2	4:20	G
	20	2:10							6	8:20	I

*See No Decompression Table for repetitive groups

Depth (feet)	Bottom time (min)	Time first stop (min:sec)	70	60	50	40	30	20	10	Total ascent (min:sec)	Repetitive group
			Decompression stops (feet)								
	25	2:00						2	14	18:20	J
	30	2:00						5	21	28:20	K
	40	1:50					2	16	26	46:20	N
	50	1:50					6	24	44	76:20	O
	60	1:50					16	23	56	97:20	Z
	70	1:40				4	19	32	68	125:20	Z
	80	1:40				10	23	41	79	155:20	Z
150	5								0	2:30	C
	10	2:20							1	3:30	E
	15	2:20							3	5:30	G
	20	2:10						2	7	11:30	H
	25	2:10						4	17	23:30	K
	30	2:10						8	24	34:30	L
	40	2:00					5	19	33	59:30	N
	50	2:00					12	23	51	88:30	O
	60	1:50				3	19	26	62	112:30	Z
	70	1:50				11	19	39	75	146:30	Z
	80	1:40			1	17	19	50	84	173:30	Z
160	5								0	2:40	D
	10	2:30							1	3:40	F
	15	2:20						1	4	7:40	H
	20	2:20						3	11	16:40	J
	25	2:20						7	20	29:40	K
	30	2:10					2	11	25	40:40	M
	40	2:10					7	23	39	71:40	N
	50	2:00				2	16	23	55	98:40	Z
	60	2:00				9	19	33	69	132:40	Z
	70	1:50			1	17	22	44	80	166:40	Z
170	5								0	2:50	D
	10	2:40							2	4:50	F
	15	2:30						2	5	9:50	H

Depth (feet)	Bottom time (min)	Time first stop (min:sec)	Decompression stops (feet)							Total ascent (min:sec)	Repetitive group
			70	60	50	40	30	20	10		
	20	2:30						4	15	21:50	J
	25	2:20					2	7	23	34:50	L
	30	2:20					4	13	26	45:50	M
	40	2:10				1	10	23	45	81:50	O
	50	2:10				5	18	23	61	109:50	Z
	60	2:00			2	15	22	37	74	152:50	Z
	70	2:00			8	17	19	51	86	183:50	Z
180	5								0	3:00	D
	10	2:50							3	6:00	F
	15	2:40						3	6	12:00	I
	20	2:30					1	5	17	26:00	K
	25	2:30					3	10	24	40:00	L
	30	2:30					6	17	27	53:00	N
	40	2:20				3	14	23	50	93:00	O
	50	2:10			2	9	19	30	65	128:00	Z
	60	2:10			5	16	19	44	81	168:00	Z
190	5								0	3:10	D
	10	2:50						1	3	7:10	G
	15	2:50						4	7	14:10	I
	20	2:40					2	6	20	31:10	K
	25	2:40					5	11	25	44:10	M
	30	2:30				1	8	19	43	63:10	N
	40	2:30				8	14	23	55	103:10	O
	50	2:20			4	13	22	33	72	147:10	Z
	60	2:20			10	17	19	50	84	183:10	Z

RESIDUAL NITROGEN TIMETABLE FOR REPETITIVE AIR DIVES

The quantity of residual nitrogen in a diver's body immediately after a dive is expressed by the repetitive group designation assigned to him by either the Standard Air Table or the No-Decompression Table. The upper portion of the Residual Nitrogen Table is composed of various intervals between 10 minutes and 12 hours, expressed in hours: minutes (2:21= 2 hours 21 minutes). Each interval has two limits: a minimum time (top limit) and a maximum time (bottom limit).

Residual nitrogen times, corresponding to the depth of the repetitive dive, are given in the body of the lower portion of the table. To determine the residual nitrogen time for a repetitive dive, locate the diver's repetitive group designation from his previous dive along the diagonal line above the table. Read horizontally to the interval in which the diver's surface interval lies. The time spent on the surface must be between or equal to the limits of the selected interval.

Next, read vertically downwards to the new repetitive group designation. This designation corresponds to the present quantity of residual nitrogen in the diver's body. Continue downward in this same column to the row which represents the depth of the repetitive dive. The time given at the intersection is the residual nitrogen time, in minutes, to be applied to the repetitive dive.

If the surface interval is less than 10 minutes, the residual nitrogen time is the bottom time of the previous dive. All of the residual nitrogen will be passed out of the diver's body after 12 hours, so a dive conducted after a 12-hour surface interval is not a repetitive dive.

There is one exception to this table. In some instances, when the repetitive dive is to the same or greater depth than the previous dive, the residual nitrogen time may be longer than the actual bottom time of the previous dive. In this event, add the actual bottom time of the previous dive to the actual bottom time of the repetitive dive to obtain the equivalent single dive time.

Example:
Problem—A repetitive dive is to be made to 98 fsw for an estimated bottom time of 15 minutes. The previous dive was to a depth of 102 fsw and had a 48-minute bottom time. The diver's surface interval is 6 hours 28 minutes (6:28). What decompression schedule should be used for the repetitive dive?

Solution—Using the repetitive dive worksheet—

Repetitive Dive Worksheet

I. PREVIOUS DIVE:

___48___ minutes   ☑ Standard Air Table
___102__ feet   ☐ No-Decompression Table
___M___ repetitive group designation

II. SURFACE INTERVAL:

___6___ hours ___28___ minutes on surface
Repetitive group from I ___M___
New repetitive group from surface
Residual Nitrogen Timetable ___B___

III. RESIDUAL NITROGEN TIME:

___98___ feet (depth of repetitive dive)
New repetitive group from II ___B___
Residual nitrogen time from
Residual Nitrogen Timetable ___7___

IV. EQUIVALENT SINGLE DIVE TIME:

___7___ minutes, residual nitrogen time from III.
___15___ minutes, actual bottom time of repetitive dive.
___22___ minutes, equivalent single dive time.

V. DECOMPRESSION FOR REPETITIVE DIVE:

___22___ minutes, equivalent single dive time from IV.
___98___ feet, depth of repetitive dive

Decompression from (check one):
☐ Standard Air Table ☐ No-Decompression Table
☐ Surface Table Using Oxygen ☐ Surface Table Using Air
☑ No decompression required

Decompression Stops: _____ feet _____ minutes
_____ feet _____ minutes
_____ feet _____ minutes
_____ feet _____ minutes
Schedule used   _____ feet _____ minutes
Repetitive group   _____

* Dives following surface intervals of more than 12 hours are not repetitive dives. Use actual bottom times in the Standard Air Decompression Tables to compute decompression for such dives.

Surface interval times (h:min). Repetitive group designation at the beginning of the surface interval is read across the top; each cell gives the surface interval range (low–high); the new group designation is read at the bottom.

A	A	B	C	D	E	F	G	H	I	J	K	L	M	N	O
0:10–12:00*	0:10–2:10	0:10–1:39	0:10–1:09	0:10–0:54	0:10–0:45	0:10–0:40	0:10–0:36	0:10–0:33	0:10–0:31	0:10–0:28	0:10–0:26	0:10–0:25	0:10–0:24	0:10–0:23	0:10–0:22
2:11–12:00*	1:40–2:49	1:10–2:38	0:55–1:57	0:46–1:29	0:41–1:15	0:37–1:06	0:34–0:59	0:32–0:54	0:29–0:49	0:27–0:45	0:26–0:42	0:25–0:39	0:24–0:36	0:23–0:34	
2:50–12:00*	2:39–5:48	1:58–3:22	1:30–2:28	1:16–1:59	1:07–1:41	1:00–1:29	0:55–1:19	0:50–1:11	0:46–1:04	0:43–1:00	0:40–0:54	0:37–0:51	0:35–0:48		
5:49–12:00*	3:23–6:32	2:29–3:57	2:00–2:58	1:42–2:23	1:30–2:02	1:20–1:47	1:12–1:35	1:05–1:25	1:00–1:18	0:55–1:11	0:52–1:07	0:49–1:02			
6:33–12:00*	3:58–7:05	2:59–4:25	2:24–3:20	2:03–2:44	1:48–2:20	1:36–2:03	1:26–1:49	1:19–1:39	1:12–1:30	1:08–1:24	1:03–1:18				
7:06–12:00*	4:26–7:35	3:21–4:49	2:45–3:43	2:21–3:04	2:04–2:38	1:50–2:19	1:40–2:05	1:31–1:53	1:25–1:43	1:19–1:36					
7:36–12:00*	4:50–7:59	3:44–5:12	3:05–4:02	2:39–3:21	2:20–2:54	2:06–2:34	1:54–2:18	1:44–2:04	1:37–1:55						
8:00–12:00*	5:13–8:21	4:03–5:40	3:22–4:19	2:54–3:36	2:35–3:08	2:19–2:47	2:05–2:29	1:56–2:17							
8:22–12:00*	5:41–8:40	4:20–5:48	3:37–4:35	3:09–3:52	2:48–3:22	2:30–2:59	2:18–2:42								
8:41–12:00*	5:49–8:58	4:36–6:02	3:53–4:49	3:23–4:04	3:00–3:33	2:43–3:10									
8:59–12:00*	6:03–9:12	4:50–6:18	4:05–5:03	3:34–4:17	3:11–3:45										
9:13–12:00*	6:19–9:28	5:04–6:32	4:18–5:16	3:46–4:29											
9:29–12:00*	6:33–9:43	5:17–6:44	4:30–5:27												
9:44–12:00*	6:45–9:54	5:28–6:56													
9:55–12:00*	6:57–10:05														
10:06–12:00*															

New → Group Designation: Z O N M L K J I H G F E D C B A

Repetitive Dive Depth																
40	7	17	25	37	49	61	73	87	101	116	138	161	187	213	241	257
50	6	13	21	29	38	47	56	66	76	87	99	111	124	142	160	169
60	5	11	17	24	30	36	44	52	61	70	79	88	97	107	117	122
70	4	9	15	20	26	31	37	43	50	57	64	72	80	87	96	100
80	4	8	13	18	23	28	32	38	43	48	54	61	68	73	80	84
90	3	7	11	16	20	24	29	33	38	43	47	53	58	64	70	73
100	3	7	10	14	18	22	26	30	34	38	43	48	52	57	62	64
110	3	6	10	13	16	20	24	27	31	34	38	42	47	51	55	57
120	3	6	9	12	15	18	21	25	28	32	35	39	43	46	50	52
130	3	6	8	11	13	16	19	22	25	28	31	35	38	40	44	46
140	2	5	7	10	12	15	18	20	23	26	29	32	35	38	40	42
150	2	5	7	9	12	14	17	19	22	24	27	30	32	35	38	40
160	2	4	6	9	11	13	16	18	20	23	26	28	31	33	36	37
170	2	4	6	8	10	13	15	17	19	22	24	26	29	31	34	35
180	2	4	6	8	10	12	14	16	18	20	22	25	27	29	31	32
190	2	4	6	8	10	11	13	15	17	19	21	24	26	28	30	31

Residual Nitrogen Times (Minutes)

USEFUL CONVERSION FACTORS

psi × 0.068 = atm (or divided by 14.7 psi)
atm × 14.7 = psi
psi × 2.31 = ft. of fresh water
psi × 2.25 = ft. of salt (sea) water

ft. of fresh water × 0.434 = psi
ft. of sea water × 0.445 = psi

Water depth in ft. ÷ 33 + 1 atm = atm absolute
Water depth in meters ÷ 10 + 1 atm = atm absolute
Atmosphere absolute less 1 atm × 33 = ft. depth
Metres less 1 atm × 10 = atm absolute

cm × 0.394 = in.
m × 39.37 = in.
m × 3.28 = ft.
km × 0.621 = mi.
m^2 × 10.76 = sq. ft.
km^2 × 0.386 = sq. mi.
liters × 1.06 = qt.
1 qt. × 0.946 = 1 liter
statute mi. × 1.61 (or ⁸/₅) = km
nautical mi. × 1.85 = km
kilometer × ⅝ = statute mi.
statute mi. × 0.87 (or deduct ⅛) = nautical mi.

NAUTICAL DEFINITIONS

Nautical Mile   At any place on the earth's surface is the length of 1 minute of arc measured along the meridian through that
place.
It varies in different latitudes owing to the irregular shape
of the earth.
In practice, it is taken to be 6080 feet, which is its value
in latitude 40 degrees.

Knot   In navigation the unit of speed is a Knot, which is a speed
of 1 nautical mile per hour.

Cable	A Cable is one-tenth of a nautical mile; in practice it is taken as 200 yards.
Fathom	A Fathom is a unit of 6 feet used in sounding and recording depths of water. It is not generally used for freshwater soundings.
Shackle	A Shackle is the amount of cable between shackles in an anchor cable. As a measure it is taken to be 15 fathoms.

Wind—Direction, Speed, and Measurement

Direction	Wind direction is always specified as the direction from which the wind blows.
Speed	Wind speed is expressed in: knots by mariners and airmen; miles per hour by landsmen and coastal navigators.
Conversions	1 knot = 1.7 feet per second approx.

1 knot   = 1.7 feet per second approx.
                        = 0.51 meters per second approx.
1 mile per hour   = 1½ feet per second approx.
                        = 1609 kilometers per hour approx.
1 foot per second   = ⅔ miles per hour approx.
                        = 0.3 meters per second approx.
1 kilometer per hour= ⅝ miles per hour approx.
1 meter per second   = 3⅓ feet per second approx.

USEFUL ABBREVIATIONS

atm	atmosphere		lb.	pound
cc	cubic centimeter		m	meter
cm	centimeter		m²	square meter
cm²	square centimeter		m³	cubic meter
cu	cubic		mi.	mile
ft.	foot		oz.	ounce
gal.	gallon		psi	pounds per square inch
in.	inch		pt.	pint
km	kilometer		qt.	quart
km²	square kilometer		sq.	square
l	liter		yd.	yard

1 cubic foot of fresh water weighs approximately 62.5 lbs.
1 cubic foot of salt water weighs approximately 64 lbs.
1 cubic foot of air weighs 0.08 lbs.
1 cubic foot of ice weighs 56 lbs.

CONVERSIONS (APPROXIMATE)

Miles to kilometers . . . . multiply by $8/5$
Kilometers to miles . . . . multiply by $5/8$
Statute miles to nautical miles . . . . . . deduct $1/8$
Nautical miles to statute miles . . . . add $1/7$

TEMPERATURE

To convert degrees Fahrenheit to degrees Centigrade: deduct 32 and multiply by 5/9.
To convert degrees Centigrade to degrees Fahrenheit: multiply by 9/5 and add 32.

CONVERSION TABLE FOR APPROXIMATE VALUES OF SOME TYPICAL DEPTHS

Feet	Fathoms	Meters *
1	—	0.3048
3.2808	0.5468	1
6	1	1.8288
6.5616	1.0936	2
9.8424	1.6304	3
10	—	3.048
12	2	3.7
20	3.3	6.1
32.8	5.5	10
36	6	11
50	8.3	15.2
65.6	10.9	20
100	16.7	30.5
120	20	36.6
131.2	21.9	40

*Why meters? You may take a trip overseas in, say, European waters where the metric system is used.

BIBLIOGRAPHY

American National Red Cross, The. *Life Saving, Rescue and Water Safety.* Garden City, N.Y.: Doubleday & Co., Inc., 1974.
———. *Standard First Aid and Personal Safety.* 1st ed. Garden City, N.Y.: Doubleday & Co., Inc., 1973.
———. *Advanced First Aid and Emergency Care.* Garden City, N.Y.: Doubleday & Co., Inc., 1973.
Athletic Institute, The. *Human Performance and Scuba Diving.* Proceedings of the Symposium on Underwater Physiology, 10–11 April 1970, at La Jolla, California. Chicago: The Athletic Institute, 1970.
Bascom, Willard. *Waves and Beaches.* Garden City, N.Y.: Anchor Books, Doubleday & Co., Inc., 1964.
Bass, G. *Archaeology Under Water.* New Jersey: Humanities Press, Inc., 1974.
Bates, Marston. *The Forest and the Sea.* New York: Vintage Books, 1965.
British Sub Aqua Club, The. *The Diving Officer's Handbook.* 4th ed. London: The Riverside Press, Ltd., 1973.
Carrier, Rick, and Carrier, Barbara. *Dive: The Complete Book of Skin Diving.* New York: Funk & Wagnalls, Inc., 1973.
Carson, Rachel. *The Edge of the Sea.* Boston: Houghton Mifflin Co., 1965.
———. *The Sea Around Us.* New York: Oxford University Press, 1961.
Cayford, John E. *Underwater Work—A Manual of Scuba Commercial Salvage and Construction Operations.* Cambridge, Md.: Cornell Maritime Press, 1959.
Chapman, Charles F., and Maloney, E. S. *Piloting Seamanship and Small Boat Handling.* New York: Hearst Books, 1977.
Clark, Eugenia. *Lady and the Sharks.* New York: Harper and Row, 1977.

Council for National Co-operation in Aquatics. *The New Science of Skin and Scuba Diving*. New revised edition. New York: Association Press, 1974.

Cousteau, Jacques Yves, and Cousteau, Philippe. *The Shark: Splendid Savage of the Sea*. Garden City, N.Y.: Doubleday & Co., Inc., 1970.

Cousteau, Jacques Yves, and Diole, Philippe. *Life and Death in a Coral Sea*. Garden City, N.Y.: Doubleday & Co., Inc., 1971.

Cousteau, Jacques Yves, and Dugan, James. *Captain Cousteau's Underwater Treasury*. New York: Harper and Brothers, 1959.

Cousteau, Jacques Yves, and Dumas, Frederick. *The Silent World*. New York: Harper and Brothers, 1953.

Degn, Morgan, and Craig, John D. *Invitation to Skin and Scuba Diving*. New York: Simon and Schuster, 1965.

Drew, E. "Botany." In *Underwater Science*, edited by J. Woods and J. Lythgoe. London: Oxford University Press, 1971.

Drew, E. A. et al. *Underwater Research*. New York: Academic Press, Inc., 1975.

Dueker, Dr. Christopher W. *Medical Aspects of Sport Diving*. Cranbury, N.J.: A. S. Barnes and Co., Inc., 1969.

Dugan, J. *Man Under the Sea*. Revised edition. New York: P. F. Collier, Inc., 1959.

Dumas, Frederic. *Thirty Centuries Under the Sea*. New York: Crown, 1976.

Flemming, N. C., ed. *The Undersea*. New York: Macmillan Publishing Co., Inc., 1977.

Freuchen, Peter, and Loth, David. *Peter Freuchen's Book of the Seven Seas*. New York: Simon & Schuster, Inc., 1968.

Frey, Hank, and Frey, Shaney. *130 Feet Down, A Handbook for Hydronauts*. New York: Harcourt, Brace Jovanovich, 1961.

Greenberg, Jerry. *Underwater Photography Simplified*. New York: Seahawk Press, Inc., 1958.

Halstead, Bruce W. *Dangerous Marine Animals*. Cambridge, Md.: Cornell Maritime Press, 1959.

Heezen, Bruce C., and Hollister, Charles D. *The Face of the Deep*. New York: Oxford University Press, 1971.

Helm, Thomas. *Shark*. New York: Collier Books, 1963.

Ivanovic, Vane. *Modern Spearfishing*. New York: Contemporary Books, 1975.

Kephart, Horace. *Camping and Woodcraft*. New York: Macmillan Publishing Co., Inc., 1948.

Knudsen, J. *Collecting and Preserving Plants and Animals*. New York: Harper and Row, 1972.

Lambertsen, Christian J., ed. *Underwater Physiology.* New York: Academic Press, Inc., 1971.

Meade, James. "Killers From Beyond Time." *Skin Diver,* vol. 23, no. 1 (January 1973).

Mertens, Lawrence E. *In-Water Photography: Theory and Practice.* New York: Wiley-Interscience, 1970.

Miles, S. *Underwater Medicine.* 4th ed. Philadelphia: J. B. Lippincott Co., 1976.

Mount, T. *Safe Cave Diving.* Miami, Fla.: National Association for Cave Diving, 1973.

————. *The Cave Diving Manual.* Miami, Fla.: National Association for Cave Diving, 1972.

National Association of Underwater Instructors. *NAUI: The Complete Guide to Cave Diving.* NAUI Technical Publication Number Three, 1973.

Nesmith, Robert I., and Potter, John S., Jr. *Treasure Hunter's Guide: How and Where to Find It.* Revised edition. New York: Arco, 1975.

Peyser, R. *Corrosion of Steel Scuba Tanks.* Kingston, R.I.: University of Rhode Island, 1970.

Shepard, F. *Submarine Geology.* 3rd ed. New York: Harper and Row, 1973.

Silvia, Charles E. *Lifesaving and Water Safety Today.* New York: Association Press, 1965.

Throckmorton, Peter. *Shipwrecks and Archaeology: The Unharvested Sea.* Boston: Little, Brown, 1970.

Tilden, Freeman. *The National Parks.* Revised edition. New York: Alfred A. Knopf, Inc., 1968.

U.S. Coast Guard. *Rules of the Road: International—Inland.* August 1, 1972. Washington, D.C.: U.S. Coast Guard, 1972.

U.S. Coast Guard Auxiliary. *Boating Skills and Seamanship.* Washington, D.C.: U.S. Coast Guard, 1977.

U.S. Department of the Army. *Survival.* FM 21-76 Headquarters, Washington, D.C.: Department of the Army, October 1957.

U.S. Department of Commerce. NOAA. *Tidal Current Tables* and *Tidal Current Charts.* Rockville, Md.: National Ocean Survey.

U.S. Department of the Navy. *U.S. Navy Diving Manual.* NAV-SHIPS 0994-001-9010. Washington, D.C.: Government Printing Office, 1973.

Zanelli, L., ed. *The British Sub Aqua Club Diving Manual.* 7th ed. London: The British Sub Aqua Club, 1974.

————. *Underwater Swimming, An Advanced Handbook.* South Brunswick, Great Britain: A. S. Barne and Co., 1969.

INDEX

Abalone, 171, 210
  steaks, 190
Acoustics, 306
Air
  composition of, 24-25
  cylinders, 82-83
  duration, effect of depth on, 72
  embolism, 16, 18, 29, 36, 115, 226-27
  impure, consequences of using, 51
  lungs and air consumption, 38-39
  open-circuit scuba equipment and,
    40-41
  physics of, 37-38
  running out of, self-rescue and, 248-49
  supply, effect of exertion in calculation
    of, 29-30, 73-74, 75-77, 79, 81
  See also Pressure
Airlift tool, 154-55
Alveoli, 38
American Littoral Society (ALS), 118, 159
American Standards Association (ASA),
  166, 168
Anchors and anchoring, 265-71
  bend knot, 288
  cable lengths, 268-69
  lines, fastening, 268
  trip line, 269
  types of, 266-68
  weighing anchor, 269
Anoxia (oxygen starvation), 73, 221

Anxiety, predive, 91-92
Archaeology, underwater, wreck diving
  and, 142-59, 308
  artifacts, effects of salt water on, 155-59
  expeditions, wreck diving, 145, 148-49
  location of wrecks, 146
  plotting position of wrecks, 147-48
  recovery of wreck, 151-52
  search methods, 149-51
  sites, wreck, 148, 152, 159
  tools, recovery, 154-55
  types of, 153-54
  wooden ship (Galleon), recognizing
    wreck of, 152-53
Archimedes' principle, 15
Artifacts
  desalinization of, 158
  preservation of, 157-59
  salt water, effects on, 155-56
  See also names of artifacts, e.g., Brass;
    Copper; Gems; etc.
Artificial respiration, 256-59
Ascent
  buoyancy and, 18-19
  decompression and, 36
  emergency, 250
  free, making of, 248
  rule of thumb to figure rate of ascent at
    elevation, 138
Asphyxia, 221-22

329

Audubon Society, 118
Automatic reserve valve, 46

Backpack (harness), 42, 83
Barnacles, 209-10
Barometer, 293
  for wind indications (table), 294, 296
Barracuda, great, 205-206
Bass, 171
Bearings, finding, 276-77
  cross-bearing, 277
  line of position, 277
  relative, 276
  true, 276, 277
Bends, 226-27
  symptoms of, 116
Biology, marine, 306
Black crappies, 171
Blackout, shallow water, 220
Black seabass, 171
Bluegill, 171
Boats
  anchors and anchoring, 265-66, 268
  beaching, 281
  beam, 262
  bottom, 264
  buying, 261-66
  chartering, 261
  cockpit, 263
  collision, 285
  construction, material of, 265
  depth finder, 265
  entry and exits from, 92-93, 264
  fire on board, 284
  floors of, 263
  freeboard, 264
  galley, 264
  hull surfaces, 264
  knots, 287-88
  length of, 262
  maintenance of, 270
  motor, 262-63
  navigation equipment, 264
  pumps, 264
  radio communication, 264
  range of, 263
  ropes, 286-87
  spare parts and tools, 270-71
  speed and power, 262
  storage of, 263

stormy seas, handling in, 280
swamping and capsizing, 284
tachometer, 265
towing, 284
trailability, 265
transom, 262
Bobbing, 101
Bottom time, 112
Boyle's law, 28-30, 31, 72, 216, 225, 248
Brass, as artifact, 156
Breathing, 72
  apparatus, 10-11, 52-53
  buddy system of, 45-46, 245-46
  equipment, retaining when empty, 249-50
  gases for, 25
  hoses, 44, 83
  process, 38-39
  snorkel diving and, 74
Buddy system, 63-64
  breathing and, 45-46, 245-46
Buoyancy
  compensator (BC), 17-19, 73, 84
  control pack (BCP), 19-20
  negative, 14-15
  neutral, 15-16, 17, 18
  positive, 14-15, 16

Cable, 324
Caisson's disease. See Bends
Carbon dioxide (CO$_2$), 25
  cartridge, 18-19
  poisoning, 222
  speargun, 124
Carbon monoxide (CO), 25
  poisoning, 222-23
Catfish, 125, 171
Cave diving, 129-31
Charles's Law (a/k/a Gay-Lussac's Law), 30-32
Charts, nautical, 288-89
Chemistry, marine, 307
Ciguatera poisoning, 239-40
Circular sweep method in underwater archaeology, 151
Clams, 171, 186-87, 207
Claustrophobia, 92
Cleaner-fish, mutualism and, 119
Clouds, 300-301
  chart, 293